To Bob Batterson

Such is the way
to the stars!

Wally Kent

USS ARIZONA'S
LAST BAND

THE HISTORY OF
U.S. NAVY BAND NUMBER 22

Molly Kent

USS *Arizona*'s Last Band:
The History of U.S. Navy Band Number 22

Copyright © 1996 by Molly Kent.

Printed in the United States of America.

ISBN: 0-9654199-0-8
Library of Congress Catalog Card Number: 96-92673

Silent Song Publishing
2122 N. 49th Terrace
Kansas City, KS 66104

In Loving Memory
of the Members of the Last United States Navy Band
Ever to Serve Aboard the USS Arizona

Frederick William Kinney
Wayne Lynn Bandy
Oran Merrill Brabbzson
Ralph Warren Burdette
Harry Gregory Chernucha
Gerald Clinton Cox
Frank Norman Floege
Curtis Junior Haas
Bernard Thomas Hughes
Wendell Ray Hurley
Emmett Isaac Lynch
William Moore McCary
William Starks Moorhouse
Alexander Joseph Nadel
Neal Jason Radford
James Harvey Sanderson
Jack Leo Scruggs
Robert Kar Shaw
Charles William White
Ernest Hubert Whitson, Jr.
Clyde Richard Williams

To my family, both past and present,
and to the families of *Arizona*'s musicians.

About the Author

Molly Kent is the sister of Clyde Richard Williams, Musician Second Class, United States Navy, one of the musicians in the last USS *Arizona* band. All twenty-one members of *Arizona*'s band were killed at Pearl Harbor on December 7, 1941.

From material collected by her parents, including official and personal letters and newspaper accounts pertaining to the attack on Pearl Harbor, she has written this history of the boys who served in *Arizona*'s last band.

Contents

Preface

For many years after my brother, Clyde Richard Williams, was murdered at Pearl Harbor, I needed only to say, "My brother was a member of the USS *Arizona* band," and people would reply, "I am so sorry—that was horrible!" There was no need for me to elaborate further. Everyone knew that the *Arizona* was blown up on Sunday, December 7, 1941, at Pearl Harbor, Territory of Hawaii, when Japan conducted her sneak attack on the United States.

And everyone knew the story of *Arizona*'s band—how, when air alert sounded that morning, her bandsmen had run down to their battle stations in the ammunition hold. How they had just arrived when the ammunition in the hold exploded with a mighty blast, killing all twenty-one members of the band.

Everyone knew the band's story because the United States Navy had told us about it on April 1, 1942, four months after the attack. All the newspapers in our country ran the Navy's press release,[1] and the band's story was repeated for many years in speeches and articles.

For the past ten years, however, it has become obvious that the true facts of the band's life story have succumbed to half-truths and fables. Now, when I say, "My brother was a member of the USS *Arizona* band," people usually say, "Oh, yes, I've heard of that band. It's musicians were in bed asleep that morning!"

Our family first heard the "asleep in bed" fable on Memorial Day, 1982, when my husband and I took my mother to Pearl Harbor for her first visit to the *Arizona* Memorial. There is entombed whatever remains of her son. As we sat in the theater of the visitors' center watching their film, suddenly there was a picture of *Arizona*'s band! And there was our Clyde, looking out at us with his familiar half-smile. We were stunned.

Even more stunning to us, however, was the story the narrator was telling. How the *Arizona* band had played so well the night before and had gotten back to the ship so late that the Navy had let the musicians sleep late the morning of December 7. And how all the bandsmen were still in bed asleep when the attack began, and so they had all died!

What a picture that conjured up for us! The U.S. Navy, to which we had entrusted our beloved Clyde, being so kind and gracious to him on his last morning on earth.

And what a comforting thought that was for us! After forty-one years of struggling to accept the horror of the last few minutes of life of our *Arizona* bandsmen, we could now put them to rest in such a serene, peaceful manner. We would love to believe that story—we would like nothing better than to know that the band really was still in bed. There is certainly nothing wrong with having a morning off from duty and being able to lie abed, basking in the luxury of not having to get up yet. All of us have done that all our lives, whenever the opportunity presented itself. Yes, the picture of our bandsmen lying on their innerspring mattresses, totally oblivious, when the *Arizona* suddenly blew up and snuffed out their lives, with no warning and with no pain, is something we could live with much more easily than that which really transpired that morning.

But what hogwash! That was a United States Navy Band—not fancy members of some elite finishing school. *Arizona's* last band operated under the same rules and regulations which govern all sailors, rules which have been set down by the Navy for many years. The band had its assigned duties and its bandsmen were expected to perform them. The Navy has its own way of seeing that its rules are enforced.

Therefore, we knew that the comforting picture of *Arizona's* musicians lying peacefully in their beds until late that morning could not be true, for the simple reason that her band members did not ever have any beds on the *Arizona*.

They ate and slept in the same compartment. And they slept, not in comfortable beds, but in hammocks, which were swung from hooks each night. Their hammocks were taken down early each morning, rolled up, and stored. The tables for eating, which had been suspended from the ceiling the night before, were then lowered to the deck.

There was never any deviation from that schedule. The tables were down in the daytime—the hammocks were down at night. Never were the two down at the same time.

The Navy even furnished an alarm clock to tell the musicians when it was time to get up. That clock, in the form of the master-at-arms, stalked around carrying a big stick, the better to whack sailors on the rump when they did not jump out of their hammocks fast enough to suit him. It was a very effective system.

There was no sleeping late for the bandsmen—ever. There was no crawling back into their hammocks for another forty winks—their hammocks were just not there anymore.

As for the fable of *Arizona*'s band playing so well the night of December 6, the families of the bandsmen have known since early 1942 just where *Arizona*'s musicians were on their last night, what they did, and to whom they talked. After all, we had a vested interest in learning the true facts of the band's activities as quickly as we could. We came to realize early on that we would not receive much information from official sources, and that anything we learned would come from our hard work and from the kindness of strangers.

Not only did the band not play anywhere the night of December 6, its members were not late getting back to the ship. They were on board by the usual 1:00 A.M., as required of all unmarried sailors at Pearl Harbor.

But friends continued to return from Pearl Harbor relating the "band was asleep" fable.

Unfortunately, if we repeat an untruth over and over, year after year, it becomes firmly engraved into the history of a nation.

But what a disservice to those very talented musicians, whose only sin was to follow orders and to perform their duties as they had been trained.

Cannot we say something about how that band was famous all over the Pacific Fleet as the best military band our servicemen had ever heard?

Cannot we say something about how those twenty-one men had spent their entire lives studying and training to become the proficient band everyone so admired?

Cannot we remember them as young men who were cheated out of their lives before their lives ever really began?

Is our only memorial to that group of men to remain forever a lie?

Those men all had loving families back home who still remember them and who did not rest until they had ferreted out their story, but it seemed to me that no one else knew or cared.

Perhaps that was our fault. The families of the *Arizona* bandsmen have seldom talked to outsiders about our private grief, preferring to bear our pain in silence. The mothers wrote extensively to each other for years after the attack, pouring out their grief to one another. They were fully aware that nobody in the world who had not experienced such a loss could possibly understand the suffering they were enduring.

Gradually it dawned on me that perhaps, if the band's story was ever to be written, it would require some action on my part.

Research material was no problem. My parents preserved all my brother's letters to us from the time he entered the U.S. Navy until his death. They also saved the letters which were written to them after the attack by the parents of his fellow musicians. All this material, plus many, many articles, books, letters, and photographs pertaining to Pearl Harbor, was entrusted to me many years ago for safekeeping.

Not only did my parents preserve these papers, they also went to great lengths in the early years to search out the facts of their son's death, and to document the sources.

But how could I take on such a personally painful task?

How could I spend several years researching and writing about the intimate feelings of those boys and their families? How could I open up again the unspeakable pain and horror which we endured for so long after Pearl Harbor?

It appeared I had two choices. I could leave the *Arizona* band with the epitaph of "They were in their beds asleep" or I could muster the courage from somewhere to tell their true story.

Little by little, with much soul-searching, I developed the obsessive drive necessary to undertake such a project. I felt bolstered by some unseen force. I could almost hear my parents, long since gone, saying, "Go for it, Molly." And I could feel the band boys urging me on, assuring me that "You can do it!"

Finally, in January 1993, I surrendered and began this book.

And I was right—it took all the courage I could muster to open those many boxes of letters, written more than fifty years ago, and to start putting them into some sort of order.

I had not read my brother's letters since he first wrote them to us in 1940 and 1941. Since I moved from our hometown in January 1942, I had never read the letters the parents of the other *Arizona* bandsmen had written to my parents.

Just to read, sort, and copy those letters, written so long ago, proved extremely difficult. It was not long before I learned that it is possible to type with tears running down one's face!

In the beginning, I was grateful for my fury and indignation about the untruths being told about the band—it drove me on, when it would have been so easy to throw up my hands and say, "Enough! This is just too painful."

Before long, however, my fury dissolved into humility. Everywhere I turned, friends and total strangers were enthusiastic and encouraging. Everyone, it seemed, was eager to help. Always, if they could not answer my questions, they suggested someone else who might know, until I had a large network of people all over the country, trying to remember events that happened so long ago!

It was extremely comforting to find that so many people really did care and wanted to know the true facts about the *Arizona* band.

My pride in the band grew with each interview, as former servicemen told me how good the *Arizona* band was and how much they always enjoyed listening to it. They assured me over and over that the *Arizona* band was not only the best band in the Pacific Fleet, it was the best in the whole Navy!

I became more convinced that now it is time to tell the story of the *Arizona* band, and to tell it as accurately as possible. It is time to share the results of the research of the families of *Arizona*'s musicians.

We owe this to our twenty-one bandsmen; we owe it to their families; and we owe it to our nation's historical records.

Here, then, written in tears and with much love and respect, is the story of the very short life of the last band of the USS *Arizona*.

Acknowledgments

This book is the culmination of many searches by the families of *Arizona*'s last bandsmen, searches which began on December 7, 1941, and have remained ongoing to this day. Had it not been for those families' careful research and even more careful storage of the information they acquired, none of us would know the history of that talented group of musicians. That would have been a great loss.

Therefore, first and foremost, I want to thank all the parents of the *Arizona* bandsmen for their part in preserving the history of that ill-fated band. By exchanging information and photographs of their sons so many years ago, they laid the foundation for this book.

Especially do I thank my parents, Dick and Jane Williams, whose only son, Musician Second Class Clyde Richard Williams, was a member of *Arizona*'s last band.

Also, I thank the living families of the bandsmen, who were all so encouraging. They know firsthand our grief and were able to sympathize with me as I struggled for so long with this book.

Robert Radford, the brother of Musician Second Class Neal (Mike) Radford of *Arizona*'s last band, sent a copy of his brother's letters. I am very grateful to Bob for his assistance.

Pauline Scruggs Ellis, whose brother, Musician Second Class Jack Leo Scruggs, was a member of *Arizona*'s last band, also sent her brother's letters. Since early 1942, the Scruggs family has shared photographs which Jack had sent them with the other families.

I was also encouraged by the Reverend Kenneth Paul Bandy, brother of Musician Second Class Wayne Lynn Bandy of *Arizona*'s last band. I found the Bandy family by a miracle whose name is Dolores Bertels.

Ruth Cadwell Sanders, who was Wayne Bandy's "girl back home," sent photographs of Wayne and other members of the band which had been sent to her by Jack Scruggs' mother in 1942.

By a strange coincidence, I found Elizabeth Haas Landeweer, the stepmother of Musician Second Class Curtis Junior Haas. My husband and I had searched all over Kansas City for some person who could tell us about Curt's family, but had about given up. One day I went to the Wyandotte West Library of Kansas City, Kansas, to read microfilms of some old newspapers I had ordered regarding another bandsman. David Thomas, the head of the audiovisual department, casually asked why I was reading such old newspapers. When I told him I was working on a book about the USS *Arizona* band, David remarked that his father had gone to school with a member of the *Arizona* band. Of course, that had to be Curt Haas.

David's father, Jerry Thomas, led me to Edna Scharz. Edna contacted Betty Jane Brown Miller, a friend of Elizabeth Haas Landeweer. Thanks to all those people, I have had many delightful conversations with Elizabeth. She is a very intelligent, talented person, and I have enjoyed knowing her.

Don Hurley, the brother of Musician Second Class Wendell Ray Hurley, was also very encouraging and sent Wendell's entire photograph album. Most of our favorite photos of my brother taken at Pearl Harbor came from Wendell Hurley's father in 1942, as he shared the pictures from his son's album with all of us.

In addition to the families of the *Arizona* musicians, the assistance, interest, encouragement, kindness, and prayers of so many other people, both military and civilian, did much to ensure the completion of this book.

Personnel at the United States Navy School of Music, now no longer confined to the U.S. Navy, but training musicians for all the branches of the armed forces, could not have been more courteous. When we visited the school at Little Creek, Virginia, in 1993, the Commanding Officer was Commander Raymond A. Ascione and the Executive Officer was Lieutenant Mike Alverson. Lieutenant Alverson was very helpful in furnishing addresses of people who might assist me in my research.

Captain W. J. Phillips, who was Officer in Charge/Leader of the U.S. Navy Band, wrote a very encouraging letter through J. L. Barnes, Master Chief Musician.

I was delighted to find Doctor James M. Thurmond, who was Bandmaster-in-Charge of the U.S. Navy School of Music when the *Arizona* bandsmen attended in 1940 and 1941. He was most helpful in furnishing some of the history of the school and in asking other former bandsmen to assist me.

Nothing could have prepared me for the kindness, helpfulness, and encouragement of the men who survived the Pearl Harbor attack on December 7, 1941. At first I was hesitant to contact them, as I know how painful it must be for them to discuss that day. But they were most gracious, and I sincerely thank them. In particular, members of the Pearl Harbor Survivors Association, Inc. always found the name of someone who could help me.

I am grateful to the former students of the U.S. Navy School of Music who attended the school with the *Arizona* bandsmen. Most of the men I interviewed were also survivors of the Pearl Harbor attack, so not only did they know our bandsmen at the school, they also knew them at Pearl Harbor. It was personally a great comfort to me to talk with them, as they were the last friends our boys ever saw. They always had time to answer one more question. They sent me copies of material from their scrapbooks; they sent the names of other musicians who might help; they invariably cheered me on. They, more than anyone else, understood what I was trying to do. I want them to know how much I appreciate their kindness and assistance.

I also talked at length with other Navy and Marine musicians who were on ships or on shore at Pearl Harbor that day. Although they had attended different music schools than had the boys in the *Arizona* band, they all had heard them play at Pearl Harbor and remembered them well.

Civilians, some of whom were not even alive in 1941, have been very interested in this book, and have helped in many ways. They are:

Ramona Corbin of the Kansas City, Kansas, Office of Senator Bob Dole, who helped expedite responses from government agencies.

Lorraine Marks Haislip, Historian of the USS *Arizona* Reunion Association, who was very generous in sharing material regarding the *Arizona* band.

Many special people helped me in my unsuccessful attempts to find other families of *Arizona*'s bandsmen.

In addition to the assistance provided by Jerry and David Thomas, Edna Scharz, and Betty Jane Brown Miller, the following people helped in my search for the family of Curtis Haas: Gus Leimkuler of the North Kansas City, Missouri, High School Library; Margaret McCoy, Archivist, Unity School of Christianity, Kansas City, Missouri; my friend, Sue Logan, of Harrisonville, Missouri; and Alvina Wells of the Bates County, Missouri, Historical Society.

Robert H. McCary of Birmingham, Alabama, helped me in my effort to find the family of Bill McCary. Although I called all the McCarys in Birmingham, including Robert, we were never able to find any family connection. I thank him, however, for his courtesy in looking through all his family records for me.

Mike Kelley and Janet Dagenais Brown of the Wichita State University Library, Wichita, Kansas, and Bill Ellington of the Wichita, Kansas, Public Library, searched long for me in our attempt to find the family of Bill Moorhouse.

Terry Linville, Jackie Williams, and Richard Del Real of the Webb Sanders Funeral Home, Lindsay, California; Jane Balmer of the Lindsay, California, Cemetery; and Sue Palmer of Porter's Funeral Home in Kansas City, Kansas, all helped in my search for the family of Harvey Sanderson.

My cousins, Betty Gerow Ryan of Chicago, Illinois, and Kay Gerow Morris of Pasadena, Texas, tried very hard to find the family of Bobby Shaw.

Wanda Campbell, Jane Golden, Lawrence Houchin, Betty Mae Martin, Asa E. Streight, and Jess and Betty Winn, all present or former residents of Okmulgee, Oklahoma, helped me in various ways, as did my cousin, Frankie Morton, of Norman, Oklahoma.

Good friends Virginia and Emily Doughty of Chesapeake, Virginia, extended their hospitality to us when we visited the School of Music in Little Creek, Virginia.

Employees of the Kansas City, Kansas, Library were always willing to help. These include especially Joan Ganert of the Main Library and David Thomas, Larry Busch, and Rex Nowland of the Wyandotte West Branch.

Roderick Townley of the Writer's Place in Kansas City, Missouri, was very generous in giving me advice, as were Carolyn Riddle, Pola Firestone, and Francis X. Medina.

Many, many close friends, such as Steve and Mary Holloway, Bill and Nancy Byous, and the Reverend Ralph Culler, never tired of asking how the book was going, making sure I did not stray far from the task at hand.

Our longtime friend, Fritz Kropf, of Kansas City, Kansas, a survivor of the Pearl Harbor attack, helped me find addresses for many of the men I wanted to contact.

My friend, Sister Frances Marie Grady of Kansas City, Missouri, insisted from the beginning that I must write this book. She made me see that the project was possible, when I was not so sure.

When I went to Washington, D.C., in January 1942 at the age of twenty, I had, in less than two months, lost my brother in a horrible manner and had left home for the first time. I was only saved by some beautiful Government girls who had also left home at the same age. They were (and still are): Maggie Corder Runkle, Virginia Patton Doughty, June Cockrell Estabrook, and Angeline Calvert Pickett. I have treasured their friendship through all these years.

As I entered the mysterious world of self-publishing, I was guided and assisted by Darla Pennington, who did the typesetting for the book; Jean Staub, who did the proofreading; and David G. Plumer of Walsworth Publishing Company.

My husband was a tower of strength during this work. He was always ready to drive me to check out yet another clue, or to do some chore around the house when I did not seem to be aware of the need.

And, as always, I have been strengthened by the love and encouragement of Omer, Peggy, and Willie Kent.

Although I freely acknowledge that many people have helped with this book, such assistance merely reflects their kindness. Certainly I do not suggest that they agree with all the statements in this book.

Especially I do not want to imply that all members of the families of the *Arizona* band agree with all the statements contained in this book. We have all formed different opinions over the years about who was responsible for the Pearl Harbor disaster and how the fiasco could have been avoided.

We stand as one, however, in our sorrow and regret for the unnecessary and untimely loss of our beloved *Arizona* bandsmen.

USS ARIZONA'S

LAST BAND

Part I

THE BAND

SIC ITUR AD ASTRA

SUCH IS THE WAY TO THE STARS, OR TO IMMORTALITY.

ARIZONA BAND TROPHY—1941

CHAPTER 1

They Didn't Have a Chance!

As far as the United States Navy can ascertain, it was the only U.S. Navy Band which was formed together, trained together, transferred together, reported aboard a ship together, fought together, and died together.[1]

It was to become the best-known musical band in the Pacific Fleet, assigned to what was to become the most famous ship in the world.

Its members were equally proficient performing as a concert band, a dance band, a jazz band, or an orchestra.

They were the musicians of Band Number 22, serving aboard the battleship *Arizona* (BB-39).

Members of the ill-fated band were: Bandmaster Frederick William Kinney; Wayne Lynn Bandy; Oran Merrill Brabbzson; Ralph Warren Burdette; Harry Gregory Chernucha; Gerald Clinton Cox; Frank Norman Floege; Curtis Junior Haas; Bernard Thomas Hughes; Wendell Ray Hurley; Emmett Isaac Lynch; William Moore McCary; William Starks Moorhouse; Alexander Joseph Nadel; Neal Jason Radford; James Harvey Sanderson; Jack Leo Scruggs; Robert Kar Shaw; Charles William White; Ernest Hubert Whitson, Jr.; and Clyde Richard Williams, who was my brother.

At the time of their deaths, Bandmaster Kinney held the rate of Musician First Class; most of the other bandsmen held the rate of Musician Second Class.

Not much has been written about the *Arizona* band, and what has been written is seldom correct. The purpose of this book is to help you come to know its musicians and to understand what a terrible shock the loss of those twenty-one boys was to their families.

Unfortunately, the only way I can introduce you to the band is through these pages, since the bandsmen are no longer with us. The entire band, along with their Bandmaster, was blown up with their ship. They died together as heroes, and they deserve to be remembered forever.

When the Japanese conducted their sneak attack against the United States military installations at Pearl Harbor, Territory of Hawaii, on December 7, 1941, they wrecked havoc on all our ships, planes, and buildings. Pearl Harbor was completely devastated, with much of our property there either damaged or destroyed.

But as bad as the damage was to our national property and to our national pride, it was nothing to the damage the Japanese did to the families of the 2,403 persons who were murdered that day. Property can be and was repaired or replaced, but the men lost that day were lost forever to their families and friends waiting back home.

To us, the deceased were not just cold statistics—they were our happy, fun-loving, handsome boys, real flesh-and-blood human beings, who were cheated out of their lives by the stupidity of greed.

This book does not deal with the causes of our unpreparedness at Pearl Harbor that day, nor does it deal with the technical details of our military forces there. Not having been a member of the armed forces and not having been at Pearl Harbor that day, I cannot add anything to the excellent books which have already been written about the attack.

Rather, this book has been written from the viewpoint of a group of civilians whose lives were forevermore changed when their loved ones perished that day.

I had the pleasure of meeting all the *Arizona* band members. They were an exceptionally fine group of boys. I am only sorry that I could not have known them longer.

For more than fifty years, they have been honored as heroes. Their families have always appreciated the honors and have been very proud of them. But, like most heroes, our boys have not been alive to receive their honors, so it has been hollow glory for us. Medals, memorials, and honors, while well-deserved in this case, can never replace warm loving sons and brothers. For after all, our boys can no longer hug us, laugh with us, cry with us, talk to us—and that we have missed very much.

I am aware that the U.S. Navy calls all its personnel "men," and I am sure "old salts" will cringe every time I refer to the *Arizona* bandsmen as "boys." The Navy is always so quick to tell us that it takes boys and turns them into men. No doubt they did so in that case—certainly the bandsmen of the *Arizona* died like men.

But since much of this book has been taken from letters written to each other for many years by their grieving families, and since all those families called them their "boys," I have chosen to use the same term.

After all, they were "boys" when they left us—they never came back—so they have remained for us the age they were when last we saw them.

Most of the boys had been sailors less than a year. Nearly one half of them had joined the Navy when they reached the age of eighteen. All had requested entry into the United States Navy School of Music, and after an audition at the school in Washington, D.C., had been accepted. The audition was mandatory, since only accomplished musicians were permitted into the school. The U.S. Navy School of Music was not set up as a training school for amateurs.[2]

The boys came to the school from states on the East and West Coasts and from the Middle West—from Alabama, California, Illinois, Indiana, Kansas, Kentucky, Missouri, Nebraska, New Jersey, New York, Ohio, Oklahoma, Pennsylvania, Texas, Utah, and the state of Washington.

By the time they died, they had become a close-knit professional group, writing home to their families how proud they were of their band and of their "pals."

They were just embarking on a career in music. They dreamed they would someday be members of a big band, the likes of Glenn Miller. They were destined to be remembered always as members of a famous band, although neither they nor Glenn Miller lived to savor their fame.

Glenn Miller had his beloved "String of Pearls," but the last band of the USS *Arizona* had only its one last, final Pearl—their despised

Pearl Harbor.

Members of the *Arizona* band died together on December 7, 1941. Their idol, Major Glenn Miller, Director of the United States Air Force Band, died three years later—December 15, 1944—lost on a flight from England to Paris.[3]

The *Arizona* band's last day of life began on a beautiful sunny, calm, quiet tropical morning, and ended less than two hours later in terror, with blood, smoke, fire, explosions, pain, and death.

For their families back home, the hardest part to bear has always been—how long did they live, how did they die, and did they suffer? Although we have devoted our lives to finding the answers to these questions, we still do not know.

Caution must be used in writing about the Pearl Harbor attack, since so many books offer so many opposing opinions.

Everyone agrees, however, that without any warning, Japan attacked our military installations at Pearl Harbor on the island of Oahu, Territory of Hawaii, at seven fifty-five on the morning of December 7, 1941.

The first wave of 183 Japanese airplanes, part of a total of 353 planes, bombed and strafed our military airfields, where the airplanes were conveniently lined up in straight rows, then moved to the ships moored at Pearl Harbor.[4]

The Japanese then dropped bombs on our ships, which were also lined up in neat rows.[5]

According to some sources, the *Arizona* was hit with a 1,756.9-pound armor-piercing bomb, especially made with the capability of penetrating the decks of ships before exploding.[6]

The bomb penetrated *Arizona*'s deck, and by some twist of fate not totally agreed upon by historians now, caused her six main ammunition storage magazines at the front of the ship to explode.[7]

At the beginning of the attack, when the air raid alert, followed by general quarters, was sounded on *Arizona*, her band members ran to their battle stations in the ammunition hold several decks below, as they had been trained to do. Just as they arrived at the ammunition hold and lined up at their assigned places to ensure the shells and bags of powder stayed on the hoists going to the big guns above, the ammunition hold blew up.

In that instant, the entire twenty-one-piece band was gone.

Gone, too, were their hopes and dreams and the hopes and dreams of their families back home. For us, life as we knew it was over. Oh, we kept breathing, and we kept working, and we kept loving—but our lives were never quite so bright after that.

Eventually we regained the song in our hearts, but it was always in a minor key after Pearl Harbor.

Arizona lost 1,177 of her 1,511 men. In all, 2,403 persons, military and civilians, were killed at Pearl Harbor that day.[8]

The beautiful USS *Arizona* Memorial at Pearl Harbor, now maintained by the United States National Park Service, honors the men killed that day. Beneath this Memorial is probably the last resting place for most of *Arizona*'s bandsmen.

Part of their families' lifetime sentence has been that any mention of "*Arizona*," "Pearl Harbor," or "December 7" has always caused a lurch in our very souls. So, to protect ourselves, most of us have wrapped the memory of our boys in soft cotton and stored it in our hearts. No one who did not suffer through such a tragedy could possibly understand our grief, and we soon learned not to try to explain.

But now it is time to tell the story of the USS *Arizona*'s last band, and to tell it as truthfully as possible.

Most of the boys' parents are gone now, and their siblings are scattered all over the country. This book is possible only because many of the families of the boys kept every letter their sons wrote to them after they left home. Afterwards, as they became acquainted with each other, they shared that information. Without access to that material, I would have been hard-pressed to tell this story.

Fortunately, we used the long distance telephone or Western Union for dire emergencies only in those days, and other fast communication systems had not yet been invented. It is thanks to our depression-induced frugality that most of our communication was done by letters, and that those letters were kept all these years.

While they were attending the U.S. Navy School of Music in Washington, D.C., some of the boys who lived on the East Coast took

friends to their parents' homes for the weekend. After they graduated and went around to California, one of the boys whose family
lived on the West Coast did the same, so some of the parents had met
some of the boys. Some of the boys' sisters and mothers had visited
them, either in Washington or in Long Beach, California. My parents and I had gone to Washington in May 1941 for the band's graduation from the School of Music, so I had met *Arizona*'s band boys at a
dance and at the dock when they embarked on their destiny.

But none of the parents had ever met any of the other parents
before their sons' deaths. After December 7, they became a close support group for each other. In the absence of official word, the parents
shared every bit of information they could uncover regarding their
sons' last hours. And we finally came to know how our musicians
died—know, but not to understand. Never did we understand.

Much has been written and continues to be written about that
horrible day, and the military aspects of our "Day of Infamy" have
been argued for over fifty years now, and no doubt will never be resolved.

For many years the families of the band boys could not understand why our government was so taken by surprise and why our
musicians died so tragically. Some of the families accepted the verdict that Admiral Husband E. Kimmel and Lieutenant General Walter
C. Short were somehow the only two persons who allowed Japan to
sneak in uncontested and destroy our military installations. Others
felt that the heads of those two men were being offered to the citizens of the United States on a silver platter, simply to protect the
guilty.

We were a very different people in the thirties and the forties
from what we are now. We were fiercely patriotic, and we believed
our leaders to be honorable men. We trusted them. In those days,
newspaper reporters did not reveal the private, personal lives of our
leaders, and their human flaws were kept from us. So, if our leaders
deemed it to be in the national interest to keep the facts of Pearl
Harbor from us, we accepted that. We concentrated all our hatred on
the "dirty Japs," as we were being taught.

From the beginning, the families grieved because, by the sneaky nature of the attack, our *Arizona* band boys did not have a chance.

After more than fifty years of reading all I could find about the many investigations and inquiries which have been conducted as our government searched for the cause of Pearl Harbor, I am left sick with fury.

If the average citizen cannot understand the extreme rivalry between our Army and Navy, you can imagine the agony of the victims' families as we gradually learned the many reasons for Japan's success in catching us so unprepared at Pearl Harbor.

It appears that, in addition to our enemies in Japan, we in this country were saddled with the jealousy, lies, coverups, and feuds between our Army and Navy; our president and the people; our president and Congress; our Congressmen and other members of Congress; high-ranking military officers and other high-ranking military officers; Democrats and Republicans; ad infinitum.

So we were right from the start—2,403 American military men and civilians, including our twenty-one *Arizona* band members, did not have a chance!

CHAPTER 2

The Early Years

To better understand the shock and horror the sneak attack on Pearl Harbor had on this nation, it is important that we have some idea of the sort of people we were then.

When the thirteen younger members of *Arizona*'s last band were born in the "Roaring Twenties," they entered a world of optimism. Our country had just won the "War to End All Wars"—the men who had survived that madness had all come home—our country was prosperous—life was good.

Everyone looked forward to a life of comfort and joy.

The families of *Arizona*'s last bandsmen lived in states from coast to coast, half of them in small towns and half of them in large cities.

A few of the boys' families had but recently arrived in the United States, but most of the families had lived in this country for several generations.

My brother was typical of the small-town boy whose family had been in the United States for many generations. So long had our family lived here, in fact, that my brother and I had strains of the blood of the English, Welsh, Irish, Pennsylvania Dutch, German, and Cherokee Indian.

Family ties were very important then. Most people had large, extended families living nearby who visited back and forth often. With television not yet invented, we children of the twenties grew up absorbing the stories of our family heritage.

After a large Sunday dinner, we would all sit in the living room and the adults would reminisce about old times. We children loved those stories and would beg for our favorites. If perhaps the stories got a little better with each telling, we did not mind.

From our kinfolks, we learned how it was to live in the old days. We heard about life in a sod house or in a log cabin. We learned that, when you spotted Indians in the distance, riding toward you, you must run quickly to hide in the storm cellar. After we grew older, we always wondered how, on a barren prairie with no other cabin in sight, the Indians could not have figured out just where the family was hiding.

We learned about the bounty hunters who roamed through Oklahoma Territory, and how they had killed one of our relatives, only to discover he was not the man they were seeking. With barely a "Sorry, ma'am," the bounty hunters just rode off, leaving our newly-widowed aunt with several small children and a farm to care for.

We learned that, before statehood, the closest law for our kin in Oklahoma Territory was the U.S. Marshal in Fort Smith, Arkansas. By the time he arrived, the crisis was generally over, leaving either the ranch owner or the cattle rustler victorious, depending on which was the better shot.

Our knowledge of the history of our country was shaped by those stories.

Later, when he was attending the U.S. Navy School of Music in Washington, D.C., my brother derived much enjoyment from telling our family stories, only slightly embellished, to his fellow students at the school. The boys from the East Coast in particular considered Oklahoma "'Way Out West," completely uncivilized. To my brother's glee, they tended to believe anything told about our state.

Our mother's family had always lived in the South. Her family members had settled in the early 1700s in Virginia, Georgia, and Tennessee, and each generation had moved farther west, always seeking better and cheaper land.

From them, we heard stories of the Revolutionary War, the War of 1812, the Civil War, and World War I. We also heard the tragic stories of the "Trail of Tears," which had been passed down to us from a Cherokee grandmother of five generations ago.

On that side of our family, our food was Southern—our traditions were Southern—our viewpoints were Southern.

To counterbalance all our Southern heritage, our mother had married a Yankee. From our father, we inherited the blood of his Welsh father and his German mother. Our father's family was considered newcomers, having been in the United States for less than a hundred years.

Members of his family had also fought in the Civil War, the Spanish American War, and World War I. From the stories of that side of our family, we learned our nation's history from the Northern viewpoint.

Our Southern grandparents had been in Oklahoma Territory long before statehood in 1907, working for the Indians. Later, one of them had made the first land run of 1889, called the "Run of '89," and had staked out a homestead. Another grandfather had made the next "Run of 1891" and had filed a claim on the Pottawatomie Indians' land.

Our Yankee grandfather had won a land grant in Oklahoma Territory in the land lottery of 1902 and had walked from St. Louis, Missouri, to Oklahoma Territory to stake his claim on the Kiowa Indians' land.

All those homesteads had been lost through misfortune and fraud, and our grandparents were all living in Henryetta, Oklahoma, when our parents met in high school.

When World War I began, many fathers of the future *Arizona* bandsmen joined up and went overseas to fight. While our future dad was fighting in France, our future mother attended Oklahoma Agricultural and Mechanical College in Stillwater, Oklahoma, and began teaching school in rural Oklahoma.

The boys who would comprise *Arizona*'s last band were born into a world of hope and prosperity. The war was over—their fathers had good jobs—life was good.

Certainly, those were the days of naive contentment.

Their good life ended with the financial collapse of 1929.

With no laws to protect people's money, the banks simply locked their doors one day and told their depositors, "Too bad. Better luck next time."

One day a man was financially solvent—the next day he was a pauper.

All the abrupt changes in our lives scarred the citizens of the United States forever. Many people never put money in banks again—the old fruit jar under the house was safer. It had the merit of always being there when you needed it.

Even after World War II began and the employment picture improved, people who had been caught in that financial ruin were seldom able to spend money, even on things they needed. We always teased them and called them "tight," but we could certainly understand their insecurity about money.

Until the end of the twenties, my brother and the other members of *Arizona*'s last band spent their childhoods in peace, enjoying a happy, carefree life. Their families had all the necessities of life and even some of the luxuries.

But now they entered the thirties, and their families were forced to exist under unrelenting depression.

All the people of our nation were to spend the next ten years in a hand-to-mouth lifestyle. There were no jobs to be had, or if a person did find work, the pay was so minimal as to keep him eternally in debt for the necessities of life.

The boys who would become *Arizona*'s last bandsmen now set out on their relentless marches toward immortality.

As the thirties began, Fred Kinney had already been a Navy musician for four years and his future band members, ranging in age from five to fifteen years, started their musical educations.

The families of the boys, adjusting to their lower financial circumstances, were finding they really could survive with no luxuries at all!

They were strong, loving families who, by providing adequate food, clothing and shelter, nurtured their children's bodies. And by teaching them strong moral values, they nurtured their souls.

We children of the depression do not remember much "hard times" talk as we were growing up. Everyone was in the same situation, and we seemed to accept our poverty with little discussion.

Our "adequate clothing" did not include a separate pair of one-hundred-dollar shoes for each activity. We had one pair of shoes for school, one smelly pair of tennis shoes for gym, and one pair of shoes for Sunday.

The girls' clothing did not bear the logo of big-name designers. The "big-name designer" for most of us was our mother, who made all our clothes on her treadle sewing machine.

Our "adequate food" was simple, good, and nourishing. With no frozen or convenience foods, we ate fruits and vegetables when they were in season, and we canned the surplus for later. Peeling and preparing the food for canning was a time-consuming chore in which the whole family participated.

If our meals were a little heavy on beans, fried potatoes, and corn bread, we did not mind. The family ate together and talked of the day's happenings. We did not try to see how boring we could make our mealtimes with long discussions about the latest "health food" fad. Our mothers fried everything—we ate it—and that was that.

It was before food became our bitter enemy. We ate everything we wanted, and never did we feel guilty over some bite of delicious cooking.

We may have felt guilty over some things, but certainly our list of sins did not include eating good wholesome food. We were just grateful that the Lord had provided the food in the first place—never mind what it would do to our cholesterol. As a matter of fact, we had never heard of cholesterol, so it was of no concern to us.

The children of the depression were able to find pleasure and joy in the simple things.

We were all good walkers. With no public transportation in our small town, and with no automobile available to us, we always had the choice of walking or staying home.

Clyde and I started taking music lessons in the early thirties. I began on the piano and Clyde began on the violin and harmonica. Probably because the harmonica was inexpensive, lessons on that instrument were given with no charge in our public schools.

Will Rogers was an honored member of our family—not that we were kin to him or that we had even met him, but he was an Oklahoma boy who had made good, and we all loved him. Clyde started a scrapbook of the "Will Rogers' Sayings" which appeared in our newspaper each day. I still have that scrapbook.

In 1935, when I heard on the radio at my friend's house that Will Rogers and Wiley Post had just died in an airplane crash, I ran all the way home to tell my parents and Clyde. We were all stunned. Six years later, I was to repeat that run home when, as I sat in another friend's home, I heard on the radio the news of the attack on Pearl Harbor.

It was also in 1935 that our neighbor gave us a black-and-tan terrier pup. He was so tiny that we named him Dinky.

Dinky loved us all, but Clyde was his favorite person in the whole world. Those two were constant companions until Clyde left for the Navy.

When we each reached the age of eleven, Clyde and I began taking lessons on other musical instruments. In addition to the piano, I played the clarinet and string bass. Clyde, in addition to the violin and harmonica, played cornet, French horn, and baritone.

Music was our whole life. Our days literally began and ended with music. Mother played the piano and Dad played violin, the musical saw, the broomstick violin, etc. Grandpa Williams, Dad, and Clyde were all very good on the harmonica and often played together.

With Clyde and I practicing after school on all those instruments, conflicts with time schedules were inevitable. Once, when he and I were busily playing violin and piano, respectively, with each of us playing a different tune, our mother came from the kitchen to tell us to quit fighting. We laughed as we told her we were not fighting—we simply had a limited time to practice and had to do it at the same time. Through necessity, we both developed a keen sense of concentration.

There are few activities which, then or now, take more advantage of students than does the music field. A young person is expected to buy an expensive musical instrument, pay for private lessons on that instrument for years, and give up all his spare time to practice on that instrument, all for the honor of serving in the high school band and orchestra.

Few music courses were allowed during school hours. Any hint of musical notes drifting down the halls brought bitter complaints from the teachers of "more important" subjects. Consequently, marching band and concert band rehearsals were held for an hour before school began, and orchestra rehearsals for an hour after school ended for the day. Since we had to walk to and from school, it made a very long day for us.

So much time spent with the band and orchestra had the result of limiting our school friends to musicians. We were not able to participate in any school activities except music, so we did not really know the other students in the school.

The band's first duty when school began in September was to prepare for our school's football games. When the game was in town, we performed marching shows at halftime, perfecting our marching routines early in the morning on the streets of Okmulgee.

We loved the football games. We were allowed to go the games without charge (one of the very few privileges we had as musicians), and in the long Indian summers of Oklahoma, the Friday evenings were delightful. It was always a thrill to sit in our colorful red uniforms, watching the game and playing our "On Okmulgee" pep song. I thought for many years that the University of Wisconsin had stolen that march from us!

In the winter, however, those football games were not so pleasant. Under our bright red uniforms, we put on all the long underwear, heavy socks, and sweaters we could find. When we got to the stadium, we built a huge bonfire at the end of the football field and huddled around it during the game.

When it was time to perform at halftime, we reluctantly tore ourselves from the warm fire, formed up, and marched smartly up and down the field, playing our familiar marches. Only, due to all the clothes we wore under our uniforms, we did not so much march smartly down the field as we waddled along in time to the music. And since we all wore gloves, our marches were no longer very familiar. The gloves forced the clarinet and saxophone players to cover not only the appropriate keys, but also a few on each side of them, making some very strange sounds. But at that, the reed sections were more fortunate than were the brass sections. All the saliva blown into those instruments immediately froze in the valves, which would then not budge. The discordant noise coming from our band as we marched down the field would have been very hard for the few remaining spectators to take, had they not been so bundled up that they could no longer hear very well anyway.

When the football team played out of town, the band was transported in cars driven by the parents of the musicians.

In addition to the halftime shows at the football games, either the band or the orchestra always played for the school vocal concerts, the dramas, and other school activities throughout the school year.

We loved to march in parades. There was the excitement of colorful uniforms, snappy music, and cheering spectators lining the streets.

Usually, our parades were led by colorful riders on beautiful horses. The riders were dressed in their best Western clothes, and the horses sported flashy silver ornaments. Living as we did in rodeo country, the horses and riders were very popular.

Unfortunately, the band's position behind the horses created a distinct marching hazard. We were forced to watch our music, our director, and our feet at the same time, not an easy task. Any indiscretion by the horses ahead caused us to veer suddenly, even though we were not allowed to break ranks nor get out of line.

We always played "The Pilot" march during each parade, hoping the horses would take the hint and "Pile it" next to the curb!

We worked very hard all year on the selections we were to play at the high school competitions, held in the spring. The contests were held at various colleges in the state, usually on Saturday and Sunday. Transportation was arranged for us, and we spent the night in the homes of citizens who had volunteered to keep us. We looked forward to the contests, because we had friends all over our part of the state—band members we had met when our football teams played against each other.

Our band was well-known in the State of Oklahoma and we always won top awards, both for the band and for small groups and soloists. Clyde played in brass ensembles and as a soloist, winning many awards. I often played the piano accompaniment for various groups and for soloists.

One of the favorite songs which Clyde and I played together for our own amusement was "Harbor Lights," he on the violin and I on piano. We played that song so often that the words are firmly planted in my mind. Unfortunately, the song has become popular again in recent years, and whenever it is played on the radio, I think again of my brother. It is another example of the prophesy we did not understand until a few years later.

About that time, all members of our family were given nicknames. I was struggling with the required foreign language and about the only thing I learned from my two years of Latin, except for "All Gaul is divided into three parts," or words to that effect, were the words for "mother" and "father." Clyde and I started calling our parents "Mater" and "Pater," and soon shortened it to "Mate" and "Pate."

Friends who were always at our home started calling me "Molly," taken from the "Fibber McGee and Molly" radio show, and I have remained "Molly" to this day.

Clyde was given the name "Proke" by his friends, for reasons which were never explained to me. He was called that until his death, and I called him "Toke" and "Tokie." I still find it difficult to call him "Clyde."

Our home was always open to our friends, and there were usually several of them present—Reginald Carter, Vernon Carter, Frank Gross, Dick Lucas, Billy Wingate, and Jesse Winn all spent a lot of time at our house. I loved to dance, and I taught all the boys to dance. We practiced our music together—we danced—we played cards—we laughed. Years later I often told my children that we "Depression Children" had more fun with no money when we were young than they did with all their financial advantages.

Our small-town life was simple. We had no television, so there was none of the mindless sitting before the set each day, waiting for the commercials so we could speak.

Instead of television, we had our radio programs. We especially enjoyed the great comedy programs in the evenings—"Jack Benny," "Amos 'n Andy," "George Burns and Gracie Allen," "Fibber McGee and Molly," "Edgar Bergen and Charlie McCarthy," "Lum and Abner," and others.

We did not often listen to the afternoon stories, such as "Stella Dallas" and "One Man's Family." Then, as now, the daytime stories were called "soap operas." Running for fifteen or thirty minutes, the plot of the radio programs was scattered among the commercials, averaging about half plot and half commercials.[1]

By far the favorite programs for Clyde and I were "Inner Sanctum" and Lamont Cranston in "The Shadow." We would turn out the lights and sit in the dark, terrified as the door creaked open at the beginning of "Inner Sanctum." Even worse was the spooky voice which asked, "Who knows what evil lurks in the minds of men? THE SHADOW KNOWS!"

Never can visual movies equal the fright of radio programs, as our imaginations vividly filled in the details.

Late at night, we would listen to the radio broadcasts of the big-name orchestras coming from ballrooms in the large cities and picture the well-dressed couples dancing to the music. It all seemed so far removed from "Bob Wills and His Texas Playboys."

But there were advantages to our small-town life.

We were never uneasy or frightened as we walked all over town. It was even safe for girls to walk downtown late at night, attend the midnight moving picture show, and walk back home.

Our school officials ran a tight ship. We were expected to respect our teachers, as well as our parents.

Female teachers were not allowed to teach after they married. It would take World War II to change that rule.

There was no vandalism for the sake of destroying other's property. Students did not pack guns or knives to school. Any disagreement between students was settled with fists, one on one, over at the water tower after school.

We had no graffiti—the closest we came to that was "Sam Loves Susie" carved on some tree.

We lived in the middle of the "Bible Belt." Our churches taught very strict morals. They also taught us bigotry and prejudice, and it would be many years before we overcame their teachings.

I am aware that the present-day youth cannot fathom people like us. In an age when it is common to discuss on television such subjects as constipation, diarrhea, vaginal yeast infection, and any and all sexual topics, our total innocence, bordering on ignorance, must seem strange indeed.

The most risque we ever became was when we sang the following words to the tune of Dvorak's "Humoreske":

> *Passengers will please refrain*
> *From flushing toilets on the train*
> *When the train is moving, we thank you.*
> *When the train is in the station*
> *We encourage constipation,*
> *When the train is moving*
> *So may you!*

I never hear "Humoreske" performed without smiling as I think of our group of friends and how funny we thought we were. In fact, we were funny, and we all laughed a lot. We had a great innocence and joy of life that is denied young people today.

CHAPTER 3

1940—The Year of Decision

The younger boys of *Arizona*'s last band graduated from high school in May 1940. For Oran Brabbzson, Ralph Burdette, Harry Chernucha, Gerald Cox, Bernard Hughes, Bill McCary, Alex Nadel, Bobby Shaw, and Clyde Williams, it was a bittersweet time. Offsetting the excitement of finally escaping from school was the knowledge that they would probably not be living in their hometowns among their families and their best friends much longer.

It was time to make an important decision.

The older boys had already been struggling with their decision for several years. Wayne Bandy had been looking unsuccessfully for employment; Frank Floege and Neal Radford had been working on farms; Curt Haas and Bill Moorhouse had formed their own dance bands; Wendell Hurley, Emmett Lynch, Harvey Sanderson, and Ernest Whitson had been working; and Jack Scruggs and Charles White had entered college.

It was an uneasy time for our nation. Hitler had been swallowing up countries in Europe for several years now, and many people thought we would soon be at war.

Judging from the ongoing battle between Congress and President Franklin D. Roosevelt, it seemed inevitable that a universal military training bill would soon be passed. Although the youngest draft age most often mentioned was twenty-one, more and more boys were enlisting. Their decision was made easier by the lack of jobs all over the country.

For most of the Class of '40, it was obvious that, for them, there would be no American Dream of graduating from high school, attending the college of their choice, finding gainful employment, marrying well, and living happily ever after.

One by one, each of the future *Arizona* bandsmen made his fatal decision. Once set into motion, nothing could avert his fate. From then on, everything conspired to insure that each boy would be in the right place at the right time to take his place in history.

In Okmulgee, Pate and Clyde had been discussing Clyde's future for months.

Having served in the U.S. Army in France, with the daily grind of cooties, dysentery, poison water, poison gas, and filth, Pate was determined that his son would have it better. Since he worked at the post office, he was able to talk at length with the recruiting officers of the Army, Navy, and Marines.

He and Clyde finally decided that my brother's best option would be to join the United States Navy School of Music. That would require a six-year enlistment, but the first two years would be spent at the school, attending what would amount to a conservatory of music. When they considered that the six-year enlistment would be only two years longer than a four-year college education, it didn't sound so long.

They forgot to take into account the complete lack of personal freedom attached to that six-year enlistment.

So Clyde wrote to the Navy to request an application form for its School of Music.

We soon found that the requirements for joining the U.S. Navy School of Music in 1940 did not leave much to chance. The brochure read:

Information Regarding Enlistment and Application for The United States Navy School of Music

Applicants for enlistment for the U.S. Navy School of Music must be:
    Native-born or fully naturalized citizens of the United States.
    Not less than 18 years of age when enlisted.
    Under 25 years of age when enlisted.
    Of good character.

Mentally qualified.

Not less that 63 inches in height.

Of proportionate weight to age and height.

Graduate of high school, or have an equivalent education.

Unmarried, and remain so during course of instruction.

They must also:

Enlist in the United States Navy for a period of six years.

Pass a rigid physical examination.

Qualify in a General Classification Test.

Furnish authentic evidence of age.

Secure written consent of parent or guardian if under 21 years of age.

Furnish list of former employers, or school teachers, or references from at least two responsible persons.

Have no police record (except minor infractions not involving moral turpitude).

Have no juvenile court, reform school, or prison record.

Pass satisfactorily a musical examination at the U.S. Navy School of Music on the following subjects:

(a)   Sight-reading.

(b)   Technic.

(c)   Tone.

(d)   Attack.

(e)   Rhythm.

(f)   Phrasing.

(g)   Memory.

All enlistments are made for general service. No promise or assurance can be given an applicant that he will be assigned to any particular detail or duty after completion of course.

The length of the course is two years. Upon completion of this period of instruction, a student is graduated from the school, and transferred as a member of a twenty-piece organization to a ship in the United States Fleet.

Subjects taught at the U.S. Navy School of Music consist of the following: Solfege (ear training), Harmony, Theory, Ensemble, Private Instruction on Major and Minor Instruments, and Band, Orchestra and Dance Orchestra Training."[1]

The Navy went on to explain the rate of pay and details regarding retirement and enclosed an application to be returned to the School of Music.

Clyde and I laughed hysterically when we read those requirements. We decided that Jesus Christ Himself would not have been eligible to join that exalted school!

All during the year of 1940, the future *Arizona* bandsmen sent to Washington for the U.S. Navy School of Music information sheet. None of the boys had any trouble qualifying—they were all above-average in physical and mental attributes.

One by one they made their decisions—they sent in their applications—they settled down to wait.

My brother's last year of high school was a very happy time for him. He had finished all the required subjects for graduation, so his workload at school was light. As usual, he spent most of his time with music.

Having been baton twirler for several years, Clyde was now the head drum major for the school band. He was playing solos in concerts and contests, as well as playing in brass sextets and other ensembles, often winning first place at the music contests. He was first-chair cornetist in our school band, and he played the trumpet call over the school loud speaker to signal the beginning of each day.

Clyde also played in other school bands and in the local junior college orchestra, which often played concerts on the radio.

With his sunny disposition and his keen sense of humor, Clyde was popular with his classmates. Like his hero Will Rogers, Clyde had never met a man he didn't like. He was a talented, handsome boy, six feet tall, with beautiful eyes and long eyelashes.

His personality was noted in the Will of the Class of 1939, which read "Jesse Winn leaves all his wisecracks to Clyde Williams" and "Jack Simpson wills his talkative manner to Clyde Williams."[2]

Even now, when he has been gone for more than fifty years, Clyde's school friends become tearful as they talk about him. They tell me how much they loved him and how much they have always resented his early death.

Living next door to us for the past several years had been the Carter family. Reverend W. A. Carter was an official of the Nazarene Church, and he and his wife and their six children were all good friends of ours. Their son Reginald and Clyde were especially good pals and spent much time together, often double-dating.

Down the street a block was another Carter family. Reverend W. M. Carter was also a Nazarene minister and was a brother of our next-door neighbor. He and his wife's son Vernon was also a good friend of Clyde's.

In May, after a year of music and fun, Clyde graduated with honors, receiving special recognition from the State of Oklahoma for having been neither absent nor tardy during his entire school years. He certainly earned those awards, as I had seen him get up and go to school when he was very ill with tonsillitis. Our parents finally had his tonsils removed, and he was in very good health after that.

Clyde was also awarded a letter in Fine Arts for meritorious achievement in Instrumental Music, listing Drum Major and Cornet Trio. This award was signed by Lewis K. Moffatt, Director, and Guy B. Blakey, Principal.

Our high school newspaper, the *Okmulgee Torchlight*, printed the Senior Class Prophecy:

> *Clyde Williams, who was better known as "Proke" when he blew those awful tones on his trumpet every morning at the start of school, is now leader of the most "sought after band" in the nation. His motto is "Swing and Slide with Happy Clyde."* [3]

None of us can read that prophecy, printed eighteen months before Clyde's death, without a shudder.

My brother did indeed become a member of a very famous band. But at what a price!

CHAPTER 4

Enlistment

When my brother graduated from high school in May 1940, he would not be eighteen years old and eligible for enlistment in the U.S. Navy for four more months. He spent the month of June gathering up the requirements for his application to the U.S. Navy School of Music.

He requested a copy of his birth certificate from the State of Oklahoma. He obtained letters of recommendation from Lewis K. Moffatt, Okmulgee High School Band Director; from Merrill McMillan, Head of the Music Department of Okmulgee Junior College; and from Guy B. Blakey, Principal of Okmulgee High School.

Our dad prepared a notarized consent for Clyde to join the Navy, since it would be a long time before he was twenty-one years old. Fortunately, we did not know just how long it would be.

By the end of June his papers were ready and Clyde sent all the material to the U.S. Navy School of Music in Washington, D.C.

We crossed our fingers.

The sound of war drums was becoming louder and louder, but most of us ignored it. I do not recall any uneasiness about Clyde's future. Apparently we all believed our country was invincible and nothing could harm us.

On June 18, 1940, President Roosevelt announced to the country that a bill for Universal Government Service for all young men and women would soon be introduced.[1] And on June 22, a Gallup Poll revealed that 67 percent of Americans favored that enforced military training.[2]

In July, Congress finally approved the funds for a two-ocean Navy, and more and more political leaders were calling for an increase in military training.[3]

In July, after a month of fun, Clyde set off on his first military experience.

With the idea of getting another letter of recommendation and to maintain his skill on the cornet, Clyde had enlisted in the Citizens' Military Training Camp, asking for duty in the band.

The Citizens' Military Training Camp, or C.M.T.C., was a program set up by our government to help prepare our young men for war. Under the auspices of the War Department, the C.M.T.C. offered one month of intensive military training. The instructors were members of the U.S. Army, and the training camps were held at various U.S. Army posts.

Due to the youth of the recruits, the parents or guardians were notified when their sons arrived at the camp, and the boys' meager pay was sent directly to their parents.

Clyde was ordered to report to Fort Sill in Lawton, Oklahoma, early in July. Shortly after, we received a postcard informing us that Clyde had arrived safely and giving us his address.[4]

Clyde was indeed assigned to the band and Pate shipped his cornet to him. An article in our newspaper, the *Okmulgee Daily Times*, dated July 22, listed Clyde and Roy Reed as members of the C.M.T.C. Band, noting that Clyde was solo cornetist.[5] Roy was a friend of ours from the Okmulgee band.

Shortly after Clyde arrived at Fort Sill, he received a letter from Lieutenant Charles Benter, Officer in Charge of the U.S. Navy School of Music, dated July 11, 1940, informing him that he had received a grade of "A," or "Excellent," on his application to the school. His name would be entered on the list for the November class and he would be notified of the time and place for his physical.[6]

The "Information Regarding Enlistment" had already made it clear that any transportation involved in reporting to our district's main recruiting station and for returning home in the event the applicant failed to meet the enlistment standards was to be paid by the applicant.[7]

Since our district station was in Dallas, Clyde decided to hitch-hike on down to Texas after his month at Fort Sill was completed. While waiting for the summons for his physical examination, he could visit our kinfolks and tell them all good-bye.

With the suspense about his acceptance to the School of Music over, Clyde threw himself into Army life with gusto. He wrote that Fort Sill had dances at the post with lots of boys to dance with and asked me to come visit.

I answered that I certainly would like to, since practically every male in Okmulgee was leaving for some branch of the service. But, needless to say, with no job, no money, and no car, I never did make it to one of those dances.

We had already been officially invited to Fort Sill by C.M.T.C. officers, but we knew our ancient automobile was not reliable enough to travel that far. Since none of us was brave enough to hitchhike as Clyde did, we were never able to go.

Clyde's infrequent letters told of young, carefree boys away from home for the first time, enjoying life to the fullest.

He and a friend got into a water fight on the rifle range and were caught. They were both given special duty cleaning machine guns, but since Clyde had to practice with the band, he escaped his punishment.

That was the beginning. More than fifty years later, former sailors are still telling me how the U.S. Navy musicians were a pampered, privileged group of boys. These remarks stem from total ignorance of the duties of military bandsmen.

A bandmaster, charged with getting the most music he can from his group of musicians, must have all his bandsmen present for all rehearsals. If that means getting them excused from other duties, so be it.

But other sailors, slaving over those special duties, look over at the musicians blowing away on their instruments and turn green with envy. Not willing to spend the time nor money necessary to obtain a musical education, they consider a musician to be slacking when he is, in fact, working very hard at his craft.

The C.M.T.C. recruits at Fort Sill were given basic military training. While there, Clyde earned several sharpshooter medals. We were not surprised, as he and I were both excellent marksmen. We had always spent much time in our back yard, shooting our .22 rifle at milk bottle caps lined up on an old coal pile.

The boys were awakened at six o'clock each morning and herded through long days of calisthenics, marching, shooting guns, caring for guns, and war games. The hope of the officers was that the recruits would be so exhausted they would fall into bed at ten o'clock and drop off to sleep immediately.

But to nobody's surprise, the young boys discovered the young daughters of the officers living at the Fort and soon borrowed, not only the daughters, but also the cars of their officers.

To circumvent the ten o'clock lights-out, Clyde and his tent-mates used the time-honored "beat the bed-check" routine. He wrote in August:

> *Last Saturday night, I had a date with an officer's daughter. We are supposed to be in bed at ten o'clock, and it was after midnight when I got in the tent. In our tent, there are five cots and I sleep next to the door. Before bed check, the boy who sleeps in the middle of the tent traded places with me. His cot is partly covered by the tent center post, and he stuffed the bed so that it looked like someone was in it. When I came home, I slipped in the back way and no one knew the difference.*

After a big rain, one of Clyde's tent-mates attempted to straighten out their tent, and the whole thing fell down right into the mud. Naturally, the boys thought that was hilarious.

One has to feel sorry for those Army officers, who certainly earned their pay that summer. Trying to turn happy-go-lucky boys into killers cannot be an easy job.

Back home, Pate took a dim view of Clyde's activities. Normally fun-loving himself, he was consumed with anxiety about Clyde's entry into the School of Music and wrote him that he must behave himself! He reminded him that the most urgent thing right now was to get a good recommendation from the C.M.T.C. band director.

Although there was always something exciting happening at camp, Clyde thought it still seemed to be a dull life. He never did complain about the heat, but I know he must have suffered, spending a month outdoors in Oklahoma's summer. I wrote him how hot it was in Okmulgee and asked if he was doing all right in the heat there, but he did not mention it. We were not accustomed to air conditioning then, so it was not quite so hard on us as it would be now, when we are all so much softer.

In each letter, Clyde asked about his pet chicken and our beloved dog Dinky.

At a Divine Worship Service at the Stadium at Fort Sill on August 4, the C.M.T.C. band, under the direction of Sergeant Vito Alfredo, played several numbers.[8] The band also played a concert, which was carried on the Columbia Radio Broadcasting Station, but we couldn't find the correct station on our radio.

Clyde's enlistment in the C.M.T.C. was completed on August 7, and after shipping his cornet home, he hitchhiked to Texas to visit our mother's family.

The two weeks he spent in Texas were a good vacation for him. Not only was he with kin whom he loved and who dearly loved him, but he had finally escaped from his one-month Army career. On the envelope of the first letter he wrote us, next to the return address of "Lampasas, Texas," he wrote "AT LAST" in big letters. We knew then how very glad he was to be a civilian again.

But in the body of the same letter, after he had cleaned up and rested, he wrote: "During camp, the life seemed hard and tough, but I can see now what a good time I had."

Ah, how we tend to gloss over the bad memories and to retain only the good!

While Clyde was still at Fort Sill, our dad sent him a three-cent stamp, asking that he write him [Pate] a letter of his very own. Not long after this, I received a letter addressed to "Molly Williams," and shining on the corner of the envelope was Pate's stamp, which he recognized from some paper clip marks on it. Pate was devastated!

To think that Clyde would use the stamp he had sent him to write to someone else!

I promptly wrote Clyde that he was now really in trouble, relating to him the emergency of the misused stamp. Shortly from Lampasas came a letter addressed to "Pate Williams," in which Clyde wrote:

> *TO PATE AND ONLY TO PATE:*
>
> *Dearest, sweetest, most heartbroken, saddened, down in the dumps, Father: Even now as I write this letter, my eyes fill with tears as I realize that I have mistreated you to the utmost by not writing to you. I used your stamp to write to Molly, but I bought a brand new one just for you.*

It is obvious that we were still lighthearted and happy. If any of us had any suspicion of trouble to come, he must have shoved it back into his subconscious mind.

And there was trouble. Not only were our boys in Okmulgee all leaving for some branch of the service, some of them were already dying. In the early forties, there were many fatalities at the training camps, as a nation not ready for war tried to use antique equipment to teach her innocent boys the killing game.

In August 1940, John (Jack) Hadley Houchin, the brother of my friend Lawrence, died in an Air Corps training accident, and his body was brought back to Okmulgee for burial. The Air Corps sent Jack's buddy, Pat Collins, to accompany the body and to attend the funeral. The Houchins invited Pat to stay at their home, and at Lawrence's request, I dated Pat while he was in Okmulgee. He returned several times from his Air Corps training field in Illinois to see me, before he was transferred overseas.

Finally the letter, dated August 15, arrived from the U.S. Navy Recruiting Station in Dallas, informing Clyde that he was to report to them at nine o'clock Monday morning, August 19, for his physical and mental examination. Again, the Navy made it perfectly clear that travel to and from Dallas was to be at his own expense.[9]

We sent word to Clyde and he hitchhiked on up to Dallas to stay with our Aunt Hazel. He reported to the Recruiting Station, as ordered, and was given his physical and other tests.

And he was rejected!

Because he was a few pounds underweight, the Navy would not accept him. In this time of worship of the human body, when we embrace every fad diet that comes along, it is hard to imagine such a flap over a few pounds underweight.

A very dejected Clyde came back to Okmulgee. He had been gone for seven weeks, and we were so glad to see him, but we were all devastated about his bad news. We did not know that, since the School of Music accepted only forty new musicians a year, it was common to be rejected for some physical reason. Many of the students had to make several attempts to enlist before finally being accepted.[10]

However, Pate was not a person to give up easily. He wrote Congressman Jack Nichols from Henryetta, asking if there was anything Clyde could do to appeal the Navy's decision.

Congressman Nichols sent an inquiry to Rear Admiral Chester W. Nimitz, Chief of the Navigation Bureau for the Navy Department, which handled personnel problems. Admiral Nimitz answered that the Navy had no objection to Clyde's presenting himself for reexamination at the Navy Recruiting Station in Dallas.[11]

Clyde had already done that, reporting to Dallas October 9 to take his second physical, but again he was underweight. As was common then, the recruiting officer sent Clyde out to eat all the bananas and drink all the milk he could hold, and to hurry back to be weighed again.

All was in vain. Clyde was still two pounds underweight and one and one-half inches under the required chest measurement. He was rejected for the second time.

Unfortunately for us, his case was appealed to the Bureau of Medicine and Surgery, and the powers that be decided his slight disqualifications could be waived.

Their faith was justified. My skinny brother died just as bravely as did his plumper shipmates. And somewhere there is a cornet player who lost his chance to attend the U.S. Navy School of Music, but who lived to tell about it.

And so at last, Clyde's name was placed on the waiting list for entrance to the U.S. Navy School of Music. He was notified, however, that now the quota for cornet players for the class convening on November 1 had been filled.[12]

After his October 9 physical in Dallas, Clyde again hitchhiked back to Okmulgee. With our present crime rate, it makes one shudder to think of all the hitchhiking Clyde did. It was a common practice then, however, with only a slight chance of mishap. Before he moved to Washington, D.C., he always thoroughly enjoyed hitchhiking. "It sure is lots of fun rambling around riding with all classes of people and seeing the sights," he wrote from Texas.

Clyde had tried to find work in Okmulgee and in Dallas but had discovered there were no jobs anywhere. Now that he finally knew he would go to Washington soon, he relaxed and spent his last two months at home, visiting friends and having fun.

Reginald Carter, a year younger than Clyde, was now a senior in high school, and he and Clyde attended all the football games and school functions. Clyde also kept tabs on the band and orchestra and his many friends.

Always interested in art and drawing, Clyde now had time for his hobbies. He spent many hours patiently burning out lines and shadows on pieces of wood with his wood-burning iron, creating many beautiful pieces.

I had finally been employed in September as bookkeeper at a general clothing store, where I worked six days a week for seven dollars a week. I soon fell into a pattern of working every day and dancing nearly every night.

Although my brother and I had many mutual friends, we never did double-date. But when we got home from our dates, we would sit in the kitchen late at night, eating and talking.

For entertainment, the young people of Okmulgee went to the show (movies) or went dancing. We had several honky-tonks in Okmulgee, all featuring good clean fun. The music was provided by juke boxes, so even though we lived in a small town, away from the bright lights, we were very familiar with the big bands. Our very favorite band leader was Glenn Miller.

We always dated in groups, as most of us did not have cars. By sharing gasoline expense, the boys were able to date more often.

A date required that the boy have at least fifteen cents cash. That paid for one nickel soft drink for him and one for his date, with one nickel left over to put into the juke box. It was considered tacky to dance all evening on other boys' nickels, without contributing your share.

No matter how hot the evening in those non-air conditioned clubs, and no matter how thirsty we became, we girls knew the one soft drink was our limit!

And we did get very thirsty. Jitterbugging in the hot Oklahoma summer evenings required a lot of stamina and energy.

Oklahoma had always been a dry state, so no alcoholic beverages were served at our honky-tonks. If a person wanted to buy hard liquor, he must order it by telephone, and it would soon be delivered to his door by our local bootlegger.

We were taught by our churches that everything was a sin. It was sinful to dance, smoke, drink liquor, have sex, or go to the moving picture show. Consequently, most of our friends did not drink or smoke. To be perfectly honest, that was probably due as much to our depressed financial situation as to our morals.

Clyde and Reginald had many girlfriends in various Oklahoma towns whom they had met on band trips. They went to visit them often, whenever Reginald or his cousin Vernon could get their dad's car.

Those girls were appalled that Clyde would join the Navy and be gone for six whole years! One girl complained that she would even have false teeth by the time he returned from the Navy.

Clyde's special girl, Joan Watson, was living in Okmulgee when they first met, but she now lived in Shawnee, Oklahoma. He always stopped to see her on his way to and from Dallas, and he often hitchhiked to Shawnee to see her. Joan came to Okmulgee on November 20 to visit him.

Because now, all too fast, his last three months at home had sped by and it was November 21—Thanksgiving Day. Clyde had received his letter from the School of Music, stating he had been accepted into the December class, so we all knew he would be leaving on Saturday, November 23.

All the Williams clan met at our grandparents home in Henryetta, as usual, for Thanksgiving. There were twenty-one family members present that year. We always laughed and joked at those gatherings and everyone was happy to be together.

We missed our cousin, Richard Newton Conway, Jr., who had moved to California. Newt, Clyde, and Reginald were all good friends.

And then it was Saturday—time to tell my brother good-bye.

All over our country, in the year of 1940, that scene was being repeated, as family and friends bid their loved ones "God Speed."

For far too many of us, it would be our final farewell.

CHAPTER 5

Boot Camp and Leave

It was raining on Saturday, November 23, 1940, when my brother left home to hitchhike once again to Dallas to report for duty in the U.S. Navy. Fortunately, he did not need to carry much luggage, as he had been told that all his civilian clothes must be shipped back home when he reached Norfolk. Of course, he took his most precious possession, his cornet.

Since we were all working that day, our good neighbor, Mrs. Carter, took him to a filling station on the south edge of town, where he caught a ride immediately to Shawnee. After telling Joan Watson good-bye, he left Calvin, Oklahoma, at 6:00 P.M., catching a ride straight through to Dallas. He arrived at one o'clock Sunday morning and stayed with our Aunt Hazel until time to report to the U.S. Navy Recruiting Station on Monday morning, November 25.

There Clyde was given transportation and subsistence from Dallas to Washington, D.C., courtesy of our government. Should he fail his musical test at the U.S. Navy School of Music, the government would furnish his transportation back home.[1]

Clyde was pretty impressed with his first trip by Pullman. He thought the prices in the diner were higher than during the war. He was, of course, referring to World War I, as our dad had told us about diner prices during that time. Certainly Clyde and I had never eaten in a railroad dining car!

I know very well his feelings as he got off that train and walked through the huge station out onto the streets of Washington, as I was to take that same walk fourteen months later. He was the usual small-town tourist who had never traveled very far from home, staring at buildings which were even larger than the ones in Tulsa!

The first thing he noticed was how much dirtier Washington was than either Tulsa or Dallas. Washington was more than one hundred years older than any town in Oklahoma, and the difference was immediately apparent to us.

Clyde made his way to the Washington Navy Yard and reported to the Navy Recruiting Station on November 27, 1940, his official date of entry into the Navy.[2] They fed him, gave him a bed in the barracks, and instructed him to appear at the School of Music the next morning for his musical test.

There he met Boatswain's Mate James M. Thurmond, USN.

Recently I asked Dr. Thurmond if he realized how very terrified those new recruits were. He replied that it was just the Navy way.[3]

The "Navy way" was for a small-town boy, conspicuous in his civilian clothes, to be told to "SIT." Boatswain Thurmond then placed a sheet of music on a stand before his victim and ordered him to "PLAY."

It was the most important tryout in the recruit's life!

First-chair musicians in high school soon become accustomed to competition, since any band member at any time can challenge him for the first-chair position.

But that! On that tryout hinged the recruit's whole career. Not to pass the test meant he must either go back home or enter the Navy as a regular seaman.[4]

But after Thurmond tested Clyde for sight-reading, ability, dexterity, etc., he pronounced him eligible for the School of Music.

We soon received a postcard from Clyde, dated November 28, telling us that he had passed his musical test and was ready to sail for some place in West Virginia. Our grasp of geography was a little weak in those days. We did not travel much and with no television, our world was pretty much restricted to the area around us. Clyde was to capitalize on that lack of knowledge later, when he told the boys at the school about the wild Indians in Oklahoma.

Apparently someone straightened him out about the West Virginia part, as he added, "P.S. I sail at six o'clock to Norfolk, Virginia."

Clyde had seen Henry Brown that morning and reported he was looking fine. Luther Henry Brown was a friend of ours from the Okmulgee band who had also graduated from high school in May. Not having the problem of underweight that Clyde did, Henry had enlisted in the Navy a few months earlier and was already taking his training at the school.

Traveling by boat on the "District of Columbia Steamboat Company," Clyde reported to the U.S. Naval Training Station in Norfolk to begin his transition from civilian to sailor. The period at the Training Station is called boot camp, and a new recruit is called a boot. However, most sailors call boot camp "Hell on Earth."

There, boys who had been raised to believe they were as good as anyone else, or perhaps better, were soon disabused of that myth.

Boot camp was not set up for the enjoyment of the new recruits. Its main purpose was to wean young boys away from their mommies. To accomplish that, the Navy immediately stripped the recruit of all ties with civilian life.

First, he was required to buy a full set of sailor clothes, from underwear to uniforms, and to ship his civilian clothes home. The Navy did allow the recruit to pay for his new clothes in monthly payments. Since the new sailors were usually flat broke, that concession was given more from necessity than from compassion.

Next, in order to depersonalize the new boots, last names only were used, usually barked out in loud tones. Their days were filled with physical exercises and with instruction. And right away came the vaccinations, to add real illness to the boys' homesickness.

To offset the unpleasantness, the boys made new friends quickly and helped each other, in a "misery loves company" syndrome.

As usual, Clyde did not complain about boot camp. His keen sense of humor always carried him through difficult times. At least he was able to take his training in Norfolk in December, which is not to be compared with winter at the U.S. Naval Training Station in Great Lakes, Illinois.

Recruits at Great Lakes never forgot the frigid wind blowing over the lake. Nor did they ever forget being rousted out early in the morning to shovel snow off the Admirals' sidewalks.[5]

An enlisted man is soon taught humility.

Early in December, we received word from the Navy: "Your son has reported on this station and is undergoing training and instruction in the duties of the Naval Service." We also received a schedule, showing Clyde was to receive five weeks' training, then would be granted a nine-day leave.[6]

Clyde sent us his address in December, and wrote:

> *I am in Norfolk Training Station in Virginia. I have just been vaccinated for typhoid fever and smallpox. I passed the musical test and rode from Washington to Norfolk on a river boat. It's not going to be so bad here.*

That prompted Pate to write back with his usual father-son pep talk:

> *Don't take things too seriously. Just obey orders and you will get along fine. There will be things come up you won't like, but just make the best of it. I have never had a job yet that didn't have some disagreeable things connected with it, so just make the best of whatever comes along and things will work out OK.*
>
> *You stated that things would not be so bad there. Did you expect it to be bad?*
>
> *Be sure to toe the mark while you are in Virginia, because if you don't, you may not get to Washington as soon as you would otherwise....*
>
> *Go to church every Sunday....*

Clyde lost no time in sending his address to Joan Watson in Shawnee. It was a cheerful letter, in which he related how he was telling all those Easterners about the Indians who roamed the hills of Oklahoma.[7]

The new recruits arose at four forty-five each morning and went to bed at nine o'clock. Clyde remarked that he had to stand guard that night from eleven until one midnight. Later, when he was in Hawaii, he often mentioned one o'clock midnight in his letters. We never did use that term at home, so we did not know where it came from. We assumed it was something Naval.

Boot camp was a little redundant for the musicians. All that marching in formation was old hat for them—they had learned drilling and marching on the streets of their hometowns.

Also, for Clyde, the gunnery instruction was a repeat of the training he had received at C.M.T.C. Because of the sharpshooter medals he had earned at Fort Sill, he was soon put in charge of his platoon.[8]

Like most recruits, Clyde found boot camp pretty boring. He wrote:

> *There isn't much to do here but drill and listen to officers cussing. There are as many girls here as nudists in the North Pole. I am going to have a good time in Washington, I think. Tell everyone to write.*

Back to Norfolk went another sermon from Pate:

> *I noticed you made a remark about officers cussing. That is not a good idea. If they find out you made such remarks they probably would make it hard on you. You should never make any derogatory remarks about the officers, or anything else. You shouldn't do anything to cause them to get down on you, and you will get along better.*

Spoken like a former buck private in the U.S. Army who was very familiar with what can happen to an enlisted man if an officer takes a dislike to him!

As events transpired, that was the best advice Pate ever gave his son. Heeding that advice kept Clyde out of trouble during his short one-year hitch in the U.S. Navy.

It is obvious that Pate was having a hard time believing that Clyde was finally realizing their dream—Pate's dream, as well as Clyde's—acceptance into the U.S. Navy School of Music. With the usual father's anxiety, he was trying to warn Clyde about everything he could think of which might hinder him in his musical career with the Navy.

Pate had also been figuring the leave situation. He wrote Clyde that his commanding officer had written us that he would be entitled to nine days' leave when his training was over, and advised him:

> *There would be no use in your trying to come home, as it would take you six days to make the round trip and about forty dollars. If I were you, I wouldn't take any time off now and maybe they will give you more time next December.*

We were all more prophetic than we realized. Pate wrote that letter to his son on December 9, 1940. He was correct—the Navy did indeed give Clyde more time off in December 1941.

The families back home soon learned that most of the School of Music boys had the given name of "Guy." From boot camp until their deaths, all the *Arizona* musicians mentioned "Some of the Guys and I"—"Another Guy and I"—"A bunch of Guys from the band." After it was all over, we were so sorry that our boys did not name more of those "Guys."

Clyde sent Christmas presents to us from Norfolk and sent Joan a box of candy. It arrived at her home about ten o'clock Christmas morning. She was pleased, and thanked him.[9]

He thanked me for the box of food I had sent him for Christmas. The other School of Music "Guys" (three of them) helped him eat it.

I often sent him boxes of cookies, candy, pecan meats, etc. during the entire year he was in the Navy. I'm sure I knew at the time he was being very well fed and certainly did not need my extra treats, but there was not much we could do for him. So I kept showering him with dried-out cookies and candy, and he always bragged about them and shared them with his buddies.

We all wrote him often. Mate wrote the usual mother-things— could he use house slippers and a bathrobe, or did the other boys think that was sissy? What did he want for Christmas? Was he dressed warm enough for the cold winter, and did he have an overcoat? She had forwarded letters to him from his friends in various towns around Oklahoma—had he gotten them? Had he made any friends?

We tried to encourage him, as we knew the reputation of boot camp.

Mate wrote:

> *More people have called and stopped Pate and I and told us what a swell break you got and how glad they were you got into the Navy. The people of this town are for you and expect great things of you. It might not be so hot this month, but make the best of it, for I feel like you will be OK and have a good chance after you get into Washington.*
>
> *We have to take the bitter with the sweet.*

Like most mothers, Mate always had some adage to quote in times of stress. It would be another year before she found out just how bitter it was going to be.

I wrote long letters to "Dearest Tokie," complaining that everyone was going into the service, and telling him news of hometown people he knew. On December 10, I wrote:

> *Well, congrats! On passing your test, I mean. Believe me, I'm proud to call you my brother.*
>
> *I'm saving my money to come up there as soon as I can. I want to come up before your graduation. We're all coming up in our new car (that we don't have yet) for your graduation. So be sure to save some 'purty' boys for me.*

Since I was earning seven dollars a week and our old car would not even make it to Tulsa, that was going to take some doing, but youth is optimistic!

The East and West Coast boys were not the only ones who were a little weak in geography. I wrote Clyde that, while planning our trip to Washington, Pate said we would go slowly and see the country. Mate piped up and said, "Oh, I want to see Yellowstone Park again!" And I said I wanted to see the Grand Canyon. Pate suggested we both take a refresher course in geography.

While Clyde was in Norfolk for his training, we settled into a pattern that was to last for his entire last year—we would ask him questions, which he would ignore. We would ask him the same questions in each letter, becoming more and more firm, but he continued to the end ignoring them, while complaining that he couldn't think of anything to write. I wrote: "You write the strangest letters. Why don't you tell me some news. All about camp life, etc."

Only later did I understand how tiring boot camp is for new recruits, and how very boring the whole thing is.

Having completed his five-week boot camp in three weeks, Clyde reported on Christmas Eve to the U.S. Navy School of Music.

The menu for the Christmas 1940 dinner at the Receiving Station, U.S. Navy Yard, Washington, D. C., conveyed a message of cheer from the Commanding Officer and Officers of the Receiving Station and wished the crew and men of the Service Schools a Merry Christmas and a Happy New Year. The following menu was listed:

CHRISTMAS DINNER

* * * * * * * *

Cream of Pea Soup

Assorted Olives		Soda Crackers
	Oyster Cocktail	
	ROAST YOUNG TURKEY	
	Walnut Dressing	
Giblet Gravy		Cranberry Sauce
	Baked Pineapple Ham	
Candied Sweet Yams		Riced Potatoes
Asparagus Tips		Creamed Cauliflower
Hawaiian Salad		Sweet Dressing
Parkerhouse Rolls		Butter
	Coffee	
Hot Mince Pie	Fruit Cake	Pumpkin Pie
	Ice Cream	
Assorted Fruits	Hard Candy	Mixed Nuts
Cigars		Cigarettes[10]

All of us can remember our first Christmas away from home and can relate to Clyde's feelings. As usual, he did not complain, but there he was in a strange city, spending Christmas Eve with strangers!

His sorrow about missing his first Christmas at home was mitigated somewhat by the news that he had just arrived at the school in time to receive a fifteen-day leave.

Clyde immediately sent Pate a telegram:

> *Got fifteen days leave. Send thirty-five dollars. Can pay back in two months. Write details later. Merry Christmas. Clyde Williams.*

Since Clyde was now earning twenty-one dollars a month, and owed the Navy for all his new clothes, it would take him considerably longer than two months to repay that loan.

Pate rushed out to borrow the money and wired it to Clyde on Christmas Day. Gone now was all thought of how he should stay in Washington and maybe get more leave next December—our Proke was coming home!

That is, since his telegram only stated that he had gotten fifteen days' leave, we certainly hoped he was coming home! Pate wrote the same day, telling Clyde he had wired him the money and advising him about the new government rates on railroads of one cent per mile for servicemen, and was he coming home?

Clyde indeed meant he was coming home, and he arrived January 1, 1941, for our delayed Christmas celebration! Never did food taste so good to anyone as it did to him, when he could eat his favorite foods again and be with his family! We laughed at that Navy Christmas menu—such a lavish spread, when all the boys wanted was to share the simple fare of their families back home.

Clyde tried to see everyone he knew on his leave. He, Reginald, and Vernon Carter went out on dates every evening. Later, he and I met in the kitchen to eat and talk, just as we had done before he left.

We have photographs which we took on January 10, the day before our Tokie had to return to Washington, and we all look so happy. We were very proud of him in his spiffy new Navy uniform.

During his leave, Clyde hitchhiked over to Shawnee to spend the day with Joan.

Then it was Saturday, January 11, and time for Clyde to leave for Tulsa to catch his train. Mate prepared a lunch of sandwiches and cake for him to eat on his trip back to Washington.

I had been hired in the fall as bookkeeper and cashier to work until Christmas, but my boss now told me that my job was permanent. I had to work that Saturday, and when I hurried home for lunch, Clyde had already gone. I was so disappointed not to be able to tell him good-bye. Of course, now I realize that there were just too many farewells for him to handle.

Clyde had many friends in Tulsa, and a big group of them, along with friends from Okmulgee, went down to the train station to see him off.

And he was gone again.

Mate wrote Clyde that it surely was lonesome at home after he left, but she guessed she would live over it. She added:

> *Clyde, I don't know whether you ever will realize how much your Dad, Mother and sister love you or not, but maybe you do know. But Son, we do love you and we want you to make good in this world, and I know you will. Because you have already made us proud of you and I know we will always be proud of you....*
>
> *Clyde, about all your Daddie and I have lived for was for you and your education, and we feel like we have accomplished something great.*
>
> *We hope you continue to be the same sweet boy and go places with your music.*

I have always been so glad we told Clyde how proud we were of him. Too often, we wait until it is too late to tell our loved ones that simple truth.

Mate added that we were so glad to have him home and we hoped he got to come back "before he took a boat."

We were not too well up on Navy jargon in the Midwest.

It is very tempting to read signs into things which occurred then, now that we know how the story ends.

As the year 1941 began, did we suspect it would be our last year of peace?

I do not recall that Clyde and I ever discussed such somber topics. He had not yet begun his real Navy life, and I seldom read newspapers.

It is apparent from our dad's letters to Clyde that he was worried about something. We put it down to a father's natural anxiety about his son.

My biggest complaint seems to have been the shortage of dancing partners, as the boys left our small town for military service. However, the constant stream of letters and cookies which I sent to Clyde shows my uneasiness.

Certainly one of the girls Clyde had dated at Fort Sill was becoming more and more concerned. As the daughter of an Army officer, she realized the situation more than we did. She wrote him late in November, "There is so much discussion about the war."[11]

We loved each other deeply in our family and would certainly have preferred that we all stay home and maintain our life as it was.

But that was not possible for us in the year of 1941.

When my brother left Okmulgee for the last time on January 11, 1941, our family was just eleven months away from the worst horror any of us could possibly imagine!

CHAPTER 6

The United States Navy School of Music

Although the United States Navy had conducted a Music School since around 1900, they had no structured program for training professional musicians until 1935.[1] Before that date, any sailor who could play even a jew's-harp or a harmonica and who had tired of swabbing decks could apply for a position in the ship's band. The music produced by those bands was less than notable, and the duty was, indeed, soft. Those old-time Navy musicians were contemptuously referred to as "boilermakers" by their shipmates.[2]

All that changed on June 26, 1935,[3] when the United States Navy School of Music was founded in Washington, D.C. by Lieutenant Charles Benter.[4]

Charles Benter had enlisted in the U.S. Navy as an apprentice musician on March 20, 1905, becoming bandmaster of the battleship *Rhode Island* a year later. He was brought to Washington in 1919 from the battleship *Connecticut* to organize the U.S. Navy Band.[5]

A friendship developed between Benter and President Warren G. Harding and later, between Benter and President Calvin Coolidge. President Coolidge made the U.S. Navy Band a permanent organization in 1925.[6]

Lieutenant Benter served as Bandmaster of the U.S. Navy Band from its formation until he retired at the end of 1941.[7]

From its beginning, the U.S. Navy School of Music was under the direct charge of Boatswain's Mate James M. Thurmond.[8] A graduate of the Curtis Institute of Music, Boatswain Thurmond was a former member of Leopold Stokowski's Philadelphia Orchestra.[9]

James Thurmond had enlisted in the U.S. Navy in 1932 as a member of the United States Navy Band, where he played solo French horn for many years.[10]

Boatswain's Mate Thurmond was a very serious musician who tolerated absolutely no show of artistic temperament from his students. He was proud of the quality of music his students produced, but he kept his students humble. According to him, his school was designed to "put iron in the soul, steel in the muscles, and seafaring sense in the head."[11]

Thurmond's assistants were all highly trained musicians and, like him, tough taskmasters.[12] Many of the private instructors at the school were members of the big Navy Band stationed in Washington.

The location of the school did, indeed, keep the students humble. The school was given space on the third floor of the oldest building in a corner of the old Washington Navy Yard. The building was mostly taken up by the carpenter shop.[13] That old, dingy building showed the enlistees immediately just what the Navy thought of its musicians. The school was so crowded that students had to stand in line for hours to get a practice room. In the summer, the rooms were unbearably hot.

Qualifications for entrance into the U.S. Navy School of Music, as set up by Boatswain Thurmond from the beginning, were made deliberately stringent.[14] The enlistee must first pass a written test and a strict physical examination. In May 1941, Thurmond regretfully stated that four out of five musicians got no farther than the physical examination, where they were turned down for entry into the school.[15]

If an enlistee made it through the mental and physical tests, he must report to the school, where a stiff musical test was given to determine his qualifications to enter the school. The school did not teach a boy to play an instrument—the boy must be able to play at least one musical instrument proficiently before he was allowed to enter the School of Music.[16]

The musical test was given by Lieutenant Benter, Boatswain Thurmond, or by an instructor of the enlistee's particular instrument. Upon acceptance, the enlistee was sent to the U.S. Naval Receiving Station in Norfolk, Virginia, for the infamous boot camp military training.[17] If he were not accepted, the Navy would either pay his way home or accept him into the regular Navy as an Apprentice Seaman.[18] Upon completion of boot camp, the recruit returned to the School of Music where, if he were lucky, he would be given a "boot leave" to go back home to visit his family and friends.

When the musician returned to the School of Music from Norfolk or from leave, he became a member of the large School of Music massed band, which practiced several times each week. They were assisted by their instructors and by older musicians from the big Navy Band, who sat in on rehearsals to give the new students confidence and to encourage them to play out boldly.[19]

Although the bandmasters-in-training took turns directing the massed band, gaining valuable experience, the principal director was Boatswain's Mate Thurmond. His task was to sharpen the students' concentration and musical skills.

One of Thurmond's favorite tricks was to tap his baton for attention, signal the band to begin a selection of music, then abruptly direct "stop" after only one or two bars.[20] Only trained musicians can understand the total horror of playing several notes alone after the director has motioned the band to cease playing. A player soon learned to watch his music with one eye and his conductor with the other, which was, of course, the purpose of the maneuver.

On the first Monday of each month, Thurmond conducted tryouts. Taking the players of a particular instrument up to the auditorium, he sat them in a row and, one by one, placed sheet music before them, ordering each of them to play the music by sight. All of us who have ever played in a band know that test well, and the terror we felt as it came closer and closer to our turn. Depending on how well the musician did on his sight-reading test, Thurmond positioned him in the chairs, with the best player sitting in first chair.

Later, he assigned them to their permanent twenty-piece bands by the grades they had earned on their tests.[21]

By that method, musicians moved up in the chairs as they became more proficient, ready to be assigned to bands which would soon ship out.

Musicians who needed more experience and training were left in the massed band until they were deemed ready to become members of a permanent band.

The new recruits were also enrolled in classes in solfege (ear training), harmony, musical theory, and history, and were turned over to instructors for private lessons on their major and minor instruments.

Until they were ready for their permanent twenty-piece bands, they were divided into small groups of musicians. Those groups rehearsed several hours each day. Any student who had a talent for singing was also coached in various singing groups.[22]

Many of the recruits at the school were professional musicians, some with college degrees. In 1942, Thurmond stated that two-thirds of the students at his school had college training, four had M.A. degrees, and several were recruited from "name" orchestras. His students were fully able to fill a position in any good professional band. They did not pick a career in the Navy for the money to be earned—they joined the Navy with the rate of Apprentice Seaman, which paid twenty-one dollars a month, just as did any other recruit in the Navy. The inducement for joining the Navy School of Music was the opportunity to play their beloved music on a full-time basis and to be paid for it, however small the pay.[23]

Further education in the musical field was also an inducement to the young boys entering the school. Thurmond was extremely proud of his courses of study and of his teachers. He believed a student could get a better musical education at the U.S. Navy School of Music than he could at some private conservatory, because of the strict discipline which was enforced. There was absolutely no cutting of classes and no wasting of time in the classes.[24]

When the first members of *Arizona*'s last band entered the School of Music in 1940, the school had been in existence for five years. By the first of May 1941, fourteen twenty-piece bands had graduated. Until the spring of 1940, the musicians enlisted for six years, attended the School of Music for two years, were assigned to a Flag Command ship at their graduation, and served the remainder of their enlistments on the same ship as members of the same band.[25]

As musicians in a fleet band, they certainly got their wish to play lots of music. Bands stationed on a ship had to be extremely versatile, since they must cover the gambit in types of music played. Thurmond was well aware that his fleet bands might be required to play martial music in the morning, jumpin' jive at high noon, symphony at night, and fill in with vocal efforts ranging from intricate choral work to barbershop quartets. To accomplish that, before they graduated all musicians were required to play several instruments, enabling the twenty-piece band to switch easily from symphony orchestra, military band, concert band, dance band, and jazz orchestra.[26]

Once stationed on a ship, the bandsmen were responsible for all the music played on the ship and for additional performances played on shore. The bandsmen were also assigned areas of responsibility to be carried out if and when the ship was in danger. Their duties varied according to the type of danger facing the ship, whether such danger stemmed from enemy ships or from enemy airplanes.[27]

The bandmaster of each band was an older Navy musician who had been chosen to return to the School of Music for bandmaster training. To qualify, the prospective candidate must have served in a fleet band, maintained a good record, attained the rating of First Musician, and have served no more than fifteen years. At the end of his training, he was given his own twenty-piece band and was sent out with it to a ship assignment.[28]

The bandmaster was in total charge of the band—he lived, ate, and slept with his musicians in the band compartment, and spent all his working time with them as they practiced and performed for their shipmates, both on the ship and on shore.[29]

Occasionally, an opening came up in a band already at sea. Those openings were filled by asking first for volunteers. If no musician volunteered, Thurmond chose a student for the assignment.

The Navy School of Music operated on a shoestring before World War II. Thurmond printed his own music on a condemned set of photo equipment renovated by one of the students. The boys did much of their own arranging and composing, and sometimes professional civilian orchestras donated arrangements to them.[30]

The school was ever mindful that it was new, and therefore still on trial. Since Congress was always searching for ways to cut the national budget, the school did not dare ask for more money.

The music teachers knew, better than anyone else, that funding for the Arts is usually the first to go in any cost reduction.

Students reporting to the school brought their own personal instruments. At the insistence of Musician First Class Fred Kinney, bandmaster of the last *Arizona* band, most of the members of his band replaced their instruments with newer, more expensive instruments and were still making payments on those instruments when they died.

At the beginning of May 1941, there was an enrollment of 217 young musicians, more than one hundred under par, and recruits were being admitted at the rate of about ten a week.[31] That compared to about forty musicians admitted for the entire year before the war speedup.

With war tension increasing and with our government building up our armed forces faster and faster, the need for musical bands was increasing rapidly. Plans were made to ship out eight bands in May 1941, and to ship out eight more bands the following November. Because of the shortage of musicians at the school, some of the bands would not carry the full compliment of twenty musicians. Most urgent was the need for flute and French horn players. Few of those 160 musicians had completed the two years schooling they had been promised when they enlisted.[32] Band Number 21/22, which would become *Arizona*'s last band, was caught in the speedup.

After the war began, the course was shortened to one year or less.[33]

Lieutenant Charles Benter retired at the end of 1941, and Bandmaster Charles Brendler was appointed leader of the U.S. Navy Band.[34] Boatswain's Mate Thurmond was appointed Officer-in-Charge of the School of Music.[35]

By June 1942, the school had expanded somewhat, with an enrollment of 250 musicians. Thurmond was still Boatswain's Mate and had thirty assistants. By then the school had graduated 800 musicians.[36]

By the time Thurmond retired from the school in 1949 as Lieutenant, he had trained and shipped out 150 twenty-piece bands.[37]

The School in 1940-41, when the *Arizona* band attended, was a far cry from the present U.S. Navy School of Music. Moving to spacious quarters at the Little Creek Naval Amphibious Base, Virginia, in 1964, the school now trains nearly 600 musicians a year for the Navy, Marine Corps, and the Army. The two-year course has been shortened to twenty weeks of intensive training. Musicians still start at the bottom, however, and take many years to work their way up in the ranks.[38]

A musician or an artist is one of the best bargains the military can get. The rate of Musician is still one of the few jobs in the military in which you must be qualified before you are ever accepted. Most of the applicants have spent nearly ten years in hard study on their musical instruments and have spent a great deal of money becoming proficient on them.[39]

Unlike the average seaman, who depends on the Navy to teach him a trade, musicians and artists bring their trades and talents to the Navy.

Periodic efforts to close the School of Music and thus save the cost of maintaining it have been blocked so far by intelligent people who realize what a big boost to the morale of servicemen a structured program of music provides.[40]

The future *Arizona* bandsmen began arriving at the school in 1940. Any idea they had that the school was going to be a snap was immediately disabused when they were issued the "Rules and Regulations of the United States Navy School of Music."

The sixteen-page booklet, entitled "Excerpts From 'Station Orders, Receiving Station, Washington, D.C.' and Standing Orders of the Navy School of Music and the Navy School of Music Barracks," was signed by Lieutenant Charles Benter, USN, Officer-in-Charge, Navy School of Music, and approved by Lieutenant A. J. Benz, USN, Executive Officer of the Receiving Station.

Nothing was left to chance.

According to the "Rules and Regulations," students were to wear the uniform of the day at all times and the proper way to wear that uniform was spelled out in detail. The School of Music students were not to wear dungarees, nor could they enter or leave the Navy Yard in civilian clothes.

Most of the students soon rented lockers outside the Navy Yard in which to keep civilian clothes.

The students were responsible for washing their own uniforms and underwear. There were laundry facilities available to them at a charge, but most opted to use their money for better purposes—such as liberty. Because of that, strict rules were spelled out for when and where clothes could be washed and hung up to dry. Emphatically, the toilet rooms were not to be used for laundry purposes.

To the new sailors, mothers began to look more and more like angels!

Lest the students get the idea they were as good as anyone else, they were firmly instructed on the use of the toilets, or "heads," in the school building:

> *The Head on the main floor will be used by instructors and First Musicians only; that on the second floor will be used by students.*
> *The heads will be kept neat and clean at all times.*

That should have given the students a clue as to how long it would be before they made their First Class rating, since it would appear that the First Class Musicians were all so old they could no longer climb the stairs.

The students took turns standing watch over the school building and over the barracks where they lived. Orders were explicit regarding the watches and regarding procedure in case of fire.

It was at the U.S. Navy School of Music, during fire drills, that *Arizona*'s bandsmen first learned to run directly to the scene of danger, as ordered. They all learned that lesson very well, and they were to put it into practice on December 7, 1941.

Classes were convened and dismissed by bugle calls, and there were bugle calls for "Fire Call," "Attention," and the favorite, "Pay Call." Of special interest to my brother and the other cornet players was the instruction that all students must know the various bugle calls and all cornet players must be able to play those calls.

Since the school building was too small for their needs, strict rules were laid down. There was to be no smoking, no relaxation, no leaving personal possessions lying around, and no defacing of the building or equipment. Specific regulations covered music books, personal instruments, and government instruments.

Practice on their musical instruments was mandatory. The students were required to study at least one-half hour in preparation for their next recitation classes. They must practice one hour each day on their major instrument and a half-hour on their minor instrument. The school was available for practice each week day from noon to one o'clock, and from four to ten o'clock. They were not allowed to practice after 10:00 P.M. on any day, nor could they begin practice before noon on Sundays.

Students were required to sign the practice roster as they entered and left the building. The man on watch then verified the signature and noted the time. Each student was required to have a minimum of fourteen hours individual practice on each bimonthly report.

Liberty was the most important part of the students' lives. When out on liberty, they were prohibited from going beyond forty miles from the Navy Yard without special permission.

Obtaining that special permission practically required an Act of Congress. Their request must be made on the form provided (naturally), and must be submitted via:

The First Musician in Charge of that section or band.
The Bandmaster-in-Charge.
The Chief Master-at-Arms.
The Officer-in-Charge.
The Executive Officer, Receiving Station.

The request would have had to be very special indeed to warrant spending so much time satisfying all those requirements.

First-year students were permitted to leave the Navy Yard every Wednesday afternoon from four-thirty until midnight. They were also free to leave from eleven on Saturday morning until seven-thirty Monday morning.

That included the boys in the future *Arizona* band, since most of them spent only a few months at the School of Music. Those months at the school were the only times during their entire Navy career that they were off duty on weekends.

The School of Music students were instructed to use the Eleventh and "O" Street Gate, showing their liberty cards to the sentry on duty as they left and returned.

Each section of thirty musicians was assigned the duty in turn. Duty required that they rotate all the watches and to sweep and clean the barracks and the school.

Finally, in the cover letter of the "Rules and Regulations," students were given strict orders to familiarize themselves with the contents of the enclosed sixteen pages of orders and to govern themselves accordingly.[41]

Altogether, a good school—a serious school—a tough school.

A school which could go far toward helping students obtain their goal of a career in music. They all told themselves that, to reach that goal, they could put up with a great deal of unpleasantness.

Which they did.

CHAPTER 7

The Band Is Born

When *Arizona*'s last band was born in January 1941, it was as U.S. Navy Band Number 21 of the U.S. Navy School of Music in Washington, D.C.

When it died on December 7, 1941, it was as U.S. Navy Band Number 22.

At its birth, student-bandmaster Frederick William Kinney, Musician First Class, USN, was appointed leader of Band Number 21. He had been brought to the U.S. Navy School of Music in 1940 for training as a bandmaster.

Band Number 21 was his first and last band.

Kinney had enlisted in the Navy in 1926 at the age of sixteen. He was born in Ashland, Kentucky, but was now from Bremerton, Washington. He had been a baritone player in the fleet bands.

He was married and his wife Betty was with him in Washington.[1]

Although formed in January, Band 21 did not begin rehearsing together as a unit until March 30.[2]

There was no sense of urgency—the band was scheduled to ship out at the end of November,[3] giving their new leader plenty of time to shape his new band into a professional unit.

The members of Band 21 were certainly not idle, however. Until their permanent band was fully organized, the students were loosely formed into groups. They rehearsed with both the massed band and with their separate groups. In addition to those rehearsals, they attended classes, took private lessons, did their preparation for the next day's classes, and practiced on their major and minor instruments.[4]

Kinney set out to form the best band he could possibly gather from the ranks of the students at the school. He was still switching the members of his band until just before graduation on May 23. By the time they shipped out, he was pleased with his musicians and proud of his new band.[5]

The members of Band Number 22 at graduation in May were:

WAYNE LYNN BANDY, Seaman Second Class, played cornet and was a singer in the band. He was born in Broken Bow, Oklahoma, but was living in Waynesville, Missouri, when he entered the Navy.

He enlisted in the U.S. Navy in September 1940 at the age of nineteen.

Wayne excelled in swimming, tennis, and softball. He was a minister's son and was a gentle, quiet boy.[6]

ORAN MERRILL BRABBZSON, Musician Second Class, played French horn. He was from East Meadow, Nassau County, Long Island, New York.

He enlisted in the U.S. Navy in September 1940 at the age of eighteen.

Oran played football and tennis, and was a boxer and wrestler.

Oran was called "Buddy" by his family. After the band left Washington, Oran was named "Buttercup" by the boys in the band, because of the severe seasickness from which he suffered each time the ship went to sea.[7]

RALPH WARREN BURDETTE, Apprentice Seaman, played French horn. He also was an excellent cornet player, but switched to French horn at the request of the School of Music.

He was from Plainfield, New Jersey.

Ralph enlisted in the U.S. Navy in February 1941 at the age of nineteen.

He had a sunny, pleasant disposition.

Because Ralph was six feet tall and still growing, he was called "Chow" (short for "Chowhound") by the boys in the band.[8]

HARRY GREGORY CHERNUCHA, Seaman Second Class, played clarinet and saxophone in the band. He was from North Merrick, Nassau County, Long Island, New York.

He enlisted in the U.S. Navy in January 1941 at the age of eighteen.

He was of Russian descent and was a short, tough wrestler. Before enlisting, he had won the State of New York wrestling title for his weight of 130 pounds.[9]

GERALD CLINTON COX, Apprentice Seaman, played clarinet, saxophone, electric Hawaiian guitar, and Spanish guitar in the band. He also played the violin, although he did not have that instrument with him on the ship.

He was from East Moline, Illinois.

Gerald enlisted in the U.S. Navy in February 1941 at the age of eighteen.

He was called "Jerry" by his family.[10]

FRANK NORMAN FLOEGE, Apprentice Seaman, played clarinet and saxophone. He was from Harvey, Illinois.

He enlisted in the U.S. Navy in March 1941 at the age of nineteen.

Frank was an orphan who had lived most of his life either in orphanages or in foster homes.[11]

CURTIS JUNIOR HAAS, Seaman Second Class, played clarinet, saxophone, and flute in the band. He also was one of the singers and wrote some of the musical arrangements. He was from North Kansas City, Missouri.

He enlisted in the U.S. Navy in November 1940 at the age of twenty-one.

Curt was a quiet, talented boy.

He was called "Buster" by his family.[12]

BERNARD THOMAS HUGHES, Apprentice Seaman, played trombone in the band. He was from Athens, Pennsylvania.

He enlisted in the U.S. Navy in February 1941 at the age of eighteen.

Bernard's greatest desire was to play in a big-name band, especially in Glenn Miller's.

He was called "Bee" by his family.[13]

WENDELL RAY HURLEY, Seaman Second Class, played clarinet, saxophone, and Hawaiian guitar in the band. He was from

Marion, Indiana.

He enlisted in the U.S. Navy in November 1940 at the age of twenty-one.

Wendell was an expert baton twirler and taught twirling in high schools in Indiana, Michigan, and Illinois before enlisting in the Navy.

Because he was an outgoing, happy boy who was fond of the ladies, he was called "Casanova" and "Lady Killer" by the boys in the band.[14]

EMMETT ISAAC LYNCH, Musician Second Class, played bass drum in the band, and also played the piano. He was from Louisville, Kentucky.

He enlisted in the U.S. Navy in April 1940 at the age of twenty-four.

Emmett married Lorraine Lee Sisk in February 1941.

He was a tall boy with red hair and was called "Rusty" and "Red."[15]

WILLIAM MOORE McCARY, Seaman Second Class, played the tuba in the band. He also played cornet, piano, flute, and almost all the other musical instruments. He was from Shades Mountain, Alabama, near Birmingham.

He enlisted in the U.S. Navy in September 1940 at the age of sixteen.

Bill was a member of the Birmingham Concert Orchestra, and was the drum major for a local band.

He was interested in deep-sea diving and had invented a diving helmet when he was a child.

He was called "Billie" by his family and was called "Swede" by the boys in the band.[16]

WILLIAM STARKS MOORHOUSE, Musician Second Class, played cornet in the band. He was born in Wichita, Kansas, but was raised in Erie, Pennsylvania.

He enlisted in the U.S. Navy in September 1940 at the age of eighteen.

Bill was an excellent golf player and swimmer.

He was called "Bill" by his family.[17]

ALEXANDER JOSEPH NADEL, Apprentice Seaman, played cornet in the band and wrote many of the musical arrangements for the

Arizona band. He was from Astoria, Long Island, New York.

He enlisted in the U.S. Navy in April 1941 at the age of nineteen.

He played with the New York Symphony and for operettas in the New York City area.

He was called "Alex" by his family, and "Swoose" by the boys in the band.[18]

NEAL JASON RADFORD, Seaman Second Class, played baritone in the band. He was from Newark, Nebraska.

He enlisted in the U.S. Navy in October 1940 at the age of twenty-five.

Neal had a writer's talent for describing his Navy experiences and for seeing the humor in the band's situation.

He was more than six feet tall and was built in proportion. He loved all sports, particularly football.

He was called "Mike" by his family and "Frick" by the boys in the band.[19]

JAMES HARVEY SANDERSON, Seaman Second Class, played clarinet and saxophone in the band. He was from Lindsay, California.

He enlisted in the U.S. Navy in October 1940 at the age of twenty.

He was a tall boy with a pleasant disposition.[20]

JACK LEO SCRUGGS, Seaman Second Class, played trombone and accordion in the band, and was one of the vocalists. He also wrote some of the arrangements for the band, and played the piano and baritone. He was born in Hanford, California, and was raised in Long Beach, California.

He enlisted in the U.S. Navy in December 1940 at the age of twenty-one.

He was a gifted poet.

He was called "Scrooge" by the boys in the band.[21]

ROBERT KAR SHAW, Seaman Second Class, played trombone in the band. He was born in Fort Worth, Texas, and was raised in Pasadena, Texas.

He enlisted in the U.S. Navy in November 1940 at the age of eighteen.

He was called "Bobby" by his family.[22]

CHARLES WILLIAM WHITE, Apprentice Seaman, played snare drums in the band, and also played the piano and was learning to play several additional instruments. He was born in Salt Lake City, Utah, and was raised in Bountiful, Utah.

He enlisted in the U.S. Navy in March 1941 at the age of twenty-one.

Charles was a happy boy with an outgoing personality.[23]

ERNEST HUBERT WHITSON, JR., Apprentice Seaman, played bass horn and string bass in the band. He also played the piano. He was from Cincinnati, Ohio.

He enlisted in the U.S. Navy in March 1941 at the age of twenty-three.

Ernest was older and more settled than the other members of the band. He was called "Ernie" by his family and the *Arizona* bandsmen.[24]

CLYDE RICHARD WILLIAMS, Seaman Second Class, played cornet in the band. He also played baritone, French horn, and violin. He was a baton twirler and a former drum major for his high school band. He was born in Henryetta, Oklahoma, and was raised in Wetumka and Okmulgee, Oklahoma.

He enlisted in the U.S. Navy in November 1940 at the age of eighteen.

Clyde was six feet tall with a slender build. He was a happy, fun-loving boy with a keen sense of humor. He was fond of swimming, diving, tennis, and art.

Clyde was called "Proke" and "Toke" by his family and friends, and was called "Okmulgee" by his friends at the School of Music and by the musicians of the *Arizona* band.[25]

When Band Number 21/22 left Washington on May 26, headed for the *Arizona*, only nine of its musicians had been members of Kinney's band from its beginning. They were: Brabbzson, Chernucha, Haas, McCary, Moorhouse, Sanderson, Scruggs, Shaw, and Williams. Three more musicians had been assigned to the band when they arrived at the school—Burdette at the end of February and Floege and Whitson in April.

Those twelve musicians weathered cut after cut as Kinney honed his band to his satisfaction.

Eight musicians—Bandy, Cox, Hughes, Hurley, Lynch, Nadel, Radford and White—almost escaped their fate. Those boys were originally assigned to other bands and remained safe until late in May. But just before graduation, they were moved into Kinney's band to replace more fortunate students who were transferred to other bands.

Thus, Band Number 21/22 was not fully organized until late in May. Its members were young—nearly one-half of them not yet in their twenties.

But Kinney had done well with his horse trading. All his bandsmen had excelled in music in high school. They had won awards in their state competitions. Most of them had played in other bands and orchestras, in addition to their high school bands. They all played several instruments.

They had often performed in their hometowns. They had played or sung in churches and for civic functions. Haas and Moorhouse had formed their own professional dance bands.

Almost half of them had attended college, majoring in music.

So, although Kinney's boys were young, they had gained a great deal of musical experience, even before they entered the Navy.

The musicians in the last band of the USS *Arizona* graduated from the School of Music on May 23, 1941—they shipped out on May 26—they went aboard the *Arizona* on June 17—they died on December 7, 1941.

This is their story.

CHAPTER 8

Winter in Washington

The musicians in *Arizona*'s last band have been gone for a long time now, but thanks to their families, we still have their letters and photographs. From these letters, we have a clear picture of *Arizona*'s bandsmen, their friends, and their days at the U.S. Navy School of Music in 1940 and 1941.

Each member of the future *Arizona* band reported his assessment of the school to his family back home. The impressions varied from student to student, of course, depending on his personality and on his age. It was interesting for me when, in recent years, I interviewed the living alumni of the school and saw how they have forgotten the negative things which bothered our *Arizona* boys then. For most men, the only time that life in the armed forces seems like fun is after they have been out for awhile. Then memory sands over the rough places, leaving only happy remembrances.

John W. Crawford, a student at the school in 1940, remembers that, coming from a small town in Pennsylvania, he felt his world was about to open up.[1]

Most of the students were disappointed by the grubby appearance of the buildings assigned to the School of Music, but they wanted to succeed so much that they vowed to overlook that unfortunate aspect.

However, many of them never did come to terms with all the regimentation and boot polishing which go with "Life in the Military."

The new students were surprised to find that, although they had thought the musicians at the school would spend all their leisure time talking about music, on the contrary, about all they talked about were their leaves and their women. In other words, those talented, dedicated musicians were just like the regular "guys" back home.

Certainly the laundry situation made an immediate impression on the students. Neal Radford mentioned in a letter home that he had just finished washing out a couple of suits of underwear—strange activity indeed for a farmer.

Washington is a cold, damp city in the winter, and for people not used to such a climate, it can be very uncomfortable. Thanks to the erratic heating system in the ancient barracks, the new sailors were often either too warm or too cold at night. The two white blankets furnished them were not adequate at times, and they complained bitterly to each other and to their families.

The buildings of both the school and the barracks were old and, since DDT was not yet available, full of bugs.

Many areas of Washington still had outhouses behind the homes, and that lack of modern plumbing did not help the sanitation of the city. Having endured the "Great Depression" for ten years now, our country was sadly lacking in public improvements.

Neal Radford had a special talent for observing life and a poetic way of describing his impressions to his family back home.

He thought the Potomac River, which bordered the Navy Yard on the south, would be deep enough to float a battleship, since it was dredged out frequently. And the road beside the Potomac River reminded him of one of the roads back home.

Living in such a beautiful city as Washington did not impress the students at first. They were homesick for their old towns and their old friends. Radford missed the open spaces and the freedom of the farm in Nebraska. He and another baritone player, Kunzeker from Humboldt, Kansas, often walked the four miles down to the substation, just to get away for awhile.

Because weather is the most important thing in a farmer's life, Radford mentioned Washington's weather in every letter he wrote his parents. He was always concerned with how their crops were faring.

He was amazed to observe that, when builders wanted to put down a lawn of bluegrass in front of a completed building, they did not just scatter seeds on the ground, but went out into the country, peeled up the grass, and hauled the sod in on trucks.

The new students at the school were shocked at first with their tough teachers, but most came to admire them and to appreciate their help. Of course, being young and irreverent, they promptly dubbed Bandmaster Thurmond "Jungle Jim." I never did ask Dr. Thurmond if he was aware the students called him that, but I think we can safely assume he was.

The students did not casually give out respect to their leaders— certainly that had to be earned. Although their opinion of some of their instructors was unanimously low, they were all impressed with Jim Thurmond. In spite of the "Jungle Jim" title they gave him, they all wrote that he was the best director under whom they had ever played, and that he really knew how to draw the music out of a bunch of "guys."

Whenever the big Navy Band was out on tour, Thurmond would take a group of musicians from the school to play the Navy Band radio broadcasts in Washington. The boys wrote that Thurmond always received nothing but praise for their music.

A direct result of the Great Depression was the loss of beauty from our lives. When money becomes scarce, the first thing to go is the Arts. And when people cannot support our actors, dancers, painters, writers, photographers, and musicians, our world becomes very dull and colorless.

Unable to sell enough tickets to pay expenses, our large symphony orchestras had no choice but to disband. Many of those professional musicians then joined the Navy and were assigned to the School of Music as instructors.[2]

William E. Bohuslaw, a student at the school when the *Arizona* bandsmen attended, still remembers the instructor with whom he and Oran Brabbzson studied. Fred (or Frank) Palmer had played French horn with the Boston, Philadelphia, and Chicago symphonies before he enlisted in the Navy and was an outstanding teacher.[3]

Also remembered by the students was Manyonona (Manny), the baritone instructor. To improve their sight-reading, Manny required his baritone players to sing their parts,[4] which caused much merriment among the students—behind Manny's back, of course.

Some of the other instructors at the school were H. A. Heard, who taught tuba; Ralph Mack, who taught conducting; and Jim Thurmond, who taught harmony.[5]

Thanksgiving Day, November 21, 1940, was the first family holiday most of the students had ever spent away from home. Bandy, Brabbzson, Haas, Moorhouse, Radford, and Sanderson had all returned from boot camp in time to celebrate Thanksgiving at the school. Of those, only Brabbzson lived close enough to go home.

Describing their Thanksgiving turkey dinner, Radford said they had everything you could think of, even including candy, nuts, cigars, and cigarettes. He commented that the Navy must think that made up for the "measly twenty-one bucks they give us." When he compared the Navy cooking to the cooking of the women back in Nebraska, the Navy cooks lost the contest, but he thought the Navy's pastries were excellent.

Later, when Scruggs arrived, he echoed Radford's assessment of the food, which they all thought was better than that which they had been served in boot camp.

As Scruggs said, when you were served turkey or chicken at the Washington Navy Yard, you could tell what it was and not have to guess. Scruggs, like Radford, thought the Navy had the best bakers anywhere.

Late in November, Radford had a chance to escape his impending fate when he, along with ten other baritone players, were called up to the Adjutant's office. The band on the battleship *New York* needed a baritone player, and the Adjutant asked for a volunteer to fill the vacancy. To Radford's intense relief, Nichols, who had been at the school about six months, stepped forward. Had nobody volunteered, the Adjutant would have appointed someone, and none of them wanted to leave all their new friends at the school.

And Radford lost his chance.

Early in December, twenty of the older bandsmen were sent with President Roosevelt on a long cruise down to Panama and back. They all came back with their sea bags stuffed with cigarettes. At that time, when ships were at sea, no tax was charged on cigarettes. Brands such as Lucky Strike sold for six cents per pack, and cheaper brands sold for three cents per pack.

None of the future *Arizona* bandsmen went on that cruise.

On December 17, having been at the school for about six weeks, Radford was getting better acquainted with more of his fellow musicians and was liking it better each day.

Uppermost in the thoughts of all the students at the end of 1940 was boot leave. The school scheduled two fifteen-day leave sections, the first to begin on December 15 and the second to begin on December 30.

Bandy, Brabbzson, Haas, Moorhouse, Radford, and Sanderson had all returned to the school from boot camp in time to go on first leave; however, only Brabbzson and Radford were actually granted leave.

Brabbzson had no problem with transportation, as he lived close to the school.

Radford immediately asked his parents for a loan so he could buy a train ticket. He told of one student who had hitchhiked to Youngstown, Ohio, in nine hours, while it took him ten hours to return to Washington on the train.

However, just as he was ready to start home, Radford became ill with a chest cold and fever and was sent to the U.S. Naval Hospital.

Regulations spelled out the procedure for reporting any illness, but the students were shocked to learn that reporting those illnesses resulted in their being sent to the hospital.[6]

At that time, people went to the hospital for serious illnesses only—illnesses which often ended in death.

Radford learned his hospital lesson the hard way. He vowed then and there that he would have to be pretty sick ever to go to sick bay again. He was disgusted that what he considered just a bad cold had caused him to miss Christmas at home. Although he could still have taken first leave, leaves began on Sundays, and the Naval Hospital only released patients on Tuesdays and Fridays, so by the time he was released on Tuesday, he had already missed two days of his leave.

Other School of Music students who were in the hospital that December were Turner from Oklahoma and Kantely from California, prompting Radford to remark that the Western boys were not yet used to the damp climate.

Having nothing to do except lie in his hospital bed all day, Radford described his surroundings in a letter to his parents. The Naval Hospital at Twenty-third and "E" Streets, NW, was built on a big hill about three miles from the Navy Yard, on the outskirts of Washington. It overlooked the Lincoln Memorial, Bolling Field, and the big bridge which crossed the Potomac River into Virginia. On a clear day, you could see Arlington Cemetery across the river. The riding stable was near the hospital, and Radford spent much time looking out his window, watching the horsemen. Having been raised on a farm, that had a definite fascination for him.

The Navy was building a new hospital in Bethesda, Maryland, about twelve miles from the Navy Yard. Radford heard it was to be twenty-two stories high and would have no stairs, using automatic elevators, which the sailors would run themselves.

As is true with most servicemen (and the rest of us, for that matter), Radford complained about the shortage of food in the hospital and how the patients made up for that by raiding the icebox down in the galley. Their food came from the kitchens of the Navy Yard, but the icebox at the hospital was kept full of milk and fruit juices, which he said the patients used to keep body and soul together.

Bandy, Hurley, Radford, and my brother, Clyde Williams, were granted fifteen-day leaves in the second leave section beginning on December 30, 1940.

Bobby Shaw did not return to the school from boot camp until January 1, 1941, so he barely missed out on the second leaves.[7]

Bandy hitchhiked home to Missouri and returned by bus to the School.[8] Hurley,[9] Radford, and Clyde all went home and returned to Washington by train.

After his disappointment over missing Christmas at home, Radford was looking forward to being home on New Year's Day, 1941. He planned to be sitting right beside the radio in his parents' living room when Kennie Raknig kicked off for Nebraska against Stanford in the Rose Bowl. He complained that the Washington newspapers did not give the Rose Bowl game much publicity. He thought the papers in Washington were still rubbing it into their pet team (the Washington Redskins) for losing 73 to 0 to the Chicago Bears.

Fortunately for Radford, he did arrive in Nebraska in time to listen to the Rose Bowl football game on the radio. Unfortunately for him, Stanford beat Nebraska 21 to 13 in that 1941 Rose Bowl game.[10]

As soon as the students returned to the school from boot leave, they started planning their next leave, which would be granted just before their band shipped out.

After his leave, Radford wrote his family: "It sure was swell to be seeing you folks again...but it was kinda nice to get back to work again."

It was not until my brother returned from leave that he had a chance to spend much time at the school. Now things were getting down to normal and he began his studies in earnest. Reveille was at 6:00 A.M., but Clyde skipped breakfast and slept until seven-thirty. That was not conducive to gaining the weight the Navy required, and photographs taken later at the beach in Hawaii show that he never did put any meat on his ribs.

The students went to school from eight until eleven o'clock, had their noon meal (chow), and rested (crapped out) until one. They then attended school until four, after which they were free for the rest of the day.

After I read that, I wrote Clyde several sarcastic letters, telling him how sorry I was for his tough schedule. Since I was working six days a week, and my noontime siesta consisted of walking more than a mile home for lunch and then walking back to work, his hours sounded pretty soft to me!

Of course, all those practice hours still had to be worked in after school.

Clyde was assigned classes in solfege and harmony on Monday and theory on Wednesday, taking his private lesson on Friday afternoon.

At last it was explained to him that "solfege" was a method of singing syllables instead of words to music. The course was designed to train the musician's ear to identify a particular note.

Strict emphasis was put on teaching all types of music, from classical to modern dance music. The old military bands were not trained in modern music, and their music did not appeal to the young men being drafted.

Recognizing that problem, the U.S. Army announced in January 1941 that Leopold Stokowski, director of the Philadelphia Symphony Orchestra, would train an eighty-five-piece Army band in California. It was an experiment by the Army to develop more typically American music and to modernize the Army bands.[11]

Occasionally an opening occurred in the big U.S. Navy Band, stationed in Washington. To qualify for transfer to the big band, a student at the school was required to play both a wind and a stringed instrument. Although my brother was qualified, he never entertained any idea of trying to transfer. The Navy Band was composed of older men, and Clyde wanted to stay with his younger friends.

And they were making friends at the school. Getting used to people from so many different regions of the country was sometimes amusing.

It is hard for us to understand how very little we knew then of other areas of our country. Thanks to the Great Depression, few of the students at the school had ever traveled very far from home.

My fun-loving brother immediately took advantage of the boys' lack of knowledge regarding Oklahoma. The very name "Oklahoma" conjured up for the other students pictures of all the Westerns they had ever seen at the movies.

Once, when a student noticed the postmark on one of Clyde's letters from home and exclaimed about the length of time it took the letter to reach Washington, Clyde told him that was because all of Oklahoma's mail had to be taken by Pony Express to the border. In fact, Clyde told them, he himself was working for the Pony Express when he joined the Navy. The boys were horrified that he would give up such an exciting job just to join that dull Navy!

Clyde's stories about the Indians in Oklahoma also grew wilder and wilder and, except for the Midwestern boys, his new friends swallowed all his tales. Fortunately Bandy, who was also from Oklahoma, never did give him away.

Clyde had great fun writing his friends back in Oklahoma what he was telling the other students about our state.

It was about that time that my brother acquired the reputation of being "Windy."

Church service was mandatory for all students who were in the barracks on Sunday morning.[12] One Sunday morning in December, Radford wrote his mother that in a few minutes, the school would make him go across the street and confess all his sins, of which he said he had none.

The third Inauguration of President Franklin Delano Roosevelt on January 20 was a high point for the School of Music students. A large contingent of musicians from the school marched in the Inaugural Parade that day, including Clyde, Shaw,[13] and McCary.

Clyde had told us when he was home on leave that he would march in the parade, so Mate listened to the radio broadcast of the ceremony and pictured her son marching along, blowing his horn.

Radford and Don Harbin went downtown that day to watch the parade. Radford complained that, although they wore all the clothes they owned, they nearly froze to death.

There were five or six bands, including the Army, Navy, and Marine Bands, plus a band from the School of Music. The School's Drum and Bugle Corps also participated, and Radford thought they were "pretty nifty." Later, Lieutenant Benter called the school to congratulate them on their appearance in the parade.

Billie McCary, who had been turned down for entrance to the School of Music because he was only sixteen years old, was being held at the Receiving Station in Norfolk.

Because McCary had attended the Georgia Military College for one year, he had been appointed drill sergeant of a platoon at the Receiving Station. In a competition held at Norfolk, McCary's platoon had won first place. As an award, the platoon had been brought to Washington to parade in review before the president. While in Washington, McCary went over to the school to try out again for entrance, and was finally accepted.[14]

His fate was sealed, not only because he was very gifted on several musical instruments, but also because the school needed more bass players to fill out the bands it would soon ship out.

Also marching in the parade that day were cadets and midshipmen from the Army and Navy Academies—namely West Point and Annapolis. There was a show of the Army's mechanized units, such as tanks, armored cars, troop trucks with guns behind them, etc. For two hours, the sky was filled with about 350 Army and Navy planes, plus one group of thirty-six flying fortresses. Radford said the noise was terrific.

Perhaps we can be forgiven if we are less than enthusiastic about that Inauguration Parade. We can only wonder where all that military power was less than a year later when the *Arizona* and the other ships needed it so desperately! I have always wondered if, after our fiasco at Pearl Harbor, President Roosevelt and the big military brass stationed in Washington ever thought of those boys who had marched in that parade to honor them in January and who had died so horribly for them in December.

On January 25, a band from the School of Music played for President Roosevelt's press conference at the Willard Hotel. Again, we are grateful to Neal Radford for his description of the event.

After spending all Saturday afternoon getting his clothes ready, Radford attended the press conference as a member of a twenty-one-piece band. The plan was to present a rerun of the Inauguration Parade for the president. The twenty-one-piece band was split into three seven-piece German bands and they marched across the room playing "Anchors Aweigh." One band began, then after eight bars, another band began, and after eight more bars, the third band began. Radford thought it would be like the "rounds" they sang in school at home, but their bandmaster assured them it was the way it should sound.

The press conference went off as planned, except that the president was not there. Instead, a "guy" was there to represent him. Radford thought it was a very nice program, anyway.

Some actors, including Preston Foster, performed. Everyone was dressed in formal attire. Radford judged the price of tickets for the affair would have been at least fifty bucks a pair.

After they played, the band was sent to another room, where they were served sandwiches and beer. Radford couldn't help adding that they were given one "ten-center" beer apiece.

Things have not changed much over the years since then. At formal affairs, it is still champagne for the guests, beer for the band, and water for the waiters.

By the end of January, the school was getting more strict with the students, adding drilling with rifles to their other duties.

Harry Chernucha and Jack Scruggs finished boot camp and arrived at the school at the end of January. It is hard to imagine a more different pair of boys than those two. Not only were they from direct opposite ends of the country—Chernucha from the East Coast and Scruggs from the West Coast—but they were direct opposites in personality.

Where Scruggs was a serious musician, given to writing poetry, Chernucha was a short, tough fighter who had just won the 1940 State of New York wrestling title for his weight.

Therefore, Chernucha was warmly greeted by the students at the school. There was fierce competition at the Navy Yard in various sports and games, and the School of Music often finished at the top in baseball, boxing, and wrestling.[15]

Chernucha was promptly put on the wrestling team, and J. E. "Duke" Bolen, Jerry Wentworth, and Frank W. Schwarz, all students at the School of Music then, remember wrestling him at the Navy Yard.[16]

Despite their differences, Chernucha and Scruggs became good friends, as did all the members of the future *Arizona* band.

Although all the students mentioned the Captain's inspection in their letters home, Radford, as usual, wrote the best description:

> We had Captain's Inspection yesterday (Saturday February 8). That means we had to march out on the drill field and stand at attention while the Captain of the Yard walked up and down our ranks and looked for "chow marks" on our uniforms, loose or missing buttons, unshined shoes, etc.

> *After that, we came back in the barracks and stood by our*
> *lockers while he looked them over. If he had to speak to us*
> *about anything, Jenky Joe would take some liberty away from*
> *the culprit.... He caught one guy with a flat hat that fit him*
> *like a gunny sack.*

The constant complaint from the students was the lack of money.
Beginning as an Apprentice Seaman at twenty-one dollars a month,
a student advanced to Seaman Second Class after four months, with
the pay of thirty-six dollars a month. After ten months total service,
the student was usually raised to Musician Second Class, which paid
fifty-four dollars a month.[17]

To qualify for each of these pay raises, the student must pass a
written test, and hope he would be included in the allowed quota for
promotions.

Later, advances came very slowly, if at all. Usually, if a musician
wanted to get a very high rate, he would have to transfer out of the
Musician field to another branch of the Navy. Musicians were assumed to be willing to starve for their art, and were paid accordingly.

They were paid on the fifth and twentieth of each month. Clyde
told me that sailors were always broke. Since I was making seven
dollars a week, I could relate to that.

By the time they were paid, many of the boys were already in
debt for the entire amount they received. Most of them were sending
money home for various reasons—repaying the money they had borrowed to go home on leave, making payments on the new instruments they had been required to buy, or assisting their folks
financially. Some of the boys had taken out life insurance, and the
payments on that required much sacrifice.

Clyde mentioned money in every letter he wrote us for the rest of
his life. While he was still paying our dad back for the loan for his
train ticket, he either mentioned that there was a money order enclosed or explained why there was not a money order enclosed.

A favorite pastime for all the boys was dreaming of what they
would do when they began drawing thirty-six dollars a month.

Radford figured he could then afford to buy a new euphonium horn and pay it out at twenty dollars a month.

Shooting craps and playing poker were the fastest ways for a new sailor to part with his money. After several sessions with the big boys, most recruits gave up that luxury.

Some sailors who were better able to manage money did quite well by lending out a dollar, with two dollars payable on payday. Radford, being older and more settled, was sometimes able to lend money to the students. He said the guys were usually pretty dependable about paying their debts on payday.

With no locks on their lockers, petty theft was a real problem. The students complained about the loss of cigarettes, tobacco, and money. Radford always had to hide his Bull Durham tobacco a few days before payday, as all the "moochers" came out of the woodwork.

Even more insulting to Radford was the time he left several pieces of his mom's fudge in his locker while he went over to the school to practice. When he returned, he was shocked to find the fudge was gone. He told his mother that her fudge must have been very good to tempt a guy into stealing!

Radford was also incensed that, while he was at boot camp, some guy had traded a seven and two-thirds size blue flat hat for his brand new seven and one-eighth size hat. He was going to have to spend a buck and a half to get another one, as he could not get the hat altered, nor could he find a student who would trade with him. Small town boys did not expect such thievery then, as it was not yet the common practice it is today.

And yet there seemed to be no problem with the students' expensive musical instruments and musical arrangements. After his initial examination in Washington, each student left his personal instrument on a shelf at the school while he went to Norfolk for boot camp. It was always still there when he returned.[18]

All the musicians at the school donated fifty cents to Navy Relief and to other causes each year. Such donations were termed "voluntary." When faced with choosing to part with fifty cents or losing their next liberty, all of them chose the former. Consequently, there was always 100 percent participation.

When the band assignments began in January and February, the sobering thought occurred to the students that they would soon go separate ways from their new friends.

Radford was assigned to Band 20, which meant there had been twenty bands formed at the school since its beginning in 1935. His good friend Don Harbin was assigned to Band 17, which was due to ship out in May.

Rumor had it that Fred Kinney's Band 21 would go to the West Coast. Scruggs hoped the scuttlebutt was true, since his family lived in Long Beach.

Scruggs, who was an excellent piano and accordion player, in addition to the trombone, began taking classical piano lessons as his minor instrument. Kinney told him he would play trombone in the concert band and piano in the dance band. Kinney was fortunate to get Scruggs in Band 21, as there was a shortage of good piano players at the school.

When Clyde first wrote us that his band would ship out in November, Mate and Pate were alarmed. She wrote right back that she and Pate would rather he stayed in school, at least until November, so he could have that much more training.

She also asked him if he would get to come home before he shipped out in November. We all asked that question of the *Arizona* bandsmen for the rest of their lives—when do you get your next leave?

Even before Clyde came home in January, we had started planning to go to Washington to visit him. Mate and Pate were to figure how to buy a new (to us) car, and now that my job was permanent, I was to begin saving my money for the gasoline.

After we heard that Clyde would not stay in the School of Music for his promised two years, we discussed going to Washington in November to attend his graduation. However, after Clyde told us his graduation would be held in the Sail Loft where, he was sorry to say, no visitors were allowed, we reconsidered.

Since we could not attend his graduation ceremony anyway, we went back to our plan to go to Washington in June, when the weather would be better.

Clyde was corresponding with many friends back home, telling them he was glad to get into the school because he could really learn music. He always added, "It isn't too easy here, though it sounds easy enough."

He wrote our cousin Betty that they did not have a bugler at the barracks, as they did at the school, but that the bell was ringing for them to go over to the school, so he hurriedly closed his letter with:

> *Yours 'till my ship sinks—Clyde.*

Why did he write that? Premonition? How can we tell?

Joan Watson complained to Clyde that his letters were not very long.[19] I had been telling him that since he first left home.

A friend of his in Tulsa wrote that everyone was mad at him because he had not written to them.[20] Never one to sit alone when he could be talking to someone, Clyde did not spend too much time writing letters. For that reason, they all became even more precious to us.

We tried to keep him up to date on all his friends who were leaving Okmulgee.

In February Clyde had a throat infection and was sent to the Naval Hospital. Mate told him we were so thankful for the good care he was getting. I sent him a get-well card which stated: "Hope you'll soon be well again! May you and your bed soon come to the parting of the ways—And may you soon be smiling through happy healthy days!"

My wish for Clyde and his bed to come to the parting of the ways was to come true in May, when he graduated from the school. After he left Washington, my brother never again had a bed.

In February, Radford remarked that those musicians were the damnedest guys to get sick he had ever seen. There were at least ten of them in the hospital all the time, and in the last week, there had been three appendectomies.

On February 8, Emmett Lynch and his girl went over to Hyattsville, Maryland, to get married.[21] Lynch and Lorraine Lee Sisk had gone together for some time, but the rules at the School of Music prohibited marriage of the students. Apparently, he had finally obtained permission from the school to marry.

John Crawford got into trouble for some minor infraction and was put into the brig on bread and water for several days. Since the brig was near the bakery at the Navy Yard and since John had many friends, he did not suffer unduly.[22]

Efforts were made to entertain the sailors at the Navy Yard, and the music students were included in those events. Radford was impressed with a magician who appeared at the Receiving Station and described his various tricks. He also sent home a program for a symphony concert he had attended.

Dances were held for the sailors every Friday night, and the nurses gave a tea dance for the enlisted men of Washington on Sunday afternoons. I immediately made big plans to attend both events when we visited Washington.

Scruggs was scheduled to play in a band for church on Sunday, which he thought would be fun.

Mate heard that the music war was over and she hoped we would now be able to hear the Navy Band on the radio again. She asked Clyde to let us know if he ever played on the radio, so we could listen to the program.

Reluctant to admit that her son was now grown, Mate continued to caution Clyde about bathing regularly and keeping his socks clean, "not to mention your teeth!" She did not know the sort of environment her son had entered. Military men enforce their own standards of cleanliness, often to the dismay of the victim!

Both Radford and Scruggs described the "Shower Parties" given in the barracks for new students. It was the usual high jinks which college men consider funny—unless, of course, they were one of the victims. It was all good "clean" fun, however—none of the vicious hazing one hears of today. The only *Arizona* bandsman I know who was caught in one of those "showers" was Scruggs, and he was let off lightly, having only to sweep the hall.

The families continued to send packages of food to our boys. Despite the slow mail service, the dehydrated food was an important link with home. According to Clyde, "The candy tasted swell and it wasn't too soft or too hard. Thanks again for the pecan meats."

Radford thanked his mother for the candy and picture album. He added: "Boy, that stuff sure was nifty. Harbin and I ate what we could hold and passed out the rest. The guys sure thought my mom could make fudge."

Along with all the young people in our nation, the students at the school were getting restless. Radford was "fed up" with the school at times, considering it pretty dead. He wished he could ship out in the spring to some place where something was happening.

He was soon to get his wish.

CHAPTER 9

Spring in Washington

With her famous cherry blossoms and other plantings, Washington, D.C., is beautiful in the spring, and the spring of 1941 was no exception. The students of the U.S. Navy School of Music spent their liberties sightseeing and searching for girls, not necessarily in that order.

Unfortunately, there was a distinct shortage of female companionship for sailors in Washington. Consequently, Larry Conley considered himself extremely fortunate when he met a Sweet Young Thing while out on liberty.

Larry Conley had arrived in Washington in September 1940 and had met Oran Brabbzson at a bus stop. Both boys had just enlisted and were reporting to the School of Music for their musical examination. They had both passed the test, attended boot camp together, and had become good friends at the school.[1]

On that particular spring afternoon, Conley escorted Sweet Young Thing to the soda fountain at a nearby drugstore and they exchanged telephone numbers.

After their chance meeting, they met several times, always at the soda fountain and always in public.

One day, as the students were going about their business, the peace of the school was shattered by the arrival of a squad of Federal Bureau of Investigation agents, along with Naval Intelligence officers, all demanding to see Conley!

Conley was taken to an interrogation room, where the grim men suggested strongly that he come clean about the whereabouts of Sweet Young Thing.

Since the girl had been sitting at the soda fountain when Conley last saw her, he found it difficult to answer any questions about where she might be.

An extremely bewildered Conley finally pieced together the story.

SYT had departed from the tender loving care of her parents and had forgotten to come home. The attention of the FBI to a routine missing-persons case stemmed from the fact that she was the daughter of a United States Senator.

Conley had entered the picture when her parents found his telephone number in her desk drawer.

The fact that Conley barely knew the girl and certainly did not know she was missing made it hard for him to confess. One can only wonder how he was supposed to have smuggled her into the heavily-guarded Navy Yard.

Nevertheless, after the interrogation, Conley was slapped into the brig, presumably so he would have time to remember where he had stashed SYT.

While Conley was confined to the brig, Fred Kinney visited him in an effort to cheer him up. Kinney assured him that, since he was innocent, he had nothing to worry about and should remain calm. They would find SYT anytime now, and Conley would be sprung from the brig.

Of course, Conley was about as calm as any of us would be who found ourselves in the clutches of the FBI!

But Kinney was right.

After Conley spent the weekend in the brig, the authorities found Sweet Young Thing and returned her to her loving parents. She had indeed run off with a sailor, but fortunately for Conley, not with him.

Conley never forgot Kinney's kindness to him.[2]

Along with our hometown newspapers, Mate also sent some of my brother's civilian clothes to him. In March, he bought some more civilian clothes from a boy who was shipping out, and was hoping to buy a new civilian suit. Mate wrote, "I dreamed of seeing you all dressed up in a new suit with a new hat. You looked so nice."

Another portent of things to come?

I did not realize the significance of all those civilian clothes he was buying until we visited him in Washington. Clyde did not want to distress our parents, but when he and I were alone, he told me how most civilians in that town had nothing but contempt for servicemen.

Often fancy nightclubs in Washington refused entrance to men who were wearing military uniforms, although, when caught, always maintained that they showed absolutely no discrimination against men in uniform.[3]

The actions of the fancy hotels did not bother the students at the school, since they had no money to participate in such affairs anyway. But the attitude of the civilians hurt them very much. Those musicians were extremely talented and were highly regarded in their hometowns. Now people considered them scum, and that was a bitter pill for them to take.

Since the homes of "nice" girls were not open to them, the sailors kept civilian clothes in a locker away from the Navy Yard. Regulations forbade them from wearing their civilian clothes in the Navy Yard, but they could put on their "civies" after they left the Yard and change back to their uniforms before they returned to the Yard.

In civilian clothes, the sailors could be accepted by Washingtonians as persons who might come up to their social standards.

Unfortunately, *Arizona*'s last bandsmen did not live to see how highly servicemen would be regarded by those same people by the end of the year.

First-year students were given liberty every Wednesday evening from four o'clock until midnight. They also were free from noon on Saturday until seven-thirty Monday morning. Clyde spent his liberties with Jimmy Campbell from Florida. Jimmy played baritone in Kinney's band, and the two musicians planned to ship out together.

Clyde and Jimmy tried to see everything they could in Washington, as well as Alexandria and Arlington, Virginia.

In March, they spent the weekend in Warrenton, Virginia, a small town lying at the foot of the Blue Ridge Mountains about fifty-five miles from Washington. There they met a lot of nice young people, both boys and girls. From then on, they spent nearly every weekend in Warrenton, taking the bus over and back.

When they got back to Washington, they usually had only enough money left for bus fare back to the Navy Yard. Invariably, Clyde opted to spend his bus money on doughnuts and coffee, and walk back to the Yard. Although Jimmy still had enough money for his bus fare, he always chose to walk with Clyde. When I asked him why he didn't just ride on back and leave Clyde, Jimmy just grinned and said it was more fun to walk with him and preach all the way back about how Clyde must learn to manage his money better.

Radford spent many weekends with Don Harbin's family. The Harbins lived in Riverdale, Maryland, about seven miles from Washington. Radford also spent liberties with Coody.

Scruggs toured the gun shops which made the big guns for the ships and found it very interesting. He and Haas often went out on liberty together.

The Naval Hospital was still conducting a brisk business. Clyde wrote, "There have been five men sent to the hospital from the Music School with the measles. They might have to quarantine us."

Later he added another boy to the measles list, and told of a boy who had broken out with the chicken pox.

It must have occurred to the Navy then that their new recruits were a trifle young!

About that time, Clyde started sleepwalking again, something he had not done since he was a child. Sleepwalking was an extremely serious offense in the eyes of the Navy and was grounds for discharge. The Navy took a dim view of the possibility of one of its sailors walking in his sleep some night and strolling off the end of his ship.

Consequently, all Clyde's bunkmates in the barracks went on full alert to guard him. They slept lightly, always ready to chase him down and put him back into his bunk. He was never caught, but in hindsight, a medical discharge would have been a much better fate for him than the one which lay ahead.

The school continued to operate with little money. It is hard to imagine any branch where the Navy required more from its recruits than that of its musicians. In addition to insisting they replace their instruments with new ones, the Navy also required the students to purchase their own solo music. Scruggs asked his folks to send his trombone and piano solo music. He thought there was no use buying more music when he already owned so many pieces at home.

One can picture the scene if the Navy told its enlistees, "You will begin as an Apprentice Seaman, so be sure to bring your own mops, buckets and scrub brushes."

Only musicians would put up with such nonsense.

Disillusionment was setting in now for the students. Some resented all the menial tasks to which they were assigned, which cut into their practice time. Others thought they could have gotten a better musical education elsewhere. Most of the students were disturbed by the politics common in military life.

For those boys who did not like the school, their six-year enlistment must have stretched out before them into eternity!

One story making the rounds of the school was that Deems Taylor, a music critic in Washington, D.C., had written in his column that Bandmaster Benter surely followed the Navy Band well. Whether true or not, the story caused much glee among the students.

The school was still being remodeled, with the students doing much of the work, instead of practicing and studying. Some resented that bitterly.

They were homesick; they were tired of the confinement of the school; they wanted to go home on leave.

Most of the students, however, were still enjoying school and life. They were philosophical, telling themselves that at least they had a job in the midst of the depression.

Clyde could not believe he had been in the Navy nearly half a year. The time was going fast, because he was young and because, in spite of the heavy schedule at school, he was having fun.

If we can believe his letters, he was still his usual bubbly self. He wrote that the school was a swell place and that he felt he was going to learn a lot more about music. Again he explained that "solfege was the training of the ear so you can give the name of a note when it is played. If you hear a trombone hit a note, you can tell what note it is and play it on your instrument. This will come in handy, I know."

Toward the end of April, the sailors changed into their summer white uniforms. They were much cooler, but the boys hated them because they were so hard to keep clean.

Not all the planned entertainment for the new sailors was appreciated. One evening everyone in the Music School who did not have the duty was lined up and marched over to hear the Navy Band Symphony Concert. When they reached the concert hall, it was discovered that the concert hall was full, with no room for the students. As they were marching back out of the Marine barracks gate, one lady was heard to exclaim, "Oh dear, isn't it too bad that the boys have to go back without hearing the concert!"

From far back in the column of marching sailors came the voice of the ever-present class wit, "Lady, we don't *have* to go back—we *get* to go back!"

Hushed snickers were heard all up and down the line!

By far the most popular entertainment at the Navy Yard that spring was the view from the northeast corner of the Yard, where the School of Music was located. A girl just across the street forgot(?) each night to pull her shades down before she started undressing. There was always a large group of appreciative sailors standing on that corner each evening, taking in the view.

Sports competitions at the Yard also were popular. On April 18, the Receiving Station played a game of baseball against the Air Station. Daniels from the School of Music pitched for two innings before he gave up eight runs. Daniels was a tall, rangy boy from Hastings, Nebraska, and was a good friend of Radford's.

The School of Music continued to send the students out to perform. A group of singers, with Scruggs accompanying them on the piano, went up to "some swanky place" and sang for the Pan American Convention. Vice President Henry Agard Wallace was in attendance.

The next week, the same group sang for the Naval Engineers banquet. Scruggs said it was *the* banquet of the year and was lousy with gold braid. There were ninety-nine tables, with eight or ten persons seated at each table. That time, instead of playing the piano accompaniment, Scruggs sang with the group and they were accompanied by the big Navy Band.

Parades were a big part of life at the school. One Saturday the whole school marched in a big Army Day parade carrying, not their instruments, but guns and bayonets.

Later the school sent a 100-piece band to march and play in a safety parade. My brother participated in that parade.

In the spring of 1941, a distinct sadness lay over our nation. So many of our young people were leaving for military service that we were beginning to see that the life we had known up to now was changing, possibly forever. We still did not know how big that change would be.

Our nation was in the bewildering process of getting ready for war with little or no equipment and with green recruits. Our friend Dick Lucas wrote Clyde from the Air Corps in Texas:

> *Recruits are coming in here so fast that there are no older noncommissioned officers down here. The First Sergeant of our company has only been in the service four months.*
>
> *Our recruit drill is simple. We catch KP and Guard duty about once a month, but I was bugler for my company for awhile before it was disbanded, so was exempt from KP and Guard.*[4]

Whether we admitted it or not, war was getting closer.

The Foreign Policy Association reported that the U.S. Navy had "attained a virtual war footing" and that "it becomes increasingly clear that this country may have to participate in naval warfare with the ships it now possesses." The Association praised the rapidity and efficiency with which the Navy had been brought to a state of mobilization.[5]

Secretary of the Navy Frank Knox, while commissioning our new battleship *North Carolina*, told the nation that she was but one of a new line of ships to be added to Uncle Sam's fleet. He said that would give the United States unchallenged supremacy of the high seas.[6]

And we believed.

There was a flurry of building in Washington. Radford observed that, like the last war, the laboring man could tell his boss to go to hell and go down the street a block and get another job.

That may have been true in Washington, D.C., but certainly not in Oklahoma!

The School of Music was now taking in musicians faster and faster.

The boys at the school were getting restless. Radford asked his parents about their opinion of the war situation. He hoped the ship he was sent out on got convoy duty. He said he would like to see a damn good battle once, commenting that lots of guys had been in the Navy twenty years and returned without ever seeing a battle.

In six months, Radford would be present when his ship participated in a damn good battle, but he would not see very much of it.

In a step toward preparing for war which directly affected the School of Music, the Navy removed all pianos from its ships. The purpose of the move was to hold down the amount of flying splinters if the ships were hit by enemy fire.

As a result of that action, Scruggs lost his position as Band 21's piano player. Therefore, he sent for his accordion and his accordion music, promising to repay his family for the postage at the rate of two bucks each payday.

A few days later, he asked for some of his piano solos also, such as "Park Avenue Fantasy," "Marti Gras," etc. He had been told by his piano teacher to get some solos, so he thought he might as well use the solos he had already purchased before he left home.

What with students buying their own instruments and their own music, one would hardly figure that for a United States Navy band, would one?

As each of the future *Arizona* bandsmen completed four months of service, he took the test and was promoted to Seaman Second Class, which paid thirty-six dollars a month. Although they hoped the higher rate would enable them to save money, they still had their debts to pay off.

It was late in April before Clyde finally finished repaying the loan for his train ticket to come home on leave. From then until his death, he continued to send money home each payday, and Pate kept a meticulous record of his loans, so he could send him money when he finally got his next leave.

Clyde wrote me, "Boy, that is a joke about you going through your pay quicker than anyone you ever saw. You've never seen a sailor then. He's broke an hour after he gets paid (if he is lucky)."

Mate and I both had birthdays in April. Clyde wrote late in April that he was sorry he did not send us anything for our birthdays, but that each time, he did not even have bus fare into town. He promised to make it up to us sometime. I wrote him that we celebrated Mate's birthday on April 3. We had a cake, but I told Clyde it was not any fun without him.

After he checked on the long distance telephone rates, Radford told his folks that the first time he had three bucks to spare, he would give them a ring.

Late in April, he did call his girl back home and reported to his mother that the cost was two dollars and ninety cents for three minutes.

Rumors about shipping out kept the students and their families on edge. Both Clyde and Scruggs heard that Band 21 would ship out in November. Clyde and Henry Brown were scheduled to ship out at the same time, but not on the same ship nor to the same place.

It was said that Radford's Band 20 was to ship out the first of July, and would be sent to the *New York* or to the *Arkansas*, battleships which were operating in the Atlantic Ocean.

Gerald Cox was granted his boot leave in April. He told his parents it appeared he would get his two-year training on a ship, instead of at the School of Music, as he was due to ship out soon.[7]

Since the bands which were shipping out were always given leave before they went to sea, the families back home were getting very eager. Every letter back and forth between *Arizona*'s future band members and their families concerned the fervent wish on both sides that they could see each other soon.

Radford suggested that his folks just climb into their new V-8 and drive to Washington.

He added, "The scenery here sure has that back in old Nebraska beat, but between you and me, that place would look darn good to me now."

June Brabbzson went to Washington from her home in Long Island, New York, to visit her brother Oran.[8]

According to Scruggs, rumors were still flying that they would go out before the end of the year, possibly to the West Coast. He said if they did not go to the West Coast, he did not know when he would ever see his family again, as he did not expect any leave.

Radford particularly wanted to see his girl and his family again before he left, but he wrote that it looked as if they would not get any leave before they shipped out. Even if he did get a leave, he didn't think he would have the dough to come home, anyway. He was tied down completely by the payments on the life insurance he had taken out. In order to pay it up to date, he had to save twenty dollars of the thirty-six dollars he was earning.

As it turned out, all his sacrifice to pay those life insurance premiums nearly went for nought.

On April 16, the four bands which were shipping out were granted leave. They were scheduled to go aboard their ships when they returned from leave.

Back home, things were getting pretty dull in Okmulgee, with so many of the boys being drafted or enlisting in the service. I still complained about the shortage of boys and tried to figure how I could move to Washington to work. It seemed to me that all the boys were having great adventures while I, a lowly girl, was stuck at home.

On the envelope of one letter to Clyde, I drew a picture of a lady sitting in her chair knitting, surrounded by her bird cage and her cat, which was playing with the ball of yarn. Under the picture, I put "Life Here is Very Exciting !" Although I was still going out dancing nearly every night, all the boys I was dating were just good friends.

On another envelope, I drew a picture of a man with a long beard, leaning over on his cane, with a baby crawling beside him. I wrote under it "There Are Still Plenty of Men Here."

I was still asking Clyde's opinion of the boys I was dating. I had always done that when he was home, and I told him how much I missed his comments about my friends.

I wrote him news of the Okmulgee High School band. The band was getting new hats, and I added: "I wish I were back there, don't you? We would be working on the contest numbers about now." The band had been such an important part of our lives and now that it was spring, we missed it terribly.

The lack of music in my life was particularly depressing for me. When our local band went to Shawnee to play for contest, I wrote Clyde, "It really makes me sad 'cause I couldn't go to the contests. You have band work still, but I don't have anything! When I come up there, can I play in the band so I can say I played in the Navy Band?"

We were landlubbers, with no idea of the restrictions of the U.S. Navy.

Mate wrote her son:

> *Sometimes I just nearly pass out thinking of you being gone, then I get to thinking what would you do if you were here? And of the wonderful chance you have in your music. Also the fact that you have to have a special training in something in order to get anywhere in life, so I brighten up. And am glad you are where you can get a better education.*

Now that it was spring in Washington, Clyde asked us to send him his tennis racquet. He said there was a court next to the barracks.

Our grandparents Williams had their fiftieth wedding anniversary on April 25 and all the family got together in Henryetta. It was really sad, with all the boys in the family gone now. We wrote Clyde about the party and gave him the news of our family.

Even our family dog, who had lived with us nearly ten years, was affected. One cool evening, I decided to borrow Clyde's leather jacket. When I got it from the closet to try it on, our dog Dinky, smelling Clyde's scent on the jacket, nearly went crazy. He was beside himself, leaping into the air and whining. I felt so sorry for him, as I knew how very much he, too, missed Clyde.

In April, I began asking Clyde for a photograph of him, taken in his uniform. I asked for that all the time he was still living, but I never did receive one. I always felt sure he did have his portrait taken in Hawaii, but although I tried very hard after his death, I was never able to find the photographer.

Reginald Carter, Clyde's best friend back home, summed up the situation for all of us, when he wrote Clyde:

I miss you.[9]

On Saturday, April 12, the day before Easter, a tragedy occurred in the Carter family next door which totally devastated all of us. Their seven-year old son Charlie and a six-year old neighbor boy managed to shut themselves up in an old unused icebox and suffocated. It was late in the day when we went home for supper that we learned the boys were missing and that all the parents were out searching for them. Their sisters found them shortly after we arrived, and we called the ambulance.

Mate and Pate spent the next day cooking for the Carter family. I stayed with my friend Kay Kennedy for several nights, so some of the relatives of the Carters could use my bedroom.

We all took off work to attend the funeral on Monday, and I wrote Clyde a long letter, describing the tragedy and the funeral.

Of course, Pate had seen death at the front in the Muese-Argonne forest during World War I, and both he and Mate had lost family members during their early years as children of homesteaders.

But it was the first time Clyde and I had been faced with the death of someone close to us. We were not yet familiar with tragedy. We did not witness bloody battles and horrible crimes every evening on television, so our compassion had not yet been dulled.

Mrs. Carter told me they could not have made it without us, and Mr. Carter told me he just felt as if he were smothering all the time.

I could not comprehend such extreme grief then, but our turn was to come soon. And years later, when my husband and I lost our only son, I thought of the Carters and of my parents, and then I understood.

That whole experience really bothered me. It was a long, long time before I could step into a closet or any closed area, and I had trouble eating and sleeping for quite some time.

Clyde was devastated. He loved those people so very much, and he was so very far away. He wrote, "I never was so shocked in all my life as I was when I read about Charlie dying. That is the hardest way to go, they say. I'll bet Mrs. Carter is plenty broken up about his death. I wish there were something I could do, but I don't know of anything I could do. Give the Carter's my sorrow and tell them I wish I could have done something."

We could not possibly have known it then, but that was the first of three tragedies we and the Carter family were to face together, changing our lives forever. And although we tried very hard to help each other, in the long run, each of us had to find our way through that dark valley alone.

At the school, some of the boys received five days' leave for Easter weekend. Since that was not enough time for Clyde to come home, he and Jimmy Campbell planned to go to Jimmy's home in Florida. They thought they could get a ride each way on a fruit truck which made deliveries to Washington from Florida.

That, of course, drew another sermon from Pate, who was still expecting disaster. He thought five days was too short a time to make the trip to Florida and that the truck rides were too uncertain. He also reminded Clyde that he had just finished his probation period.

It turned out to be a moot point, as Campbell's parents moved to Virginia Beach before Easter. The two boys spent their leave with Jimmy's parents, but in Virginia, not in Florida.

All during the month of March, while we still thought Clyde would ship out in November, we continued making plans for our trip to Washington. We finally worked out our finances, and on March 3, Pate bought a 1936 V-8 Ford sedan for his car and two hundred sixty dollars. Clyde offered to lend Pate money each month to help make the car payments, and Mate told Clyde that, with all of us helping, we were going to be able to make the trip.

Clyde was delighted. He said it would be good to see all of us again, and told me I would meet all the guys at the Friday night dance at the Navy Yard.

Pate arranged for his vacation to run from June 8 to 28. We planned to go to Washington, then to Niagara Falls, and on up to Toronto, Canada.

I was excited and looking forward to seeing Clyde again, going to the Navy dances, and to meeting his friends from the school. I asked him about the appropriate clothes to wear back East.

With trying to buy some clothes for the trip and saving for the gasoline, I was even more broke than usual. I asked Clyde to keep praying that we got to come.

Now two of our aunts began saving their money to go to Washington with us.

But early in April, Clyde told us there were now complications. Because of the increase in Navy personnel, four more bands, in addition to the four scheduled to leave in May, would leave in June. If that were true, Clyde would ship out in June, as Band Number 21 was the third band on the list.

He suggested we stand by for more definite news, and to keep our fingers crossed. He added: "How many are coming up here? Bring everybody. This town will hold them."

None of that helped our plans any. Mate wrote Clyde that she hoped he did not leave in June because first, we wanted to come up and second, we wanted him to have more schooling. The school was what all the struggle had been about.

She consoled herself that she had been told Clyde could go back to the school once in awhile. She added, "My son, hitch your wagon to a star and strive for it."

Clyde was never to return to the School of Music again, nor was he ever to reach his star.

That is, we mere mortals do not think he did.

Clyde actually answered my questions about the Navy Yard dances, reporting that the girls did not wear formals to the dances, and that he had not seen any girls wearing slacks in Washington. However, he said it was still cold there and had snowed all day.

He said the guys danced every kind of way under the sun, so I could take my pick of the style of dancing.

Also, he told me Daniels wanted a date with me when we came up, and that he thought Daniels was OK. But he warned me that I must watch everyone I was with in Washington.

Something had happened to that sweet, innocent boy from the small town in Oklahoma. He no longer trusted everyone he met.

Clyde suggested that when we got to Washington, we could all go to New York some weekend. We would have time to go, because he could get off from Friday afternoon to seven-fifteen Monday morning.

He thought we would be able to get up to Washington before he left, but warned that the sooner we came, the better chance we would have to catch him still there.

That added an urgency to our plans, but still we did not give up the idea of the trip. Apparently all those obstacles only made us more determined to see Clyde before he left.

At the beginning of April, Pate was becoming worried about our trip, and wrote Clyde that he doubted we could get the money together in only two months. But by the end of April, he had decided we would try to see him before he shipped out.

I have often wondered why my parents and I made such an effort to make that trip to Washington. It is obvious we did not have enough money for such an undertaking, but we kept right on planning for it anyway.

What force was pushing us to keep struggling, and what kept us from simply giving up?

CHAPTER 10

Graduation

By May 1941 people were getting more nervous about the possibility of war. President Roosevelt was urging us to buy Defense Bonds, even if, as he put it, it meant giving up some customary comforts and luxuries.[1]

Only a man who had been wealthy all his life would make such a suggestion. The depression had taken care of our "customary comforts and luxuries" long ago. But somehow, we did as he asked.

Most of our uneasiness centered around the war in Europe. People were anxious about Hitler and what he planned to do next. Even "Aunt Lizzie" Deevers, celebrating her 110th birthday in Oklahoma, expected the Germans to come over and attack the United States at any moment. She figured when the Germans got to Sapulpa, Oklahoma, she would get into the war, since she could "shoot the hat off your head and never touch you."[2]

We did not worry too much about Japan, because newspapers were still telling us that our Navy was stronger than ever.[3]

But some military men were telling us that the United States should beat Japan to the draw. They warned that the U.S. Naval Fleet was the only thing which stood between Japan and the Philippines, Singapore, and Malaya.[4]

Belatedly, our nation's leaders thought that perhaps we should cease aiding and abetting our enemies and took steps to tighten our national security.

The Washington Post announced on May 14 that they would no longer print lists of transfers of officers and would restrict news of movements of ships and of Marine Corps and Reserve units.[5]

Naval Intelligence asked Congress for authority to apply rigid censorship on photographs of ships, Navy Yards and bases, and of airplanes and equipment being manufactured for the Navy.[6]

Apparently it was still legal for Japanese spies to run all over Pearl Harbor, snapping photographs of our military installations and ships.

On May 18, the War Department announced that the greatest mass flight in history had occurred "last week," when twenty-one flying fortresses made a secret trip to Hickam Field in Hawaii. The War Department added that other air armadas were being groomed for flight to Hawaii soon.[7]

The flight of Army bombers was staged to call the world's attention to the one hundred million dollar defense program on the Islands which the United States was rushing to completion. The Army said smugly that when the fortifications were completed, Hawaii would be the strongest base in the world.[8]

The Washington Post ran a two-page feature article about the School of Music on May 4. Featured were several photographs of instructors and of small groups of students.

One band was pictured in its entirety—Fred Kinney's Band Number 21.[9] Moorhouse, Burdette, and Shaw sent a copy of the article home, and that photograph was to become very important to the families of the *Arizona* bandsmen.

Three weeks later, when Band 21 graduated, nearly half the musicians shown in the photo had been replaced for various reasons and Kinney's band had become Band Number 22.

Whether their transfer was due to illness, personality clashes, or other reasons, most of the boys who were taken out of soon-to-be *Arizona*'s last band still remember the bitter disappointment they felt when they had to leave their friends in Band Number 21.

Six months would go by before they realized that their transfer had been, in the strictest sense, a matter of life or death.

Dr. Walter Wehner, formerly a student at the School of Music, survived the war, earned his doctor's degree, and became a college music instructor. He was originally assigned to Band 21. Because Bob Clark, a clarinet player at the school, was sent to the big Navy

Band, Wehner was taken from Band 21 in March to replace Clark in Band 20. Wehner still remembers his acute disappointment.[10]

William Harten originally played trumpet in Band 21.[11]

Howard G. Hare played drums in Kinney's band until he became ill and was transferred to another band.[12]

Casper Gerace, a cornet player, left Kinney's band late in May.[13]

As I interviewed men who had attended the School of Music with the *Arizona* musicians, I was surprised to find how many of them still remember *Arizona*'s bandsmen.

Henry Brown and Clyde were friends from their Okmulgee High School days. Jim McCulloch was also a good friend of Henry Brown's.[14]

James Montgomery was a friend of both Clyde and Radford and he remembers them well.[15] Both Clyde and Radford mentioned Montgomery in their letters home.

Paul Holdaway was also a good friend of Radford's in school.[16]

Wendell Hurley went to Pennsylvania several times to visit the family of Kenneth Lobien. Lobien was assigned to Band 20.[17] His family wrote Hurley's family several times after Hurley's death.[18]

Roger Snyder's family lived about 100 miles from the school. Snyder had a girl back home, so he went home every weekend. Because of that, he did not know many of the boys at the school, but remembers Bandy, Moorhouse, and Radford very well.[19]

Richard Duryea knew Harvey Sanderson at school and they went on many liberties together.[20]

Dr. Walter Wehner was a friend of Floege in school and has remembered him with sadness all his life.[21]

Lieutenant Colonel Frank G. Forgione remembers my brother from school.[22]

Gerald Wentworth knew Chernucha in school, as did J. E. "Duke" Bolen.[23]

Frank Schwarz knew Sanderson and Chernucha.[24]

Many alumni, such as Mike Palchefsky, although they no longer remember *Arizona*'s musicians by name, have thought of them all these years, always with a shudder and a "There, but for the Grace of God, go I" murmur.

After Bands Number 11, 12, 13, and 14 returned to the school from leave, they graduated and shipped out at the end of April. When those bandsmen left for their leaves, some thirty musicians from the school replaced them in the funeral detail. They played for all the funerals of deceased officers who were buried at Arlington Cemetery. As Radford reverently expressed it, "We have to play for every damn officer that they plant over there."

The musicians were taken by bus to Arlington Cemetery, about six miles west of the Navy Yard. Rather than considering it a gloomy task, the young boys turned it into a school holiday, yelling and whistling at every female they saw on the way over there and back.

Once arriving at the funerals, however, all horseplay was abandoned, and the musicians showed nothing but respect for the bereaved families. It is too bad that respect has been lost today.

Wearing their dress blue uniforms and white leggings, they played "Lead Kindly Light" and "Abide With Me" just outside the church, then played three different funeral marches as they led the procession from the church to the grave site, where they played "Nearer My God To Thee."

Ever the artist, Radford commented, "Those little white stones all lined up on the green grass sure make a pretty sight."

The coffin was carried to the church in a regular funeral coach and from the church to the grave on a black wagon pulled by seven white Army horses.

The number seven would soon play an important part in the lives of Band Number 21.

Impressed by the number of gold braids who attended the funerals, Radford commented that officers were the only ones who rated a band to play at their funerals. He observed that guys like him would only have the Seaman Guard shoot over their graves.

He was mistaken.

None of the students who performed at those funeral services day after day could have foreseen the deaths of twenty-two of their fellow musicians seven months later. (One musician from the band of the *West Virginia* was also killed on December 7.) Nor could they have foreseen how twenty Musician Second Class sailors and one

Musician First Class, along with the other *Arizona* sailors killed that day, have had bands, speeches, flowers, and honors heaped upon them for more than fifty years.

Nor has there ever been any lack of gold braid at their memorial services. What passes for their graves has been visited by dignitaries from many countries, and the presidents of our own country have gone there many times to pay their respects.

There are few military officers who have been given as much honor after death as has the fallen crew of the *Arizona*.

In May 1941, when they had finished their work, the funeral detail from the school watched about 170 soldiers from Fort Myer as they drilled on horseback. Fort Myer, just to the west of Arlington Cemetery, was a cavalry post then, and the sailors admired the handsome horses and the skillful riding.

Sunday, May 11, was the first Mother's Day most of the students had not spent with their moms, and they all tried to do something special for them. The mothers of the *Arizona* band boys were to treasure their sons' thoughtfulness for the rest of their lives.

Clyde sent Mate a Mother's Day telegram, which she always kept.

Any student who lived close enough to go home received leave from Friday evening until Monday morning.

Radford wrote his sister a few days before Mother's Day to tell her he would call his mother on Sunday evening, and asked her to have their mom home by then. It would take three of his remaining four bucks, but he figured one buck would buy his Bull Durham until payday. He did complete his call to his mother, and both enjoyed it very much.

Wendell Hurley hitchhiked with Kenneth Lobien to his home in Lehighton, Pennsylvania, to spend the weekend with the Lobien family.[25]

Early in May, Band Number 21 knew they would ship out soon, but they did not know when. Nor did they know to which ship they would be assigned.

Kinney was still exchanging his musicians all during the month of May. Caught in the last-minute shuffle was Jimmy Campbell, my brother's best friend at the school. Jimmy was pulled from the *Ari-*

zona band and assigned as a replacement in the band at Guantanamo Bay, Cuba.

In what would be my brother's last chance for life, he went to the office and requested transfer to that same band, but his request was denied.

Clyde and Jimmy were very disappointed. After planning for months to ship out together, now they were to be sent to different parts of the world. Neal Radford was moved into Kinney's band to replace Campbell, and it was settled.

Campbell would live. Radford and my brother would die.

Now the war news began to sound serious.

Radford commented that one thing he did not like about shipping out was that his family would never know where he was, because the sailors' letters would be censored "until this mess is over with."

Finally, on May 8, word came down from on high that they would ship out on June 2, a month earlier than they had expected. They would be assigned to the *Pyro*, an old ammunition ship, and would be stationed on the East Coast.

That was not very welcome news to Band 21. They had heard that the *Pyro* "went all over hell and was never in one place very long." Kinney told them not to worry—he thought they would just be transported by the *Pyro* to some battleship or cruiser in the fleet.

Kinney was correct to tell his boys not to worry. So long as they remained Band Number 21, they were safe.

But all that changed a few days later.

When the original Band Number 22 was assigned to the *Arizona*, its bandmaster requested a transfer to the *Tennessee* because he had a relative on that ship. There was nothing wrong with his request. At that time, the Navy honored requests from relatives to serve on the same ship, whenever it was possible.

However, that policy was discontinued after the cruiser *Juneau* was sunk by the Japanese on November 14-15, 1942, at Guadalcanal. Serving on her were five Sullivan brothers, all of whom were killed. Our nation reacted with such horror to the story of their mother's inexpressible grief that the Navy no longer allowed relatives to serve on the same ship.

Kinney was certainly not willing to exchange bands with his fellow bandmaster. After he had worked so hard to put together such an outstanding band and had spent so much time perfecting it, he had no intention of giving it up.

So the numbers of the two bands, Band Number 21 and Band Number 22, were reversed.

And just that quickly, Fred Kinney and his boys were handed their death sentences.

Tennessee's bandmaster did not serve with his relative, after all. According to Betty Kinney, he was surveyed out of the Navy for a physical problem just before the bands left Washington, and another bandmaster was assigned to the *Tennessee* band.[26]

Tennessee was anchored in front of *Arizona* at Pearl Harbor on December 7, 1941. She also suffered extensive damage, but fortunately all her band survived.

On May 16, word again came down from on high. Kinney's band, now called Band Number 22, would ship out on May 26 and would board the *Lassen*, which they were told (erroneously) was a cargo ship. They were also told they would go to Panama, then to Pearl Harbor, Territory of Hawaii, for transfer to the battleship *Arizona*.

Arizona's home port was in San Pedro, near Long Beach, so Scruggs would be home whenever the ship was in port.

With graduation so close, Kinney insisted his bandsmen purchase the best musical instruments available. Nearly all his boys bought new instruments, either in Washington or on the *Arizona*.

Burdette, with the help of his parents, had bought his new French horn when he arrived at the school. They paid three hundred dollars for his horn, which was a small fortune in 1941.[27]

Radford bought a new baritone horn in Washington so he could ship out with Kinney's band.

Now, just as they were leaving, the musicians were moved into brand new barracks. They were on the third floor of a just-completed building, with a beautiful view of the Anacostia River.

Apparently the Navy cooks were still doing a good job of filling up so many starving young boys. Radford described one meal as a "fairly good chow" of beefsteak, mashed potatoes, creamed peas, greens, pear pie, and ice cream. The lemonade they were served twice a day was a mixture of tea and lemonade.

Petty theft was still a problem. Radford lost a buck to some light-fingered student, and Harbin lost five dollars. Radford made his usual comment about artists who were not too good to steal another guy blind.

A group of singers from the school, accompanied by Scruggs on the piano, sang at the "swankiest hotel in town" for "a big intellectual group." The Secretary of Agriculture was there, as well as the British Minister "Sir Campbell or something." Scruggs said he never ate such fancy stuff in his life.

Although four bands were granted leave and four bands were not, the school did lighten up on the bandsmen who were shipping out. They did not have any classes nor have to put in so many practice hours. After practicing with their bands for six hours, they were free after four o'clock for liberty. Unfortunately, most of them had no money with which to enjoy those special privileges.

With liberty every night, the boys wanted to see the sights before they left Washington. Since he was flat broke and payday was not until the next Friday, Radford immediately wrote home for a loan of three or four "bucks."

Washington was a good liberty town, as the movie houses featured personal appearances by big-name dance bands. For forty-four cents, one could see the movie and then be entertained with a live band concert. For the same amount, one could see the striptease at the Gayety Burlesque Theater.

The weekend after Mother's Day, Radford went with Montgomery to visit his parents in New Jersey. They fished in the ocean for two days, visited the boardwalks along the New Jersey coast, and had a great time.

Besides Cox, only one other future *Arizona* bandsman went on leave in May. Ernest Whitson was granted an emergency leave to visit his mother, who was very ill. Fortunately, when he arrived, she no longer needed another blood transfusion and was feeling better.[28]

Arizona's new band was one of four unfortunate bands which was not granted leave, so only a few of its other musicians were able to go home before they shipped out.

We never did understand why the Commanding Officer of the school did not see to it that all the bands were given leave before they left. Especially in the case of *Arizona's* bandsmen, that last leave would have meant all the difference in the world to their families later on.

It is hard to believe that the bands' departures were so urgent that their members could not have been spared for two weeks to go home to tell their families and friends good-bye. It is unfortunate that same sense of urgency did not prevail in Pearl Harbor later in the year.

Now the boys began planning their next leave.

Radford heard that one good thing about being in the band was that they usually got leave when the ship went into dry dock. They all hoped *Arizona* would need much repair and need it soon.

The Graduation Ceremony on Friday, May 23, 1941, was very impressive. The Sail Loft at the Washington Navy Yard was packed with students from the U.S. Navy School of Music. Rear Admiral George T. Pettengill, USN, Commandant of the Washington Navy Yard, presented the diplomas and addressed the class. Also participating were Commander R. A. Dyer, USN; Lieutenant Commander H. D. McIntosh, USN; Lieutenant Commander W. H. Rafferty, Chaplain, USN; Captain Charles Benter, USN, Officer-in-Charge of the United States Navy School of Music; and Captain Taylor Branson, USMC, (Ret.), former leader of the U.S. Marine Band.[29]

Eight extremely competent twenty-piece bands and eight very good bandmasters graduated that day. Very few of the students had completed the two years' schooling they had been promised when they joined the Navy. All were rushed out to Flag commands of the fleet to be part of the Navy's planned entertainment program. So many men were joining the Navy in one jump ahead of the draft that steps must be taken to bolster their morale. Even the Navy realized you cannot keep a sailor away from home for over a year without giving him some diversion. The foremost reason, of course, for their planned entertainment programs—music, sports, contests, etc.—was the Navy's desire that its sailors sign over for another six-year hitch at the end of their enlistments.

The eight graduating bands, their leaders, and their assignments were:

Band Number 15, First Musician J. A. Simpson, the light cruiser *Honolulu*.

Band Number 16, Bandmaster L. R. Luckenbach, the battleship *California*.

Band Number 17, First Musician T. G. Carlin, the battleship *West Virginia*.

Band Number 18, Bandmaster M. V. Spencer, the heavy cruiser *Indianapolis*.

Band Number 19, First Musician L. J. B. Breaux, the battleship *Texas*.

Band Number 20, First Musician H. B. Beauregard, the battleship *Wyoming*.

Band Number 21, First Musician F. B. Donovan, the battleship *Tennessee*. Donovan was replaced by James Lamar Smith before the band left Washington.

Band Number 22, First Musician Fred W. Kinney, the battleship *Arizona*.[30]

The musicians in the graduating bands had gone to school together for some months; they had played in the same bands; they had gone out on liberty together. Now graduation meant separation from their good friends.

Arizona's musicians knew they would not see their friends who had been assigned to the *Texas* and the *Wyoming* for a long time, since those bands were scheduled to go to the Atlantic Fleet. The other six bands, however, were leaving soon to join the Pacific Fleet, so *Arizona*'s bandsmen hoped they would see the members of those bands in Pearl Harbor.

After graduation, the new *Arizona* band was transported on the ammunition carrier *Lassen* to meet its ship. The new *Tennessee* band was transported on the ammunition carrier *Pyro* and arrived in Hawaii in August.[31]

Bandmaster L. B. Luckenbach escorted the new bands for the *Honolulu, California, West Virginia,* and *Indianapolis* to the West Coast. They left Washington by train on June 4 for San Diego, California.[32]

And so the school days for the graduating musicians ended. It was time to assume the job for which they had joined the Navy.

Their families back home had no reason to doubt that the Navy would protect and care for their loved ones.

For the families of the musicians headed for Pearl Harbor, however, that trust was misplaced.

CHAPTER 11

Our Trip

Despite all the changes in my brother's proposed departure date, we clung stubbornly to our belief that we really were going to Washington to visit him. We had been planning and saving for that trip from the very moment Clyde entered the Navy in November 1940. At that time, we thought we had two years to work out our finances.

That changed in February 1941 when he wrote that he would probably ship out in November. That gave us only a few months to buy another car and to save enough money for our travel expenses.

Undaunted, Pate and I made arrangements to take our vacations from June 8-29, and we prayed a lot.

But then Clyde wrote us on May 8 that Band Number 21 was due to ship out June 2 on the *Pyro* and that he would no doubt be gone by the time we got there. He was so disappointed, and we were devastated!

But we did not come from pioneer stock for nothing. That was one battle the United States Navy was not going to win! They could bar us from the graduation exercises, but they could not bar us from seeing our Clyde before he left!

Consequently, the more changes the Navy made, the more determined we became to travel to Washington. If the Navy would not give our Clyde two years at the School of Music, if the Navy would not give him leave before he shipped out, and if the Navy would not keep him at the school until our vacation began, so be it.

We would just change our plans again.

I dashed off a letter to Clyde. On the envelope was a drawing of a sailor waving from the deck of the USS *Pyro* and a girl waving from a car marked "USS *V-8*." Under the drawing was a triumphant "We're coming anyway!" I added:

> *Cheer up ! The trip isn't ruined to hell after all. We're leaving here May 18 and will be there May 21. If anything unexpected turns up, will let you know. We can stay there until you ship out. Don't tell anyone, but I'm going to stow away on your ship and go, too.*

We did not know that Kinney's band had been reassigned to the *Arizona* instead of the *Tennessee*. And I had no way of knowing that it would not have been the first time a female had stowed away on *Arizona*.

By the time we received word about the June 2 shipping-out date, we had only a week to get ready. But on Sunday, May 18, we threw our clothes into the car and headed for Washington.

When we left Okmulgee, Clyde's shipping-out date had been changed yet again. He would not be in Washington until June 2, but was scheduled to leave on May 25. We did not know that when we left, but we did realize we had better forego all the side trips we had planned and hurry on up to Washington.

Reginald Carter wrote Clyde on May 18 to tell him that we had just left. His letter shows just how uneasy we all were, when he wrote:

> *Good about you. That is, if you don't get bumped off near China.*
> *Good luck to you on the ship.*[1]

Our financial picture was helped considerably when our friend Docia Hatcher accepted our invitation to go to Washington with us and to share expenses. Her two daughters, Kathleen and Vivian, were working in Washington, and Docia welcomed the opportunity to visit with them.

Nothing about our trip materialized as we had planned, but depression people were used to disappointments and had learned to make the best of circumstances. We could easily settle for second best, or even third or fourth.

I have only scattered memories of our drive to Washington. We had talked so much about going that it was hard to believe we actually were on our way. I do remember how we all enjoyed the scenery as we motored along.

There were not big super highways then, but on the other hand, there was not so much traffic. The tourist courts in which we stayed each night were not to be compared to the luxury motels of today. They were simply small cabins sitting in a row, and we did not feel they were any too clean.

After all the difficulties connected with our trip, it is not surprising that we arrived in Washington in the midst of a record heat wave.[2] Air conditioning for automobiles was still many, many years away.

Our first task in Washington was to find Arlington, Virginia, where Docia's daughters lived.

None of us ever forgot the lovely lady riding on a beautiful horse, who calmly pointed out to us that we were happily putt-putting up the wrong way on a one-way street. After Pate got turned around and we saw we would get no tickets nor injuries, we all laughed uproariously for blocks.

When we finally arrived at Kathleen's home, she and her husband insisted we stay in their basement. They had arranged cots for sleeping and a hot plate for cooking, and it was all very clean and cool. We were grateful for their kindness, as the tourist courts were far away and not nearly so clean nor safe.

As a matter of fact, it came as a definite miracle for us. We had left Okmulgee with more faith than money, and their thoughtfulness made our trip considerably less expensive.

We called Clyde immediately at the school to tell him where we were, and he came out to Kathleen's home Thursday evening.

After all my planning for five months to go to the Friday night dance at the Navy Yard, it turned out Clyde had the duty Friday evening and must attend his graduation ceremony. We, as mere mortals, were not allowed in the Sail Loft for the ceremony.

Clyde brought his friends Jimmy Campbell and George Wedin out to our temporary home on Saturday, and Mate cooked pork chops for us all on the hot plate in the basement. We took pictures and visited with Kathleen and Vivian all afternoon.

That evening, the boys took me downtown to see a movie. I enjoyed the beautiful theater we attended and the happy, jolly boys who accompanied me.

Sunday morning Clyde and I went around Washington, seeing the White House, the Washington Monument, and other points of interest.

Then Clyde took me to Mother Steed's for dancing. Most of the *Arizona* band boys were there, having come to meet me and to tell Mother Steed good-bye.

Mother Steed was an amazing woman. She was Mrs. J. Nathaniel Steed, formerly Miss Emma C. Baum. At the time I first met her, she was about seventy-five years old. Her husband, a native of North Carolina, was retired.

She was a fifth-generation Washingtonian, and had worked for eighteen years as secretary of the Episcopal Home for Children. During World War I, at the age fifty-two, she had left that job to go overseas with a Red Cross unit, where she worked at a base hospital at Dijon, France. During that war, Mother Steed lost the sight of one eye while serving her "boys."

At the end of World War I, Mother Steed devoted her life to helping servicemen. She established and ran a canteen at 1015 "L" Street, NW and another canteen in Georgetown. She assisted veterans in getting hospitalization and compensation, always difficult for veterans after any of our wars.

Mother Steed lived in Falls Church, Virginia, and made the one-hour bus trip each day to operate her club. She served the boys lunch daily, scrounging for donations of food and money to keep the club running.[3]

Just ten days before we visited the Service Club, Eleanor Roosevelt and Mrs. Curtis Shears, president of the Women's National Democratic Club, were hostesses at a silver offering tea at the club. Proceeds from the tea were to be used to enlarge the canteen. It was pointed out that the nominal charge to the servicemen for overnight lodging did not pay the full cost of the upkeep at the club.[4]

The boys did not need the food so much as they needed the love and concern she gave them. Most servicemen who were stationed near Washington knew Mother Steed, and she nurtured thousands of them—lonely, weary, homesick boys who welcomed a kind word from a woman who reminded them of their mother.

Two months after Pearl Harbor, needing a larger club, Mother Steed opened the Servicemens' Club No. 1 at 306 Pennsylvania Avenue, NW. Having started with a coffeepot and two cups, by 1945 she was serving forty thousand servicemen each week, with four hundred hostesses volunteering their time to dance with the boys.[5]

After I went to Washington to work in January 1942, I spent many evenings at Mother Steed's, dancing with her boys. Several of my friends met their future husbands at her club.

But that was later. Now Clyde took me to Mother Steed's Soldiers, Sailors, and Marines Club at 1015 "L" Street, NW, and there were the boys from the School of Music! Of course, they gave the big rush to their pal's sister, and I danced all afternoon with first one sailor and then another. Finally, I told Clyde I just had to sit down, as I was about to drop! He was horrified, and begged me please to keep dancing with his friends. He explained that it was the first time since they had left home that most of the boys had been with a decent girl, and that I reminded them of their sisters and their girls back home. Of course, when I heard that, all pain and fatigue left, and I did not sit down all afternoon. What a thrill for a young girl— a long, long stag line, ready to cut in and dance.

Although I do not remember each boy personally, I can still envision that sea of happy faces with which I was surrounded that afternoon. They were all still laughing about their boring graduation and about having to go forward and shake hands with Lieutenant Benter, who was not their favorite person.

That was when I heard the Deems Taylor story. I do not recall any comments about Fred Kinney, probably because most of the boys did not yet know him very well.

That afternoon of dancing and talking with the Music School boys, especially the boys of the *Arizona* band, has always remained a very special memory for me. Whenever I think of *Arizona*'s musicians, which is often, I always see them laughing and joking.

While we were dancing, many of the musicians asked me to go out with them, but I refused all offers until after my brother had left Washington. That eliminated all the boys from the *Arizona* band, as they were shipping out the next day.

However, I did accept a date for the following Wednesday with J. L. "Kid" Reed, who was due to ship out a few days after the *Arizona* boys.

When I told Clyde I had made the date, he was visibly uneasy, and wanted to know immediately with whom. He thought Reed would be all right, but he told me to be very careful in that town. I was touched by his concern, and I gathered that some of the boys at the school had a reputation for loving the ladies.

After the dance, Clyde and I walked to the Chinese restaurant on Pennsylvania Avenue to have dinner. As we were walking along, chatting and laughing, I noticed that women walking past us were staring at me and looking shocked. I finally asked him why those women were looking at me in such a strange way. Clyde explained that they felt no decent girl would go out with a sailor in Washington, so the biddies thought I was a "loose woman." That made me so furious that I began staring them right in the eyes and even made some of them look ashamed.

Clyde also told me how some of the fine young civilian men of Washington would pass by in their fancy cars and shout "Uncle Sam's Chambermaids" to the sailors, and of the shoddy treatment servicemen received from the good citizens of Washington, D.C. As he talked, I could see how hurt was that sensitive, talented, kind boy.

Of course, there were exceptions. Some servicemen met, dated, and married nice girls. But usually the treatment by civilians of our men in uniform prior to World War II was not very cordial.

It is interesting how that treatment of servicemen changes drastically when our nation is faced with war, or when a town is faced with the closing of a military base. Then nothing is too good for "our boys in uniform."

I never forgot the treatment my brother and his friends received from most Washingtonians. By the time I moved there in January 1942, the war had begun and people everywhere were treating servicemen kindly. I have always regretted that the *Arizona* band boys did not ever know how suddenly, overnight, servicemen became good, decent men in the eyes of our nation's citizens, fit even for their daughters to go out with.

Since the band lived only about fifteen minutes into the war, its musicians never did know that.

Fortunately, they also did not know that they were about to give their lives for such smug, self-righteous people.

As we ate, Clyde and our Chinese waiter had a long discussion about how the Japanese were overrunning China, and what China was going to do to them. I was surprised that my brother seemed to be so very knowledgeable about the war situation in the Orient.

Japan had invaded North China in 1937 and had spent the next four years plundering, pillaging, raping, and killing innocent people in China and in neighboring countries. Japan willingly sacrificed enormous amounts of her own men, military equipment, and money to satisfy her determination to control her part of the world.

Eventually everyone in the world, including her own people, would suffer from Japan's mad pursuit of power and money.

Now, as I listened to that gentle Chinese waiter and that gentle musician talking about what those vicious little men were doing to the people of China, I felt my first chill of apprehension.

After dinner, my brother took me to the Gayety Burlesque Theater (admittance forty-four cents).

The Gayety Burlesque Theater presented a combination of scantily-clad female dancers and singers and earthy humor from comedians. The show was designed to appeal more to the male audience, of course.

The Burlesque was not the filthy trash we see today on television, but it was suggestive and funny. I could see how famous comedians got their experience on the stages of the burlesque. Looking around, I had the feeling that the Burlesque was the Sailor's Friend—a few hours of distraction from their lonely, boring days.

After the show, we went back to my temporary home.

In the movies, a scene of farewell would now unfold. I would tell my brother how very much I loved him and missed him when he was gone. He would tell me he loved me, and we would both talk about the good times we had shared in the eighteen years we had lived together.

But we said none of those things. It would not have been in character for either of us. We came from a family of talkers and jokers, whose deep feelings were usually covered up with laughter and banter.

Rather, as soon as we boarded the bus, I was overcome with such a feeling of despair that I was struck completely speechless. I tried to talk, but had to give up because I was crying so much. Trying to hide my distress from Clyde, I turned my face toward the window, not realizing he could see my reflection in the window glass. I cried all the way back to Kathleen's house and he became very quiet. Once in awhile, Clyde would ask me to tell some hometown friend good-bye for him, so I knew his thoughts were back in Okmulgee.

And so the sailor who had given up his last liberty in Washington to take his sister out and the girl who had turned down so many invitations from handsome sailors so she could spend that last day with her brother rode along in total and complete misery!

There was really no need for any words between us, so we both just sat and silently grieved all the way home.

I have never forgotten that last ride with my brother, nor have I ever been able since to say a dignified good-bye to anyone close to me.

After coming in to tell our parents good-bye, Clyde went back to the school. There, except for a few overnights at the YMCA in Hawaii, he slept on a mattress for the last time in his life.

We did not see Clyde during the day of Monday, May 26. The members of Band Number 22 were busy stuffing their belongings into sea bags, gathering up all their music and instruments, and loading everything onto a truck.

But the Navy had actually given us permission to go down to the boat dock that evening to tell the band good-bye. Consequently, at five o'clock the boys' families and friends gathered on the dock. In addition to Mate, Pate, and I, the wives of Fred Kinney and of Emmett Lynch were there. We five constituted the families of the boys.

Hurley's friend Barbara was there, and many of the boys' friends from the school had come down to see them off.

Our band boys were to board the same boat which had brought them from Norfolk to Washington—the steamboat *District of Columbia*. In Norfolk, they were to board the *Lassen*, which would take them around through the Panama Canal to Long Beach. They had been told erroneously that the *Lassen* would then take them to Pearl Harbor, where they would board the *Arizona*.

As we stood on the dock chatting with each other, still believing that everything would be fine, the bus and truck from the School of Music drove up and out stepped our boys. They were dressed in their Navy blues, and they were still laughing and joking. They were happy to have escaped school at last and to be embarking on their great adventure.

After loading their instruments and sea bags onto the steamboat, the boys came over to our little group to tell us good-bye. Still true to form, I was crying. Campbell, Wedin, Reed, and Clyde laughed at me, which gave them release from the tears they were close to themselves.

We met Bandmaster Kinney, and we thought he was a nice enough fellow. To Clyde's intense embarrassment, Mate told Kinney she hoped he would take good care of her boy, and he replied that he certainly would.

At five-thirty, it was time. The band boys went aboard the *District of Columbia* and it shoved off.

We stood on the dock and waved to our boys until they were no longer in sight. All the ladies were crying and the men had become very solemn. Gone now were their jokes and feeble attempts to cover their feelings.

We were right to be so sorrowful that day. Few of us in that group ever saw any of those twenty-one musicians again.

That tearful parting at the Washington Navy Yard was particularly difficult for our parents, as it was their twenty-first wedding anniversary.

Now they stood and waved good-bye to their pride and joy, their only son Clyde. They were sorry to see him go so far away, but they were pleased that he was embarking on his chosen career, and that he would be so closely involved with music.

Not having second sight, they could not know that on their wedding anniversary, they were seeing their eighteen-year old son for the last time.

On Wednesday, "Kid" Reed came out to Kathleen's home to take me on our date. "Kid" was also from Oklahoma, and he was very nice to me. We went on a cruise down the Potomac River and danced to a live band. I remember he went up to the band and requested they play "Tea For Two," which they did.

He was trying so hard to see that I had a good time, and I was really enjoying the band, the boat trip, the scenery, and his company, when suddenly another "spell" hit me. We were resting between dances, leaning on the railing of the deck, watching the water swirling around us, when I was suddenly overcome with the same terrible sense of dread and horror I had experienced on Clyde's last night in Washington. Again, I could not understand that feeling. I was not prone to depression—I was enjoying life too much.

But now I just stood there, unable to speak, staring down at the churning water and shaking with extreme foreboding. I don't know what "Kid" thought—since he did not know me very well, he could not have known that normally I never ran out of anything to say. But now, I simply could not speak, nor could I respond to anything he was saying to me. Eventually I recovered my speech and my wits, but the feeling of total despair lasted all the rest of the afternoon.

Since I am normally skeptical of "second sight" and other unexplained phenomenon, I never told anyone about that experience.

Six months later, when we had to go through the horror of the Pearl Harbor attack and the *Arizona* band was swallowed up in the ocean, "Kid" Reed was in the band on the *West Virginia*, tied up beside the *Tennessee*, both just ahead of the *Arizona*. I heard from him after the attack and was relieved to hear he had survived.

After the Pearl Harbor attack, remembering those experiences vividly, I became convinced that I had a premonition of impending evil, and I have never changed my mind.

After Clyde left, my parents and I spent our days sightseeing. We went to Mount Vernon, to the Smithsonian, and to other points of interest.

Our hosts obtained tickets for us to attend the Memorial Day service at Arlington Cemetery on Friday, May 30. Pate especially wanted to go to the service to honor his buddies who had been killed in France during World War I.

The Washington Post described that 1941 Memorial Day service as being held in the midst of a war-torn world. Brigidier General Frank T. Hines spoke, and we were thrilled to hear opera star James Melton sing, accompanied by the Marine Band.[6]

At that time, I could still hear a band play without crying, so I thoroughly enjoyed the music.

We felt very honored to have the opportunity to attend that Memorial Day service. Fortunately, we did not know that it would be our nation's last peacetime Memorial Day for many years. Nor did we know that the time for our own personal grieving was getting closer and closer.

After the weekend, we three and Docia started back to Oklahoma. We took a leisurely route, stopping to visit several of Pate's relatives on the way home.

When we got back to Okmulgee, a postcard from Clyde, dated May 27, was waiting for us. The "ewenty tighth" was his version of pig Latin and meant the "twenty-eighth."

> *Dear Molly, You will get this after I leave Norfolk, but I thought I'd let you know I arrived alright [sic] and got aboard my ship. We are leaving the ewenty tighth and I'll write when I get to the next port.*
>
> *Take care of everything and tell everyone "hello."*

CHAPTER 12

USS *Lassen*

Arizona's new bandsmen arrived in Norfolk, Virginia, on the evening of Monday, May 26 at eight o'clock.[1] They had looked forward to celebrating their escape from school by having some beer on the trip down to Norfolk. That salute to freedom was nipped in the bud, however, when they discovered that beer on the boat was priced at twenty-five cents a pint. It was, therefore, a mostly sober group of musicians who hit the sack at the Norfolk Receiving Station that night.

After breakfast on Tuesday, the bandsmen went aboard their first United States Navy ship.

The *Lassen* was a brand new ammunition ship which had come up to Norfolk from Mobile, Alabama. Most of her crew had been drawn from the organized reserves. The few old salts assigned to her were dubious at first about their new shipmates, always checking behind them for a mule and plow. But the salts soon came to believe the new boys would do—high praise from old seamen.[2]

The *Lassen* carried a compliment of fifteen officers and a crew of about one hundred sixty men. Her assigned home port was San Pedro, California, near Los Angeles.[3]

It was *Lassen*'s first voyage with cargo. She had been tapped by the Navy to transport *Arizona*'s new band to its ship.

As the band boarded the *Lassen*, Navy yard workers were loading her cargo and the noise was terrific.

Once aboard, the band was startled to discover she was not simply a cargo ship, as they had been told, but was, in fact, an ammunition carrier.

In talking to members of the crew the first day, the musicians learned there was enough TNT in the ship's hold to kill every man within twelve miles. Its load of ammunition weighed as much as a light cruiser.

Lassen was scheduled to stop in Cuba, Panama, San Diego, San Pedro, Mare Island (near San Francisco), and Bremerton, Washington. She would spend eleven days at Mare Island and thirteen days at Bremerton, where the band was told they would board the *Arizona*.

Eventually, *Lassen* was to be sent to England, but Radford was grateful they would not still be with her. His desire for adventure and excitement did not extend to riding a floating bomb into the midst of German submarines waiting in the Atlantic. He did think, however, that the one hundred dollars per trip which he had heard the Navy paid her sailors for such dangerous convoy duty would be nice.

Unpacking and settling in proved to be simple for the musicians. They were furnished Army cots for sleeping and lived out of their sea bags for the entire trip. Radford suggested to his family that if they wanted to know just how unhandy those sea bags were, they should try keeping all their clothes, toilet articles, and belongings in an old gunny sack for awhile.

The band played their first concert aboard a ship at noon that same day.[4] Playing a musical instrument on a ship which was rolling and heaving was a feat which took quite awhile to master.

On the same day the *Arizona* band boarded the *Lassen*, President Roosevelt proclaimed an unlimited state of national emergency for our country.[5]

The band played for colors for the first time on Wednesday morning.[6]

The ceremony for colors is an old time-honored Navy custom. When the ship was in port, the American flag was raised each morning on the fantail (at the back of the ship) at eight o'clock.

The ceremony never varied. At 7:55 A.M., the color guard and the band lined up, and the color bearers stepped up, carrying the folded American flag. Exactly at eight o'clock, the flag was raised as the band played the National Anthem, usually followed by other marches.

Everyone who was topside at that time was required to drop whatever he was doing, face the flag, come to attention, and salute the flag (or colors) until the band finished playing the National Anthem.

The colors ceremony was not observed when the ship was at sea, since all her flags flew day and night.

Except for a very few rest periods at the YMCA in Hawaii, *Arizona*'s musicians played for colors every morning the ship was in port for the rest of their lives.

Lassen weighed anchor at five o'clock Wednesday evening.[7] As she sailed away, she looked like any ordinary cargo ship. Heavily loaded as she was, she was not able to move very fast, so for protection, she was accompanied by two destroyers.

The slow cruise gave the bandsmen time to reflect on their past busy week and to become better acquainted with each other. Most of them had left their best buddies behind. Now, since they had only each other, they soon became good friends, destined to spend the rest of their lives together.

Twenty very different boys, with very different personalities, became as one. They grew from a group of strangers into the best-known band in the Pacific Fleet.

Neither from the school nor from the *Arizona* did any of the boys ever write anything unkind or derogatory about each other. Their families were later to derive much satisfaction from that.

Kinney was proud of his new band, which was already of professional caliber. In addition to their major instruments, his musicians were studying at least one other instrument. They could play any type of music, from long hair to modern. All of them had excellent music teachers in school who had written glowing letters of recommendation to the Navy. They had all won many musical awards while still in high school.

Jim Thurmond remarked many times that the *Arizona* band was the best band the school had ever sent out. He always said it was a wonderful band; its musicians were the pick of the school; and its bandmaster was the best of leaders.[8]

The Navy gained all that talent for a mere pittance.

Each band which graduated from the School of Music was supposed to receive a complete set of instruments, and replacement instruments were to be sent, when necessary, to the unit bands out in the fleet.[9] At Kinney's insistence, however, *Arizona's* bandsmen had purchased their own expensive instruments.

Only Lynch had been in the Navy for more than ten months and had advanced to Musician Second Class. Due to the wartime emergency, Haas and Moorhouse had been advanced to Musician Second Class early. Those three musicians were each paid the princely sum of fifty-four dollars a month.

Half the bandsmen were still Seaman Second Class, having been sailors for less than ten months. They earned thirty-six dollars a month. They were: Bandy, Brabbzson, Chernucha, Hurley, McCary, Radford, Sanderson, Scruggs, Shaw, and Williams.

Seven of Kinney's musicians had not even been in the Navy for four months and still held the rate of Apprentice Seaman, earning the famous twenty-one dollars a month. They were: Burdette, Cox, Floege, Hughes, Nadel, White, and Whitson.

All enlisted men started at the same pay then, and jokes were told all over our country about that twenty-one dollars a month. Even songs were written about the princely sum. At that time, however, it was twenty-one dollars more than they could have earned on the outside.

Even Kinney served as Bandmaster at the rate and pay of First Class Musician.

But Kinney was pleased. He had his first very own band. It is fortunate he did not know it would also be his last very own band.

Serving as Assistant Bandmaster for the *Arizona* band was the very talented Curt Haas.[10]

The reed men, clarinets and saxophones, were Chernucha, Cox, Floege, Haas, Hurley, and Sanderson.

Cornet players were Bandy, Moorhouse, Nadel, and Williams.

Trombone players were Hughes, Scruggs, and Shaw.

French horn players were Brabbzson and Burdette.

The baritone player was Radford.

Bass players were McCary and Whitson.

Drummers were Lynch and White.

In addition to their major instruments, Haas also played flute in the band; Whitson played string bass; Scruggs played accordion; and Cox and Hurley played electric Hawaiian guitars. Bandy, Haas, and Scruggs were singers; Haas, Nadel and Scruggs wrote musical arrangements for the band; and Hurley and Williams entertained with baton twirling.

Hurley, McCary, and Williams had been drum majors for their local bands.

The musicians could also play other instruments which they did not have with them on the ship. Burdette could play cornet; Radford could play tuba; Williams could play French horn; Scruggs and Williams could play baritone; Cox and Williams could play violin; and Lynch, McCary, Scruggs, and White could play piano. McCary could also play cornet and almost any musical instrument. Kinney himself was a baritone player.[11]

Thus, the *Arizona* band was ready for almost any unforeseen emergency, with musicians who could step in as substitutes on all the instruments.

As is usually true with artistic people, the members of the band were talented in other areas, also—Hurley in photography; Haas and Radford in writing; Scruggs in writing poetry; Williams in drawing.

Most of the boys had been active in sports—boxing, wrestling, swimming, diving, tennis, golf, football, and baseball.

The band even had its own deep-sea diver.

The happiest *Arizona* bandsman on the *Lassen* was the "baby," Billie McCary, who was still only sixteen years old. McCary had always wanted to be a sailor and a musician, and he had worked hard to obtain both those goals.

But during the summer months, while still in elementary school, Billie had devised a diving helmet from oil cans, and he spent much time under water.

To McCary's delight, he found that deep-sea divers were also traveling on *Lassen*, and they allowed him to make some dives with their equipment.[12]

Fred Kinney was an enigma. Various impressions and memories of him have been given by the boys who attended the school at the same time *Arizona*'s musicians did.

J. W. "Duke" Bolen remembers Kinney as a hard-nosed musician, a taskmaster, a dedicated, strict disciplinarian. Larry Conley thought Kinney was a fine, compassionate man.[13]

Richard Duryea regarded Kinney as perhaps the best musician at the school. He said the *Arizona* band was considered one of the best to graduate because of Kinney. Howard Hare considered Kinney a great showman, which made his band very popular in Hawaii. William Harten remembers Kinney as a nice, soft-spoken man.[14]

Mrs. George F. Kenney was the wife of a Navy musician who was a friend of Fred's before Fred went to the School of Music. She thought Fred Kinney was very strict, but was well-liked by everybody. She remembers him as quite a joker.[15]

"Red" Luckenbach, bandmaster of the *California* band which had graduated with the *Arizona* band, thought Kinney was a very good musician. He described Kinney as slender, weighing perhaps 160 pounds, and about five feet ten inches tall. He thought Kinney was a charming companion with a fine personality, an energetic and dynamic man who was very active, always bouncing around. If Kinney had lived, Luckenbach was sure he would have made a name for himself as a bandmaster.[16]

Jim Thurmond commented that Fred Kinney expected to have a symphony band with only twenty musicians. Dr. Walter Wehner thought Fred Kinney was perhaps the best director at the school.[17]

The personalities of Kinney's bandsmen ranged from very quiet to very talkative; from boys with serious dispositions to class clowns.

Some were members of large families; one was an orphan.

Some of his boys did not drink or smoke, while some could drink all night and never show the effects. Most of them fell somewhere between those two extremes.

Aboard the *Lassen*, the bandsmen's daily routine was soon established. Since they were merely passengers, they had no assigned duties on the ship. After rehearsing each morning and playing the noon concert for the crew, they found some nook where they could practice their several instruments.[18]

Their spare time was spent talking to each other and writing to the folks back home. They often discussed the good times they had just before they left Washington. My poor brother had to say he spent his last liberties with his sister!

Because of the extreme heat, it did not take the boys long to find a hammock and sleep topside beside the cannon.[19] Our family was not thrilled to hear that my sleepwalking brother was doing that.

The crew of the *Lassen* thought she carried the best of all Navy cooks. They insisted you would never hear "Boy, I'm going ashore and have a real feed!" on their ship![20] Radford agreed. He happily reported to his family that the chow on the *Lassen* was 100 percent better than it was at the school. He was pleased that all the food was put out on the table family style, and they could help themselves to as much as they wanted.

Smoking on that floating bomb was strictly forbidden anywhere on the ship except in the galley.

On Memorial Day, Friday, May 30, the band held a jam session on the top deck for over an hour. Under the beautiful tropical sunset, the band played, Scruggs played his accordion, and the whole crew joined in, singing and clapping.[21]

The next day, Hurley wrote in his diary that "the mountainous shoreline of Cuba came into view." By five forty-five that evening, they could see Guantanamo Bay for the first time. In preparation for going ashore, they filled out their passports.

On June 1, after rehearsal in the morning, the band went ashore at one-thirty for a few hours. They were startled to see how very hot it was in Cuba.[22]

Lassen left Guantanamo Bay at six twenty-five that same day. Again, Hurley and my brother swung hammocks topside to sleep. They noticed it was becoming very windy.[23]

The wind threw *Lassen* into a bucking spree which sent most of the musicians into seasickness. Although very uncomfortable, none of the boys became as ill as Brabbzson, who vomited for four days.

He was promptly dubbed "Buttercup," and "Buttercup" he remained for the rest of his life.[24]

On Monday, *Lassen* arrived in Colon, Panama Zone, where she stayed for two days.[25]

Clyde wrote us on June 4:

> *Dear Molly, This is my second day in Colon, Panama Zone. We are going through the locks later in the day, I think. We went swimming yesterday and it was fine. I am red from head to foot.*
>
> *Last night I went into Colon with some of the other guys. I went into all the stores, but no salt shakers. I don't think they knew what I was talking about.*
>
> *There are people of all kinds, blackest to the whitest. It's too hot here, so they can have every bit of it. They drive on the left side of the road here. Everything is legal here.*
>
> *So far we still have all the thirty thousand tons of ammunition that we started out with.*
>
> *We are going up the West Coast to somewhere in Washington and then over to Honolulu before we change ships.*
>
> *It is hot even during the nights, so we sleep topside. Night before last I swung my hammock on the topside and slept like a log.*
>
> *Write to me in San Pedro or San Francisco. We are going to stop in Balboa also.*
>
> *Write quick. Love & Stuff, Proke*

My hobby was collecting salt shakers, and Clyde was always looking for them everywhere he went.

Taking advantage of the two-day stop in Colon, Kinney took his band ashore to practice on solid land.

Lassen left Colon on the morning of June 5, went through the Panama Canal, and docked in Balboa Bay.[26] The trip through the Canal took eight hours.

That night, while *Lassen* was docked on the west end of the Canal, three battleships went through to the Atlantic side. Radford was startled to see no sign of life at all on the big ships. To him, it looked as though nobody was home. They had no lights showing and they did not answer any of the signals *Lassen* sent to them.

Clyde wrote on June 6:

> *Dear Molly, We are through the canal and in Balboa. I am going to see the town. None of these places have salt shakers, but I'll look around.*
>
> *Be careful and tell Mate and Pate hello. Love, Proke.*

Everyone went ashore in Balboa and went over to nearby Panama City to shop for souvenirs. Scruggs did not buy anything, as he thought the stuff was too high and that it was all made in Japan, anyway. At that time, "Made in Japan" denoted very cheap, inferior merchandise.

Radford, Cox, and my brother went into town to try their legs again and to "wet their parched throats" with some beer. As they were walking through the narrow streets, they saw a neon sign advertising "Milwaukee Beer."

According to Radford, "after breaking all existing speed records getting into the joint, sitting down and ordering three quarts of this said beer, we found some little letters on the bottom of the label that says 'Made in Panama.'"

But he added, "Being very thirsty, we did manage to get it down, but I still think they should have poured it back into the horse."

By now, the entire band was very sunburned, with blistered arms and faces. For a long time, they made various comments in their letters home about how much they disliked Panama. Radford said he never knew it could get so hot as it did there.

On June 6, *Lassen* unloaded some of her ammunition in Balboa. Scruggs wrote that so far, the bandsmen had not been required to work with the crew, because they played their music all day. Again, the band lived up to its "soft duty" image!

Lassen left Balboa that same day, headed for San Diego, California. During the entire trip from Panama, she hugged the coast, being out of sight of land for only about six hours. The trip was un-eventful.

The band spent its time practicing, as usual.

Lassen's Captain held an inspection on Friday, June 13. Radford, with his keen sense of humor, compared that Captain's inspection to the inspections they had at the school and thought *Lassen*'s was pretty easy.

They stood up on one of the hatch covers and the Captain walked through without saying a word. The former Music School students were not used to such a quiet, noncritical inspection by an officer.

Radford thought there could not have been any tackier-looking sailors anywhere. With no lockers aboard and with their clothes having been packed in their sea bags for days, everyone was pretty wrinkled. To their amazement, *Lassen*'s Captain did not seem to mind.

After inspection, the Captain spoke to his assembled crew and guests. He told Kinney how very glad he and the crew were to have had the *Arizona* band aboard with them for the past two weeks.

No doubt the band's music did help lessen the monotony for *Lassen*'s crew. A ship as small as *Lassen* would never rate a band, so it was an extra treat for her crew to have had such a good band, even for such a short while.

Lassen was not a "spit and polish" ship, and unless they were receiving a direct order, the crew was not required to salute their officers throughout the day.

In other words, *Lassen* was blessed with a very good Captain, one who did not live and breathe "by the book." That was fortunate, because otherwise that duty, with such a dangerous cargo, would have been unbearable.

Upon their arrival in San Diego at 8:15 A.M. on June 15, my brother wrote:

> *Dear Molly, California, here we are! We had a fine trip and everyone enjoyed himself. We were about five hours ahead of time yesterday, so we stopped and everybody went fishing. The officers went out in the life boats and the crew fished off the ship. Pretty soft, I'd say.*

The twelfth we saw a whale just off the port fantail. Boy, was he blowin'. All the way here, we were continually seeing flying fish and porpoises.

The roughest part of water was Windward Passage, a little ways out of Guantanimo Bay.

I think we will stay on the Lassen *until we get to Honolulu.*

Tell Pate that I haven't been paid since I left Washington and I don't know when I'll get paid. Our pay accounts are on the Arizona.

Tell Mate hello and take care of Dink.

Not much more to write about but write to me in San Francisco.

Love, Proke

P.S. All the boys send their regards.

His letter reflects the excitement of boys still enjoying their first cruise. They were all amazed that *Lassen*, loaded as she was with most of her thirty thousand tons of ammunition still intact, would simply lay to and start fishing.

But the Captain did not want to bring his ship, with her touchy load, into the harbor in the dark, so he simply anchored off the coast for the night and took *Lassen* in the next morning.

The band boys went ashore in San Diego on June 15, but their not having been paid since they left Washington put a decided crimp on their liberty.

As they got under way again, Radford looked back on their "life on the *Lassen*" and spoke for them all:

San Diego was considerably cooler than Panama.

Their life on the *Lassen* was "kinda tough." They had to sleep down in the hold with the ammunition. Since they could not leave any portholes open and did not have any air pumps, they had to breathe foul air all the time.

In other words, he reported, they had never worked less and sweated more in their lives.

He had mentioned earlier that, while they were still in Norfolk, they had heard that the Navy had already laid several mine fields outside Norfolk.

Lassen's crew told the musicians there were a lot of English warships in our ports for repair, including the British aircraft carrier *Illustrious*.

Consequently, it was becoming harder to ignore the signs of war around them. It had been simpler to remain calm at the school, when it was only talk of war. Here, cruising on a ship loaded to the gills with ammunition, escorted by two destroyers, the musicians must have wondered just what they were sailing into.

Obviously uneasy about *Lassen*'s deadly cargo just under them, they always mentioned that ammunition in their letters home.

They were right to be so nervous. *Lassen* unloaded some of her ammunition onto *Arizona* a few days later, so it was that same ammunition which, six months later, ended forever the lives of all the members of the last band of the USS *Arizona*.

CHAPTER 13

USS *Arizona*

After spending two days in San Diego, *Lassen* weighed anchor on the morning of June 17, 1941, and arrived in San Pedro, near Long Beach, at two o'clock that afternoon. *Arizona*'s new bandsmen had been told they would stay on *Lassen* until she caught up with *Arizona*. Depending on which rumor they chose to believe, that would be in Bremerton or Pearl Harbor.

They were, therefore, startled to see *Arizona* already anchored at San Pedro when they pulled in. She had arrived at seven forty-seven that morning,[1] having returned to her home port from Hawaii to give her crewmen a chance to visit their families. She was scheduled to go back to Pearl Harbor in about two weeks.

Arizona's new bandsmen lined up along the topside of *Lassen* and stared in awe at their new home. It was the biggest ship they had ever seen, and they would soon be living on her!

They had heard *Arizona* was a good ship and a happy ship. They earnestly hoped that would prove to be true.

Arizona was an old World War I battleship which had been launched on June 19, 1915, at the New York Navy Yard.[2] When her new band came aboard, she was exactly twenty-six years old.

As Commander of Battleship Division One, Rear Admiral Isaac Campbell Kidd lived on *Arizona*. The musicians had heard that Admiral Kidd was an outstanding officer.

In six months, Admiral Kidd and his new band would die at exactly the same moment. Also killed that day was *Arizona*'s Captain Franklin B. Van Valkenburgh, who had been assigned to *Arizona* on February 5.[3]

Members of *Arizona*'s old band left the ship posthaste at 9:00 A.M. to begin their seven-day leave before reporting to their new assignment.[4]

Lassen delivered some ammunition to *Arizona* at four-thirty and delivered her new band at four forty-five.[5]

It was with much trepidation that the twenty-one musicians went aboard *Arizona*. They had been told by the older musicians at the School of Music how poorly most sailors viewed ships' musicians.

However, they needn't have worried.

Normally, when a sailor went aboard a new ship, he went down to inspect his quarters and to unpack his gear. Musicians always disappeared for awhile to search their new ship for a quiet nook where they could practice their musical instruments each day in semi-solitude.

The *Pennsylvania* always caused a stir when she was in port, especially when she was in dry dock. One of her musicians had found a spot in the crow's nest where he could practice his piccolo. Men would walk by, looking up and down and around, searching for the source of those piercing notes, seemingly coming down from the very heavens.[6]

On the afternoon of June 17, however, Kinney did not give his boys any time to unpack. Instead, he took his new band topside immediately to play its first concert for the crew.

To the musicians' relief, Admiral Kidd sent word down to Kinney right away that he was very pleased with their performance.

It was the crew, however, who really gave them a welcome.

Arizona's crew was stunned by the music emanating from her new band. The band which had just departed was made up of older musicians who had not been trained to play modern dance music. Their new young band could belt out music fully as good as the popular big bands, and the crewmen were delighted.

John W. Doucett, who was Gunner's Mate Third Class on the *Arizona* at that time, still remembers the first time they heard their new band. He said they loved them immediately and could not get enough of their music. The crew clapped long and hard, and *Arizona*'s new band was pleased and relieved.[7]

Roger Snyder, who graduated with the *Arizona* band and who was assigned to the *Tennessee* band, said the ships really appreciated the new bands which were coming out of the School of Music at that time. Unlike the old bands, the new bands played not only longhair music, but also modern jitterbug and jazz music.[8] The snappy modern music played by their new band reminded *Arizona*'s homesick crewmen of their girls back home.

Kinney's band was popular with the crew for another reason. At the end of 1940 and early in 1941, *Arizona* had been sent to Bremerton for overhaul. As part of the preparations for war, all the wooden chairs and tables had been removed and the piano had been taken off. If the ship were hit by shells, wood splinters and fragments from those items would fly everywhere, causing a real danger for the men on board.

Arizona's silver service was also removed at that time and put into storage. It is now on display at the Arizona State House in Phoenix, Arizona.

In Bremerton, the crewmen of *Arizona* had been ordered to remove all their personal radios.[9] No longer able to tune in to the big dance bands, they were starved for modern dance music. And now they had their own personal band, playing music just like the big bands back home!

"Band was received with much enthusiasm aboard USS *Arizona*," noted Hurley in his diary.

The feeling was mutual. The band always loved its new ship and her crew and spoke highly of them all their lives.

Earlier, Radford had written his parents that "sailors on a battleship affectionately call it 'she' because:

1 - It takes a lot of paint to keep her looking right

2 - She always has a crowd of sailors around her

3 - She can make a hell of a lot of noise in an argument."

On a postcard picturing the USS *Arizona*, postmarked June 21, from Long Beach, California, Clyde wrote:

> *Dear Folks, This is the ship that our band is on for permanent duty. She is painted battleship grey now. She is a good*

ship and the officers and crew are all swell. They say that they enjoy our music and want us to play all the time.

I don't know where we are going, but we'll get there.

Take care of everything and I might be home this year or next.

Love, Proke

Thus began the talk of coming home on leave which was in every letter each of the boys wrote home. The scuttlebutt in the Navy is well-known, and each time we got a letter, the "scoop" was different.

As Clyde wrote our cousin Betty Gerow:

I have changed ships...now on the USS Arizona...*tied up in Long Beach, California...don't know where we are going...doesn't look as though I am going to get any leave but I may get some when I get back from Honolulu....We'll probably be there a long time unless something breaks.*

Radford especially looked forward to a few days' leave. His brother Harold was in the Army and was stationed at Fort Ord. They planned to get together for at least a weekend. But since Radford never did have a weekend off and since Fort Ord was nearly 300 miles away, the two brothers never did get together before *Arizona* left California.

After hoping for so long that they would be allowed to go home before they left California, the band boys were disappointed again. Their letters home from that point on until their deaths always contained references to their next leaves.

In a letter with no date, my brother wrote:

Dear Molly, I am now on the USS Arizona *for permanent duty. It is a battleship. The* Lassen *was an ammunition carrier.*

We will be in Long Beach for at least two more weeks. I don't know where we are going next. I may get a leave soon, and I may not, but I'm hoping for one.

> *I'm sending the pictures back and I would appreciate it if*
> *you would keep an album of pictures I send home.*
>   *I wish you would send me my camera so I can take it to*
> *Honolulu.*
>   *The trip through Panama was fine.*
>   *I can't think of anything else to write about and I am going*
> *on liberty, so G'by now.*
>   *Love, Proke*
>   *P.S. Send my mail to Clyde Williams, USS* Arizona *Band,*
> *c / o Postmaster, Long Beach, Cal.*

Radford told his folks that their address would always be "c/o San Pedro" or "c/o Long Beach," because the head boys did not want the public to know just where their battlewagons were.

The pictures my brother mentioned were the ones we had taken when we visited him in Washington. I had sent them to him, and he was returning them. I did start his photo album, as he requested, and I still have it. He took many pictures of the band boys in California and in Hawaii, which he was going to send to me for his album, but they went down with him on the ship. All the bandsmen had begun a photograph album while they were in Washington, but only Hurley sent his album home.

Shortly after the band reported aboard *Arizona*, the ship's newspaper *At 'Em Arizona* published a welcome to her new band, listing the boys' names and hometowns. The musicians all put their copy of the newspaper among the souvenirs they were saving to take home when they finally got leave. Fortunately for us all, Moorhouse sent his copy to his parents. His mother would use it later when she set out to find the families of *Arizona*'s last band.[10]

Whitson also sent his copy of the newspaper home. He circled the names of Williams, Moorhouse, and Cox and wrote beside their names that they were his best friends in the band.[11]

The musicians all ate and slept together in their living compartment, which was located on the second deck between the officers' country and the Chiefs' quarters.[12] In the compartment, they each had a small locker where they could keep their folded uniforms and underwear, their shoes, their stationery, and their personal possessions.

They were dismayed to find that, instead of the bunks they had at the school, or the Army cots they used on the *Lassen*, they would sleep in hammocks on the *Arizona*. To allow room for the sailors to walk under them at night, the hammocks were slung about six feet off the deck.[13] That caused several mishaps, as the least movement from side to side caused one to roll out. When a person sleeps in a hammock, he must learn to sleep on his back at all times, as there is no turning one way or the other.

No matter how tired or ill a sailor was, he could not hang his hammock until after seven in the evening. At that time, Chaplain Captain Thomas L. Kirkpatrick said the evening prayer over the loud speaker. All the crew was required to line up during his prayer.[14]

After evening prayers, they folded up the legs of their tables and benches and put them up on the ceiling in brackets, then suspended their hammocks from hooks for the night.[15]

The musicians were in the deck force and they did not sleep late— ever. Promptly at 5:30 A.M., they fell out of their hammocks, rolled them up, put them into the hammock bags, and stored them in bins known as nettings.[16]

The master-at-arms made sure each and every sailor in the deck force was up and dressing. He carried a stick, and any hapless sailor who was still asleep was given a big whack on his rump.[17]

Because of the age of the *Arizona*, water was at a premium. All the drinking and washing water had to be evaporated to take the salt out, so the crew was never allowed unlimited use of water. The evaporators on the ship did not work fast enough to make enough water for everyone to take a shower. They were, therefore, issued half a bucket of water three times a day by the master-at-arms.[18]

Each new seaman on the *Arizona* was required to serve three months as mess cook helpers. He was assigned to one of the various mess areas and was required to carry the food from the galley to his mess area.[19] Because the musicians played for colors each morning at eight o'clock, and played the noon and evening concerts while the crew was eating, the band was always fed first, giving rise to more "pampered" talk.

Each morning the musicians assisted their mess cook helper in lowering the tables and benches for breakfast. When the tables were ready, the seaman would bring the band's food down at six-thirty. They did not eat family style on the ship at that time, but rather were served their food in plates and tureens.[20]

Most of their day's activities were conducted in the band room on the third deck. It was there they practiced each day, tried to write letters, and visited and joked with each other.

Whenever they had time, the musicians visited with the crew of *Arizona*, and they wrote their impressions of the ship and of the impending war.

At that time, *Arizona* had a crew of about fourteen hundred men. She had four turrets of three fourteen-inch guns each, with smaller guns sticking out of every nook and corner of the ship. That was in contrast to the *Lassen*, which only carried a five-inch gun, eight antiaircraft guns, and several machine guns.

Already proud of their new ship, the musicians wrote that *Arizona* had the best record in the fleet in the last maneuvers in which she had participated in Hawaii. She had twenty-four hits out of fifty, even though it was at night.

They were all praying that the ship would not go back to Pearl Harbor, as *Arizona*'s crew told them it was the hellhole of the world. They were told that when you went ashore, all you ever saw were sailors. The only good thing their new friends could find to say about that Island was it was a good place to save money, since everything there was so expensive a sailor could not afford to buy anything.

Six months later, Pearl Harbor did indeed become the hellhole of the world, and the band and most of its new friends were dead.

After hearing the crew's comments about Pearl Harbor, the musicians told each other that after only six years of sea duty, they would be eligible for two years' shore duty. They decided the main thing would be to stay out of trouble, so as not to have a bad mark on their record. That way, maybe they could go up rapidly in the rates.

Radford hoped they would go to China, where he had heard a person could go ashore with five bucks and buy anything in Shanghai.

The scuttlebutt around the ship was that *Arizona* was going to Bremerton for dry dock to have another steel deck put on over the old one. The process would take several months so, of course, the bandsmen began planning eagerly for their leave.

Perhaps if that plan had been carried out, the bomb from the Japanese airplane would not have penetrated the deck of the *Arizona*, and most of her crew would not have died in the first few minutes.

Now the band settled down in earnest under Bandmaster Kinney.

Since the U.S. Navy School of Music had been in existence only six years, there was a constant fear Congress would shut off the funding for the school. Therefore, Thurmond had stressed to the student bandmasters that their bands were representing the U.S. Navy School of Music. They were taught that strict discipline must be imposed on their musicians, so there would be no criticism of any of the bands trained by the school. Most of the bandmasters relaxed somewhat after they left the school. Kinney did not.

As soon as the band boarded *Arizona*, Kinney became a driven man. He was an extremely gifted bandmaster, highly regarded by all who knew him. He was also very ambitious, expecting to have a symphony band with only twenty pieces.[21]

He came as close to that as anyone could have.

On June 23, the *Arizona* band played a concert for Admiral Kidd, after which they played for a dance. After the concert, the Admiral called Kinney to tell him he thought his band was the best band in the Navy.

Admiral Kidd asked Kinney to repeat the concert on June 25 for a group of friends he had invited to the ship. It goes without saying that the band graciously complied with the Admiral's request.

My brother sent us a copy of the program, on which he had written on the back, "Concert played for Rear Admiral Kidd. Clyde Williams."[22]

⚓ BAND CONCERT ⚓

at 1830 — June 25, 1941

U. S. S. ARIZONA, Flagship

Bandmaster Kinney, F. W., 1st Mus., . . . Assistant Haas, C. J., Sea 2c.

MARCH . . . . "Crosley" . . . . Henry Fillmore

SYMPHONIC POEM . . "Universal Judgment" . . Camille De Nardis
  Camille De Nardis (1840-78), although a fine conductor and composer, did
  not attain the popularity that so many musicians of his day enjoyed. The
  music loving public could not understand his fine and outstanding com-
  positions. De Nardis always depicted something of the future — never did
  his music represent the day or the past.
     First comes — "Allegro con Fuoco" — descriptive of the heavenly
  hosts, with a well developed creative, fugal form.
     Second — "Moderata Assai"— descriptive of the heavenly hosts. In this
  movement a choir of Angels descend upon the Earth sounding their trumpets — calling all Earthlings to stand Judgment before the Supreme Being.
     Third — Is a return of the first form, but far more developed; which
  intermingles with the work being done by the Supreme Power.
     Fourth — Is the "Choral" which represents the separation of Hades
  from Heaven. In this the Baritone Horn represents the Voice of the
  GRAND MASTER.
     Fifth — Representation of work well done, so a spirited "Allegro"
  brings the composition to a close.

CHARACTERISTIC . . . . "Woodland Whispers" . . . . Czibulka

SELECTION . . . . "Hall of Fame" . . . . Arranged by Safranek
  This number is what the name implies. It is made up of well known
  melodies from the works of famous composers.
     First — We hear the Introduction March to Keler Bela's Overture
  "Racoczy."
     Second — Verdi's "Celeste" (heavenly) Aida.
     Third — The brilliant "Entry of the Gladiators" by Fucik.
     Fourth — Rubinstein's well known "Melody in F."
     Fifth — Rachmaninoff's "Prelude in C sharp Minor," which carries top-
  most popularity the world over, Rachmaninoff was orignal, prolific, and
  a powerful composer.
     Sixth — "Anitra's Dance" from Grieg's "Peer Gynt Suite."
     Seventh — Dvorak's famous "Homoresque." In the last part of this
  you will hear "Old Folks at Home"; this is fitting because most of Dvorak's music is essantally American.
     For the Finale to this selection we have the brilliant "Allegro" from
  List's "First Hungarian Rhapsody."

CONCERT MARCH MILITAIRE . "My Hero" . Paraphrased - Alford
  From the "Chocolate Soldier" by Oscar Straus. This is paraphrased and
  second by Alford who inserts the ninth chord in the modern style.

⚓

The Symphonic Poem, "Universal Judgment," which the band included in its program, with its references to the "heavenly hosts" and to the "Supreme Power," is especially poignant to us now.

Admiral Kidd promptly sent down word that the concert was excellent. He was very proud of his band from the beginning, and he never did change his mind.

Arizona's band also played for a dance at the YMCA in Long Beach. Scruggs' parents and sister attended the dance and thought the boys "surely played well."[23] The Scruggs were the only family members who ever heard *Arizona's* band play.

All *Arizona's* men did not go ashore every night, so for their entertainment, movies were shown on the top deck every evening. Usually the men brought a blanket to wrap up in, as sitting up there in the open air was rather chilly.

On June 27, Clyde wrote:

> *I am still in Long Beach and don't know when we are leaving. It is a pretty good place and the beach is swell. When you were in Los Angeles, did you come over here? I think I am going over there sometime soon just to see what it looks like.*
>
> *The climate here is fine, not too hot or too cold.*
>
> *Tomorrow we are playing for a ship's dance. It starts at eight o'clock and all the guys on this ship are bringing their girls. They have these dances often while we are in port.*
>
> *I am sending an Express Money Order for ten bucks and I can send more later. I go up for Musician Second Class one month from today. I couldn't get a postal money order so I bought this.*
>
> *Tell Molly and Mate "hello" and I'll be seein' you sometime.*
>
> *Your Loving Son, Proke*
> *P.S. It's hard to think up something to say.*

Radford said they all liked the California weather much better than that of Washington, D.C., because Washington was so damp they either sweated or froze all the time.

None of the bandsmen ever mentioned any desire to go back to Washington except, of course, Lynch and Kinney, who had left their wives there.

While *Arizona* was in port in California, Shaw's sister and White's mother went to visit them.[24] Brabbzson's sister, my parents, and I had gone to visit them in Washington, D.C. Except for the Scruggs, none of the other families were able to see their sons before they left for Hawaii.

Scrugg's family invited several of the boys, including my brother, to their home for a backyard picnic. Scruggs' mother later wrote, "They were surely a bunch of fine fellows."[25]

The day after the bandsmen boarded *Arizona*, the Navy finally paid them for the first time in over a month. Although they still had not been in the Navy long enough to make much money, that payday was very welcome.

They all enjoyed the two weeks the ship was in port. The crew, with the exception of the band, was granted liberty every day from 1:00 P.M. until eight the next morning.

Most of the sailors they saw ashore were from their own ship. Radford said *Arizona*'s crewmen were really enjoying themselves after having been out in hell for four months.

Arizona was anchored in the middle of the harbor with San Pedro on one side and Long Beach on the other. A liberty boat went ashore every hour. Members of the crew lined up for inspection, both before they went ashore and after they returned. The Navy always insisted that its sailors make a good impression on the public.

The civilians in the Long Beach area were friendly to the sailors. Unlike Washington, D.C., the people who lived in *Arizona*'s home port were accustomed to Navy men.

The cruise on the *Lassen* had given the musicians the opportunity to become better acquainted with each other. Now, in Long Beach, they went on liberties together and began to cement their friendships.

They always wrote of that time as a happy experience. They tried to see all they could of the area.

Most of the musicians were excellent swimmers and divers and went to the beach nearly every day. Radford got a kick out of the breakers in the ocean, until he gulped a mouthful of salt water. After about four-thirty in the afternoon, however, it got too cold in Long Beach to swim.

Cox, Radford, and Williams often went ashore together, having become close friends on the *Lassen*. One evening, after sitting in a tavern in Long Beach, sipping their beers and listening to the radio broadcast of the Louis-Conn fight, they went to the Pike and rode on the roller coaster for about an hour. Radford reported they surely had fun.

The Pike was a well-known amusement park in Long Beach. It was big, gaudy, and noisy, and it held a special attraction for sailors, who did not see many bright lights while they were at sea.

Hurley went ashore on June 17 and spent the evening dancing at the YMCA. He thought Long Beach was a beautiful city. He wrote of the girls he met and of the dates he had, skating, swimming, and dancing.

The sailors went dancing at the "Y" and at the "Servicemen's Club."

By Friday, Hurley sadly wrote that the twenty-five dollars he had drawn on June 18 was all shot by now. Undaunted, he borrowed money on Monday and took another girl to the Pike. Chernucha and White went with Hurley on some of those dates.

Arizona's crew told the boys they would not have overnight liberty in Pearl Harbor, as they did in Long Beach, but would have to be back on the ship every night by 1:00 A.M.

It was not long after they arrived in Hawaii that they discovered they not only did not want to stay in Hawaii overnight, they did not want to stay in Hawaii at all!

CHAPTER 14

"The Land of Sunshine and Beautiful Flowers"

Arizona left Long Beach at noon on Tuesday, July 1. The crew had chosen to believe the rumor that the ship would go to San Francisco to take on more ammunition. Radford wrote his brother at Fort Ord that he would soon be in San Francisco. His brother Harold requested and received a three-day leave and sent Radford two bus tickets from San Francisco to Fort Ord.

But their reunion was not to be. When *Arizona* pulled out of the San Pedro Harbor, she headed west. That gave her crew the definite idea she was on her way to Pearl Harbor.

Wednesday an airplane brought mail out to the ship, since she was not yet more than a couple of hundred miles out.

The sea was pretty rough that day, but *Arizona* was so big and heavy that she did not ride the waves like *Lassen* did. *Arizona* just plowed through the waves and the rough sea was barely noticeable. It was noticeable to Buttercup, i.e., Brabbzson, however, who became very seasick again.

Other than Brabbzson, the members of the band agreed with Hurley, who wrote in his diary that they had a lot of fun on the trip.

That eight-day cruise across the Pacific Ocean must have been exciting for the musicians. They had time to visit with the crew and to explore the ship. They were still happy and at peace.

On her voyage to Pearl Harbor, *Arizona* was escorted by four "tin cans," or destroyers—two destroyers about three miles ahead of the battleship and one destroyer on each side and a bit ahead.

The ship was darkened each evening at sundown when they were at sea, so the band boys had to swing their hammocks before lights out. When the ship was in port, lights out was at ten o'clock, certainly a more civilized time for going to bed.

The laundry rates on the *Arizona* were pretty cheap. According to Scruggs, laundry was fifteen cents for as much as you wanted at one time. Pressing was five cents apiece, or ten cents for a suit of whites.

Wasting no time, *Arizona* conducted a general drill on July 2. When the general quarters alarm was sounded, everyone ran to his battle station and closed all the watertight doors. The doors to all the compartments were constructed so that, when they were shut and dogged down, the compartments were watertight.

Radford was impressed with the drills. He remarked that an enemy could really beat hell out of one of those ships without sinking it.

He was wrong.

During the trip to Hawaii, Scruggs wrote that the band would have a pretty good job in war. They would work in the sick bay and at the first-aid stations. They began attending classes on July 3 on how to administer morphine shots.

At the same time, the ship's doctor gave the bandsmen some rules on giving first aid during a battle at sea. The doctor told them that, if there were two men wounded, one seriously and the other only slightly, they were to fix up the one who had the least severe wounds first, so he could return to his battle station. That sounded cruel to the musicians, but the doctor explained that a seriously wounded sailor could not return to the battle, so it would be better to leave him until they had more time to attend to him. As the doctor expressed it so graphically, a man who had his guts hanging out would not be able to fire his gun anyway, so he must wait for first aid.

The musicians were still not "battle-ready." They had no idea that one man would want to kill another, nor that one nation would want to destroy another. Nor could they fathom a situation in which they must choose between life or death for a fellow sailor.

Five months later, *Arizona* would have no lack of wounded men.

On Thursday, July 3, a light cruiser joined the fleet. Radford noted that the back end of the cruiser was painted so that, from a distance, it would look like a heavy cruiser or a destroyer.

Radford wrote, "Williams, our windy trumpet player from Oklahoma, says that tomorrow, the Fourth of July, they are going to secure the guns and all hands will turn to shooting five inchers."

Apparently that was another rumor. When I asked my brother later if they had a nice Fourth of July on the ship, he replied, somewhat sarcastically: "Oh, yes, we had a swell time the Fourth. Everyone quit what he was doing and shot firecrackers. However, that was just about fifteen days ago. (Funny man.) There were some firecrackers on board, however."

From that, I assumed there were no special activities on the ship for the Fourth. Since the ship was a unit of the U.S. Navy, I had pictured a really nice patriotic program.

The musicians had not yet heard the guns being fired, but they had been told the antiaircraft guns were the ones which really hurt the ears.

Radford repeated that the Admiral seemed to think their little twenty-piece band was quite the stuff. They all hoped Admiral Kidd liked them enough to make them his own personal band, so when the ship went into dry dock, they would go ashore when the Admiral did.

On July 7, *Arizona* caught up with a couple of supply ships and escorted them to Pearl Harbor.

During the cruise, their uniforms changed to white shorts and skivvy shirts. They said that felt really good, as it was becoming hotter as they neared Hawaii than it had been in Long Beach, but not nearly so hot as it had been in Panama.

Now sleeping in hammocks was becoming more uncomfortable, as the hammocks curled up around their bodies and smothered out all the air. After the third day, some of the musicians again went up topside to sleep.[1]

The bandsmen had heard from several of their friends from the school, and hoped they would be able to find some of them after they reached the Islands. Radford remarked to his mother that there were surely some swell eggs in that bunch of 160 musicians who had graduated that spring.

He had heard that the band he was in at the beginning of his studies at the school would be assigned to a repair ship. Band 20 had gone aboard the *Wyoming* and would transfer with their Vice Admiral to the *Melville*. Those ships all remained on the East Coast. Later, Band 20 would transfer to the *Alcor*.[2] He was happy he had been switched to the *Arizona* band, as he felt he was on a better ship and in a better band.

Five months later, Radford's family would regret that transfer bitterly.

My brother heard from his friend Jimmy Campbell and wrote us, "I tried to get to ship out with Jim, but it didn't work out. He was the best friend I had in the school."

That last-minute change in Jimmy's orders saved his life. He came to see me in Washington several years later, so I know he made it at least until 1944.

Hurley twirled his baton for the crew at the band's concerts on July 5 and 6. Although one can hardly picture baton twirling on a rolling ship, Hurley wrote that he had no drops on Saturday and only two minor drops on Sunday, both of which he covered by fancy pickups.[3]

Most of the boys finally took time to write their families on July 7. There had been no point in writing before they reached Hawaii, since their letters could not be mailed anyway.

The limited water supply and the hammocks were wearing on Scruggs, who said he felt he had not had a bath nor been to bed since he left his home in Long Beach. They had been told that when the ship reached Hawaii the next day, they would get liberty at three o'clock. Scruggs thought he would just go to the "Y" and soak in a shower all day, then sleep until it was time to return to the ship.

Arizona arrived at Pearl Harbor on Tuesday, July 8.

And there it was—Pearl Harbor—the Jewel of the Pacific!

In 1840, the harbor had been surveyed by Lieutenant Charles Wilkes of the U.S. Navy, who had recommended the harbor as a Naval base. Lieutenant Wilkes wrote that the location was named "Pearl Harbor" because it was the only spot where pearl oysters could be found in the islands.[4]

My brother's next letter, sent "Air Mail," was dated July 10 and was postmarked "USS *Arizona*."

We left Long Beach before I could tell you when we were leaving and anyway, I didn't know where we were going. I am now in Pearl Harbor, Territory of Hawaii. It is about twelve miles from Honolulu and I went over there last night.

We left July first, and got here yesterday, the eighth.

I believe the country here is more beautiful than I have ever seen.

Also more Japs.

I don't know how long we are going to be here, but I think it will be two or three months.

Next Sunday some of us are going over to Waikiki Beach for the afternoon. I ought to be able to get some salt shakers for Molly here, so I'll try soon.

We are playing for an officer's birthday Thursday.

I've got to go play a concert now on the port side of the folksile, as it is nearly 1300. Mess gear is almost over and there will be some Joes and Macks out there listening.

Address your mail to USS Arizona Band, c / o Postmaster, Pearl Harbor, T. H. Love, Proke

Obviously, my brother was now becoming a sailor and was adopting the language of the Navy.

On a postcard with a Hawaiian scene, dated July 11, he wrote:

Dear Molly, This is it. Hawaii, I mean. The Isle of Dreams. It is really a wonderful country and lots of beautiful scenery all around.

I may be home around Christmas or sometime next year.

Tell Mate and Pate "hello" and ask Pate if he got the money orders from Long Beach and here. I still am holding on to the stubs. Let me know if anything goes wrong. Love, Proke

He also sent a picture postcard to one of the girls back in Okmulgee, with the same date:

> *Since I wrote you last, I have been to Cuba, Panama, and now I am in Pearl Harbor, Hawaii. It is twelve miles from Honolulu. There are more hulu-hulu dancers here than you can count. I wish you were here to see some of them.*
>
> *Next time you see Betty H. tell her that divers are pretty hard to get.*
>
> *Write soon and let me know what's new in the news. Love, Clyde*

There had been much speculation among the bands in Pearl Harbor about the new band assigned to *Arizona*. It did not take long for the other bands to discover that her new band was a superior group.[5]

The Chaplain of the *Arizona* took the band on a tour of the Islands, which they enjoyed very much. They all wrote home about how pretty Hawaii was. Scruggs said everything grew there, so it was all green, with wine-colored ground. The water was green and the breakers started way out and were big and long.

Apparently it was quite a tour on which the Chaplain took the boys. Radford said they went through Schofield Barracks, which was about twenty-five miles from Pearl Harbor.

Fortunately, Hurley took his camera on the tour, and one of his photographs shows some of the boys standing in front of their bus, looking very happy. The bus was Number 705, which was our telephone number in Okmulgee.

The musicians were paid on the fifth and twentieth of each month. They set out to see everything they could of the Islands before they started saving their money. They soon discovered why the crew of the *Arizona* hated Hawaii so much.

Our Navy considered Pearl Harbor a place of refuge and rest for its sailors and as a place for maintenance and upkeep for its ships.[6] But Hawaii was not the vacation paradise it is today. Only the very wealthy could travel to the Islands, and they stayed at Waikiki Beach in the Royal Hawaiian or the Moana Hotels.

There was not the attraction of so many scantily-clad females on the beach which you see now. As a matter of fact, there was not the attraction of any girls, scantily clad or not. All the boys could see while on liberty were sailors and more sailors!

The musicians were distressed by the lack of liberty time and by the lack of money. They soon found there was not really much to do unless a person had plenty of money, and they usually did not get off early enough in the afternoon to go swimming.

So they put their faith in the latest rumor—that they would go to Bremerton in October for overhaul and would probably get a leave of about twenty-five days.

Many of the musicians had their cameras with them. After they reached Pearl Harbor, they had to leave their cameras in a locker on shore. Our sailors were not allowed to take cameras aboard their ships.

Shortly after the ship arrived at Pearl Harbor, Kinney took his band ashore to rehearse on solid land. In a photograph one of the boys took of the band, all the musicians look very hot and miserable.

According to Scruggs: "There are a lot of guys here from the school. All the ships (practically) are right here in Pearl Harbor." Radford was pleased to run into his good friend Don Harbin one evening at the Navy YMCA. Harbin was serving in the band on the *West Virginia*. They made plans to go swimming at Waikiki Beach on Sunday afternoon. Harbin was a very good fancy diver.

Radford from Nebraska, Moorhouse from Kansas, Bandy from Oklahoma and Missouri, and Williams from Oklahoma spent much time arguing the merits of their respective football teams. Bandy was not too impressed with Nebraska's Biff Jones as a coach.

It was common knowledge among the musicians from the School of Music that Kinney had been the toughest bandmaster in the school. Now, everywhere *Arizona*'s bandsmen went in Hawaii, their friends from the school asked them how they could stand Kinney. My brother never mentioned Kinney in his letters. Most of the boys wrote that Kinney was a tough taskmaster, but that he was the best director under whom they had ever played.

And the fact remains that Kinney took a green bunch of boys, most of them just out of high school, and turned them in just a few months into the most famous Navy band in the Pacific Fleet.

It is hard to understand how *Arizona*'s bandsmen were able to get along so well together. They had absolutely no privacy—they ate together, slept together, practiced and performed together, went on liberty together. Their schedule was such that it was difficult to make friends with the rest of the ship's crew.

The lack of privacy was very critical for the musicians. Whether a singer, musician, actor, painter, writer, or dancer, creative people require solitude to rehearse, study, or just to think. Such privacy was nonexistent on the ship. The musicians certainly did not miss the School of Music, but they did miss the private practice rooms which had been available to them there.

It was a constant struggle to find a quiet spot where they could write letters. Scruggs said that everywhere he went, it was noisy. On one occasion, he was down on the third deck by the band room. Some of the boys were practicing, the motors were running, and people were rushing through all the time. It was, however, still the only place aboard where he could go to write.

Later, again trying to write, he told how a bunch of the musicians had gathered in the band room and were playing some old circus marches, fast and loud. One of the boys was shouting "Peanuts, Popcorn, Chewing Gum. Right this way to see Jo-Jo, the dog-faced boy!"

In another letter, Scruggs wrote that he hoped his family could read his letter. The ship was at sea, and he had gone up on the boat deck to write. It was pretty windy, but it was one of the few places he could go without interruptions.

About the only time the boys in the band could be sure they would not be interrupted was after they had gone to bed, and even then, they often had drills in the middle of the night.

I had asked Clyde for his schedule, and he answered:

> *Here's what we do on board a battleship. We get up at 5:30 A.M. and eat at six-thirty. At seven-thirty, we go down below to the third deck and warm up until seven forty-five. At eight o'clock, we play colors. (That's when the flag goes up on the stern-post.) We go in and those not in the dance band clean up the compartment.*

> At nine-thirty, we start rehearsal. Sometimes it is dance band and sometimes concert band. We play until eleven, and then eat our noon meal. At twelve-thirty, we play a noon concert and then go back and rehearse until four.
>
> Next comes chow. At five-thirty, we give a dance band concert until six-thirty.
>
> After that, we are free to do anything we want to, unless there is a drill.
>
> Sundays we play for church and get off in the afternoon, sometimes.
>
> In case of a fire or collision, we fall in at the sick bay as stretcher bearers. In case of an attack by air or sea, we fall in down on third deck at the ammunition hoists to send ammunition to the guns topside. When we go into actual battle, our horns will be left ashore and we will be detailed to the sick bay to take care of the wounded, pick up stray arms and legs, etc.

Scruggs wrote that the musicians were continuing to receive their first-aid classes at three o'clock each day. When they did not have class, they had rehearsal, so the band seldom got over to shore before dark.

He described their routine during an attack, when the band's battle station was down in the ammunition hold. The musicians stood along the passageways to make sure the stream of shells kept rolling.

The ship was conducting drills often. A drill began when the signal for general quarters was sounded over the loud speaker. Instantly, all hands ran to their battle stations. The drills were apt to be sounded any time of the day or night, and no matter what a sailor was doing, he must drop everything and proceed rapidly to the battle station to which he had been assigned.

During firing drills, the men up in the range finder station told the men manning the guns just where to aim and when to fire. The crew was graded after each of the drills. Radford remarked that if the men used the same speed at their general drills that they used twice a week when mail call was sounded, or that they used three times a day for chow call, the *Arizona* would have the best record in the Pacific Fleet for efficiency.

Although many of us still chose to look the other way, our nation was preparing for war. On July 11, James C. Petrillo, president of the American Federation of Musicians, ordered the 138,000 members of the Federation to play "The Star Spangled Banner" at the beginning and at the end of every musical program they performed.[7]

Arizona's band boys had been gone from home now for more than six months, and their girls back home were writing them about the dates they were having with other boys. Since there were no girls available in Hawaii for the sailors, they could only read about the good times their girlfriends were having back home. They were philosophical about it, believing that sailors make very poor husbands, especially now that they were never in the States. They thought Hawaii was no place for a decent girl, so even if they were married, they would not want to bring their wives out there anyway. Some of the married sailors did bring their wives out to Hawaii, and in most cases, that decision saved their lives later in December.

I was still complaining that all the boys were being drafted, and my brother wrote me: "I don't see why you're worrying about your dates. What if you were out here in Hawaii with nothing but Japs to look at? You had better grab someone quick, honey, before the Army does."

I answered quickly, telling him I definitely was not interested in marriage—not while I was having so much fun dating different boys and dancing nearly every night.

The servicemen were worried that all the girls would be gone when they were finally able to get back home. As my brother wrote, "It looks like I'll be among a pack of wolves when I get back there, with all the soldiers around."

When the band was in port, they played for about three dances a week and gave three or four concerts for the Admiral. With so many rehearsals and so many appearances, the band continued to improve. Bandy, Haas, and Scruggs formed a singing trio. Scruggs wrote that the crew really went for the dance band and seemed to like the trio, although he suspected they might be getting tired of their rendition of "Dolores."

On July 12, Scruggs and Shaw, both about broke, went to the YMCA to attend a broadcast being held there. Featured was an Army dance band with some singers.

On Sunday, July 13, *Arizona*'s band played for colors and for church services, as usual. At one o'clock, they gave a concert on the ship for some of Admiral Kidd's guests.

Of chief interest to the band and to the crew was one of his guests—Loretta Young. Radford airily wrote that she was "Lolly" to him.

When she and her husband came aboard, the band was playing Handel's "Largo." Loretta and her husband came over to the band and stood beside the musicians. When they finished the musical selection, they were introduced to her. She said of their playing, "That was very, very beautiful." *Arizona*'s bandsmen were very proud and all wrote home about meeting her. They continued to play for more than two hours while the Admiral's party had dinner.

After dinner, the Admiral took his guests on a tour of the ship. Loretta Young passed right by Scruggs and other musicians several times.

Later in the afternoon, as Loretta Young was leaving the ship, the crew lined up along the side, leaning over the rail to see her for the last time. One enthusiastic Marine leaned over a little too far and fell overboard!

The Admiral's concert that day cancelled Radford and Harbin's plans to go to Waikiki Beach. So after the concert, Radford showed Harbin around the *Arizona*, and then they went over to the *West Virginia*. There Harbin tried to convince Radford how much better his ship was than the *Arizona* and they watched the movie.

Each ship showed movies every night she was in port. The picture was usually pretty good, but finding a spot to place one's chair was a problem, since many more sailors stayed aboard in Pearl Harbor than in Long Beach.

Scruggs wrote on July 15 that the band had the afternoon off, at least until three o'clock, and that it was really something special for them.

Liberties were not much fun in Hawaii, where it cost ten dollars for a five dollar liberty, and where they had to be back on the ship by 1:00 A.M. They did not go uptown to Honolulu very often, since the bus fare was thirty cents round trip, and everything there was so high. They soon came to the conclusion that they might as well stay on the ship and save their money. They could buy Camel cigarettes on board the ship for six cents a pack.

Becoming discouraged about their leave, Radford told his sister she might as well kill the spring roosters she had been saving for his leave, because he did not think he would be home before October, if then.

The boys were all writing home about the movie stars they were seeing at the dances they played at the Royal Hawaiian and at the Moana Hotels. Hughes proudly wrote home that they had met Brenda Frasier at the Royal Hawaiian.[8]

My brother wrote: "Last week we played two officers' dances and one chiefs' dance. The chiefs' dance was a knockout. There wasn't a sober dancer on the dance floor." He added that he would tell us more about it when he got home.

Scruggs described one of their dances which was held on July 16 at the Officers' Club. After the dance was over, one of the officers who rode back on the *Arizona* launch with the band was slightly intoxicated and decided they needed to have a jam session on the way back to the ship. He ordered the boat stopped and told the bandsmen they could either play or stay there all night. They played.

The officer, who was only having fun, of course, held the bass drum for Lynch, and the band "went to town."

Everyone was having fun, with the possible exception of Kinney, who sat and watched the ocean spray wash over his boys' instruments while praying that the salt water did not ruin them. But one did not argue with an officer of the United States Navy!

All the participants in that impromptu jam session would die in less than five months.

Those wild, drunken parties of our troops at Pearl Harbor in 1941 which have been discussed for so many years have been highly overstated. Most of the young boys there at that time did not drink to that extent and their lack of money dampened their partying considerably.

Radford described a typical liberty. On Saturday, July 19, he, Williams, and Cox went over to Honolulu, found a nice shady spot under a palm tree in a park, and slept for about three hours. It is beyond me to imagine the total discomfort of sleeping in a hammock every night for months. Not only was it extremely hot, but it also guaranteed that the sleeper could not turn over all night. I can imagine the bliss of lying out on the grass in the shade, able to turn back and forth as one slept. After they awoke, they went to the movies, then returned to the ship about nine o'clock.

On Sunday, July 20, the band played for church and Admiral Kidd attended with some guests. The boys described Admiral Kidd as a "pretty good old devil." He stood up in church and sang with the gobs (sailors), and the Admiral's voice stood out above the voices of the others.

The singing trio had been working hard and now, in addition to "Dolores," they were singing "Walking By The River." Bandy was singing a lot of solos with the band, and Scruggs was singing a solo in "The Boogie Woogie Bugle Boy."

The boys calculated it took about ten to twelve days for a letter from the United States to reach the Territory of Hawaii. It only took three days to make the 3,900 mile trip by Clipper airplane, but an air Clipper stamp cost twenty cents, as compared to three cents for regular mail.

Clyde finally received mail from us on July 22, and his letter to me was full of comments about the hometown people I had mentioned. Sensing their extreme loneliness, the boys' sisters were writing long letters to their brothers, keeping them up to date on the latest gossip back home. The boys were always begging for more news, and Radford wrote his sister that he could close his eyes and see the things she wrote about.

The musicians were definitely homesick. All their letters reflect their sadness about their life and their eagerness to get that leave. As a matter of fact, nearly everyone in our nation between the ages of eighteen to twenty-five was sad and troubled. The depression had taught us not to expect much from life, but being young, we hoped anyway.

Few of us in the year of 1941 were where we wanted to be, and young people in love were often separated by many miles. The boys in the service were in a situation from which there was no escape, while the girls back home were equally trapped. Even if a girl could save enough money for the bus fare, she would have no funds for shelter and food after she arrived.

Our songs told of our sadness. We sang of traveling— "Chattanooga Choo Choo" and "Take the 'A' Train." We sang of loneliness— "I'll Be With You In Apple Blossom Time," "I'll Never Smile Again," "A Nightingale Sang In Berkeley Square."

Although the musicians disliked Hawaii heartily, their hatred did not stem from their hard work—they were used to that from the School of Music. And their dislike was not necessarily due to their working every day—most of us worked six days a week, anyway. Working seven days a week was just part of their job.

Their dislike of Hawaii stemmed from the total lack of girls to meet and date. Sailors were looked upon with even less favor in Hawaii than they had been in Washington, D.C.

Even some of their fellow sailors looked down on musicians with contempt. Former sailors still tell me that my brother had pretty soft duty as a musician. Such remarks stem from a total lack of knowledge of military bands and their duties.

I have always answered that, in the case of *Arizona's* band, that duty did not turn out to be so soft, after all.

Fortunately, the large majority of *Arizona's* crewmen appreciated their band and did not hesitate to let their musicians know it. That meant a lot to the boys then, and even more to their families later.

By July 23, having played three dances in a row in the past week and for yet another dance that night, the musicians were ready for some relaxation. By the time they got into the truck which was to take them back to the launch, some of the boys were feeling pretty good. They stopped the truck at a drive-in, took their instruments out, and played a jam session from the truck.

The drive-in was at a fork in the street. People rapidly began gathering, cheering and dancing in the streets. A traffic jam soon developed, but nobody cared—everyone was having too much fun.

That impromptu dance in the streets of Honolulu was not so much fun the next morning, however, when *Arizona* again went to sea. The band boys did not return to the ship until 3:00 A.M. on July 24 and had to get up at five to get under way.

In an unheard-of departure from routine, Kinney gave the band the day off. Scruggs slept from six to eight o'clock that morning, then got up to write a few letters. After he finished, he planned to go back to sleep. He said he would have to do that sleeping somewhere on the deck, of course. Never were those hammocks to be removed from their storage bins during the day!

Arizona was at sea from July 24 to August 1. When the ship was in port, the band did not stand the customary watches of four hours on and four hours off, which was required of her sailors. Rather, the band either rehearsed or performed from early in the morning until late in the evening, seven days a week.

When the ship went to sea, however, it was not always possible for the musicians to rehearse, because of the rough sea. Consequently, the band was assigned to stand watches, which were always maintained while the ship was at sea. Special watch sections patrolled the ship all night, checking that all the watertight compartments were closed. Night lights were left burning, so the men on watch could move around easily.[9]

On that cruise, Radford said they were heading south from Pearl Harbor but did not ever seem to be going anywhere in particular. He added that they were just out cruising around, spending the taxpayers' money.

It made him dizzy to think of the money it was costing to keep afloat all the ships which were at Pearl Harbor, since *Arizona* alone had a crew of more than 2,000 [sic] men.

Sunday, July 27, while at sea, the band played for church. In the afternoon, *Arizona* held a "happy hour." Both concert and dance bands played and the ship held a quiz program with prizes. That night, the band played a dance program. That comprised the band's Sunday day off!

On Monday, *Arizona* held short-range practice with the broadside guns. Her gunners shot at a floating target about half a mile away which was being drawn by a tug. Radford said he would surely hate to be on a ship at which those guys were shooting, because they did not miss.

On that maneuver, *Arizona* was accompanied by at least five destroyers, two cruisers, one aircraft carrier, and the battleship *Oklahoma*, which stayed right on the tail of *Arizona* for the entire two weeks.

Radford went up to one of the turrets during a battle drill, and thought it was the fastest he had ever seen sailors move. The groups of twenty men in each turret crew could shove a fourteen-hundred pound shell and three bags of powder into the breach in fifteen seconds. Although the big guns were not actually fired during the loading practices, the loading exercise was conducted often to increase the speed of the loaders and to make sure the loading procedure became automatic. They were expecting to fire the big guns about August 24, when they were due to conduct short-range firing. After that, they were going back to Bremerton!

Unfortunately, that was another of the going-home rumors which was to circulate among them until the day they died.

CHAPTER 15

Faded Blooms

According to Radford, *Arizona* finally returned from playing war with the rest of the fleet on Friday afternoon, August 1. Officially, she was judged to have been torpedoed twice and hit by heavy-caliber shells several more times. At the band's battle station, about a dozen men had to lie down and play "dead," because the central station phoned down to tell them their particular part of the ship had been hit by a torpedo.

Describing their battle station, Radford said they did not do anything during general quarters drill except close the watertight hatches and turn off all the air pumps. The air pumps were turned off in case of a gas attack. During the drills, the bandsmen locked themselves in their compartment and were not allowed to come out until "Secure" was passed. If they had to go to the "head" [toilet], they were instructed to use a bucket located there. Once, while locked into their battle station compartment, it became time for a meal, so the mess cooks brought them hamburgers, candy bars, and coffee. Locked into the compartment with no air, the band boys played cards or read magazines until the drill was over.

Of course, the purpose of the drills was to train the crewmen to run to their battle stations at a moment's notice. While the musicians did not actually pass the ammunition up to the guns during drills, they were in their compartment, ready to do so if the air alert turned out to be the real thing.

Radford still wanted to witness a sea battle someday, but he thought it seemed more and more unlikely he would ever actually see one. Since the band's battle station was three decks below, he decided he would have to wait until they invented binoculars capable of seeing through two feet of steel.

He was right. *Arizona* did finally have her first and last battle in December, but Radford and his fellow musicians saw only the very first few minutes of it.

Arizona returned to Pearl Harbor on August 1 at 2:00 A.M., and was tied up by nine. The boys were supposed to go on liberty that afternoon, but apparently two weeks of togetherness was wearing on Kinney. He ordered his bandsmen to clean their compartment completely from top to bottom, and they did not finish until five o'clock that evening. Since they were all broke and would not be paid until the fifth, they did not really mind missing their liberty, anyway.

From August 1 to August 14, *Arizona* was again moored at Pearl Harbor. By now, the bloom had certainly faded from the beautiful Islands of Hawaii.

Radford advised his folks that, if anyone ever told them Waikiki Beach was a good place to pay out a lot of dough to visit for swimming, they could just tell him he was a liar. Radford would a lot rather just swim in a gravel pit back in Nebraska, since every place a person stepped on Waikiki Beach, he cut his foot on a piece of coral. Also, when he was swimming out in the deep water and a wave came along, making him swallow a lot of dirty water, it made his stomach feel funny for an hour afterwards. He liked the beach on the Pike in Long Beach much better.

On the morning of August 1, a British battleship and other ships came into Pearl Harbor for repairs and painting. Radford commented that, from the looks of that battleship, she should just be jacked up and a new one run under her. He didn't believe she had seen a coat of paint in three years, since even her sides were rusty. He thought England probably did not put her ships through dry dock every year or so, as did the United States.

Radford had never seen so much painting done in his life as he had since he had come aboard *Arizona*. Everywhere he looked, there was some deck hand busy painting something or other.

The condition of the British warships was no doubt due to the fact that England had already been at war for several years. Scruggs remarked that the British warships had been bombed and were a mess.

Our Navy men rushed over to go aboard the English warships. They reported back to their shipmates who did not wish to stand in line for so long that our Navy was far superior to the English Navy.

Our sailors loved to hear the British sailors talk, and asked them anything at all just to start them talking.

The U.S. Navy threw a big program at the "Y" and invited the "Limeys" to attend. The English sailors had to get up on the stage and sing for the Americans. Some of the "Limey" sailors were Scotch, some Irish, some English, and some spoke Cockney English. All those accents were very entertaining for our boys.

At the end of the program, the English sailors stood and sang "God Save the King." The Americans stood during the song and were very silent and solemn.

On that same night, the "Y" sponsored an authentic hulu exhibition, featuring dances of the Hawaiian people from hundreds of years ago. Some dancers sat and just moved their arms and legs; some dancers used sticks and gourd rattles.

The musicians at Pearl Harbor were now being questioned by Navy Intelligence agents, who had come to Hawaii to interview former students of the School of Music. It was believed that several men on the staff of the school had been collecting the life insurance premiums at an inflated price and had been pocketing the extra money.

The musicians heard later that the culprits were eventually discharged from the Navy, but the damage had already been done. Most of the students at the school had been forced to drop their life insurance because they could not make the payments.

There was much construction being done at Pearl Harbor at that time. Scruggs wrote that they were building acres and acres of new homes for Navy people and that the houses were real nice and very modernistic.

Scruggs described the new facilities for enlisted men at Pearl Harbor. Richardson Recreation Center was equipped with a swimming pool, bowling alleys, lounges, dance floor, a big stadium, and a lunchroom. Upstairs there were reading and writing rooms and pool tables. Scruggs was especially delighted to find a piano there.

The boys thought it was all very swell, and it was free, too.

Radford described the musicians' meal time on the ship. The band boys cussed and fought over the food and stole each others dessert every chance they got. When you are eighteen years old and in an impossible situation, you manufacture your own entertainment. Radford planned to brush up on his table manners soon, since he expected to be home in a month or two.

The orchestra for church did not include all the musicians, but the members of the band took turns playing each Sunday. The orchestra on Sunday morning, August 3, was made up of nine musicians—two trumpets, two clarinets, two French horns, one trombone, one bass, and one baritone.

On August 13, the *Arizona* permitted her bandsmen and quite a few of her quartermasters to go out to Kailua Beach for an overnight party. The sailors swam and ate until dark, then the band played for the dance. When the dance ended at midnight, some of the musicians went down to the deserted beach to swim in the buff.

The next morning, the sailors went back to the ship after breakfast. That afternoon, the band played for a ballgame on shore.

Arizona went to sea again from August 14 to August 22. While the ship was at sea, my brother wrote us in an undated letter:

> *It's been a long time since I wrote, I guess, but I've been pretty busy of late. I made Musician Second Class and my pay is fifty-four dollars a month now. In ten more months, I'll be eligible for Musician First Class.*
>
> *We've been in Hawaii nearly two months now, and we ought to be headed back to the States pretty soon. We might get some leave if we go into the yards. There's no telling when we will go or where we will go. We might even go back to the East Coast.*
>
> *Tell Molly I got the box and I don't know even how to start thanking her. Everything in it is swell. I've given some of it to all the boys and they really enjoyed it too. I've still got part of it.*
>
> *We are out on the high sea now and we are going to fire the sixteen inch guns tomorrow. We are assistants to the medical department during battles.*

> *I am enclosing ten dollars in this letter for Pate. Ask him if*
> *I can get some money when I get leave for a little while.*
> *We have played two or three dances every week out here.*
> *We went on an all night trip last Friday [sic] and played for a*
> *dance.*
> *The writing is scribbly but the guys are shaking the table*
> *and the ship is pitching pretty bad. Kinda windy today.*
> *Write soon. Love, Proke*

The latest rumor was that *Arizona* would go into the Philadelphia Navy Yard for dry dock.

Radford, who always closed his letters with "So long, Mike," wrote his sister on August 17, "Well, dearie, it's Sunday afternoon and Neal is sitting on his little fanny up here on the boat deck trying his damnedest to think of something to write."

All the musicians had the same trouble. My brother could not complain about the officers or the ship, because our dad would send him another sermon. And he could not write about what the ship was doing, because the Navy was cautioning them not to divulge anything that would help the enemy. It left all the boys scratching their heads to think of something to say that they had not already said before.

The sailors wore white shorts instead of the long white pants and just a skivvy shirt instead of the white jumper. They all thought the shorts were surely more comfortable than the regular summer white uniforms which they had worn in Washington.

The lack of water was always a problem. They were still allowed a gallon and a half of fresh water a day to wash, shave, take a shower, and wash their clothes. Radford commented that, believe it or not, it could be done. To keep up, he washed a pair of white shorts, a suit of skivvies (underwear) and a hat every day.

Although Radford thought that life was pretty tough on the ship when they were out to sea on maneuvers, somehow he got a kick out of it. He had found a place to swing his hammock where an air blower sent a cool breeze over him, so what little sleep he got was at least comfortable.

Scruggs thought they were really running them around on that cruise, with drills day and night. He had given up trying to sleep in his hammock and was tired all the time. The band had a "huge coffin box" in which to keep their music, so Scruggs slept on that box every night. He said it was hard, but better than a hammock. He looked forward to getting home, so he could sleep forever.

Radford wrote of some Marines who were up in the crow's nest shooting at some little balloons with machine guns. He added the usual compliments which sailors everywhere pay to Marines (and vice versa).

Radford heard from a friend who graduated with *Arizona*'s band and whose band had been assigned to the *Texas*. That ship was now in Iceland.

On Monday, August 18, *Arizona* held her short-range practice. The last time *Arizona* had fired short-range practice, a crew from the movies was on board and filmed the exercise for the newsreels. Radford asked his family if they had seen that movie.

The four turret crews fired six salvos each at a target about a mile away. Radford said all four turret crews did really well except for number four turret, which was manned by an inexperienced crew who took too much time to load. One of the turret crews hit the target eighteen times in a row for a perfect score, and the crew of twenty men received ten dollars each as a reward.

That was the first time Radford had ever seen a gun fire where you could see the bullets from the time they left the gun until they hit the target. He was impressed with the gunners' ability to hit their target.

On August 18, the base pay for Navy personnel who were on sea duty was raised by ten dollars per month.

Now the latest scuttlebutt was that *Arizona* would go back to Pearl Harbor on Friday, August 22, and leave on Monday under sealed orders. All the crew was excited, with everybody making bets she was going back to the States for dry dock. They heard that the ship would be gone for nineteen days, which they thought would take them a long, long way from Pearl Harbor.

Radford advised his family that they should write him in San Pedro, as that would be *Arizona*'s home port by the time they wrote. He and Bill Moorhouse from Wichita, Kansas, were planning to hitch-hike home together. He said that Moorhouse could play more swing on his trumpet than he had ever heard anyone play, and he pronounced him a good kid.

Arizona had a mock air attack on August 19. Radford said the dive bombers seemed to dive down out of nowhere. He was told that the bombers were almost impossible to hit until they leveled off. There were about twenty-nine bombers in the bunch. Radford said that, from the looks of that English battleship which had been at Pearl Harbor a few weeks before, it was easy to see how the bombers could raise hell with even a well-protected thing like a battleship.

The aircraft carriers were the ships which really bristled with pom-pom guns.

Thursday night, *Arizona* took on fuel from a tanker while steaming full speed ahead, and on Friday the tanker refueled the destroyers under the same conditions. *Arizona* returned to Pearl Harbor on August 22,[1] and the band immediately began playing for dances again. They were in great demand in Hawaii, and often played for functions at the Royal Hawaiian and at the Moana Hotels in Honolulu. After the attack, the manager of the Moana Hotel wrote how much she loved the *Arizona* band boys and how much everyone enjoyed their playing.[2]

By now, the crew was totally sick of Hawaiian music. Cox and Hurley had their electric Hawaiian guitars with them and were very good on them, but the crew did not ever want to hear Hawaiian music again.

Haas, Nadel, and Scruggs were writing arrangements for the dance band. Scruggs wrote a Tommy Dorsey arrangement of "I Love You Truly," and included a trombone trio in the piece. He and Nadel both thought it was fun to write an arrangement and then hear the band play it, knowing they had written it.

Few of the families heard from the members of *Arizona*'s band the last two weeks in August. We learned later how busy they were during that period. Clyde wrote me:

I received both of your letters today and I was glad to hear from home again. I'm sorry I haven't written lately, but as usual, I have a fairly good excuse. We have been practicing for a broadcast we played last Saturday night. It was a half-hour concert. We played some pretty stiff concert numbers, but it came off 4.0 (perfect).

The radio broadcast my brother referred to was played by the *Arizona* band on Saturday, August 30, at the Honolulu "Y." The bandsmen had worked very hard to prepare for the concert, and by all reports, it went very well.

Clyde was saving all the programs of their concerts for his scrapbook, but he did not send that program home. Fortunately, Ralph Burdette sent his program and a description of the concert to his parents.

It was indeed a serious concert, as the program indicates:

Army & Navy Y.M.C.A. Honolulu
Saturday, August 30, 1941
7:15 P.M.
Concert
by the
USS *Arizona* Band
Bandmaster—Fred Kinney

Program

1. March "Anchors Aweigh" - Introducing
   "The U.S.S. *Arizona* Fight Song" .... Kinney
2. Overture - "Egmont" .... Beethoven
3. Popular Selection - "Trade Winds" .... Friend-Tobias
4. Selection - "Hall of Fame" .... compiled by Safranek
   (Well-known works of several famous composers)
   First - Introduction to "Racoozy" .... Kolor Bola
   Second - "Celeste Aida" .... Verdi

Third - "Entry of the Gladiators" .... Fucik
Fourth - "Melody in F" .... Rubinstein
Fifth - "Prelude in C Sharp Minor" .... Rachmaninoff
Sixth - "Anitra's Dance" .... Greig
Seventh - "Humoresque" .... Dvorak
Finale - "First Hungarian Rhapsody" .... Liszt
5. Novelty Number - "Schnitzelbank" .... Yodor
6. Rhapsody Moderne - "Headlines" .... Colby
An impressionistic reflection of the violent pace of modern life.
You will hear the roar of the newspaper presses as they grind
out headlines of war, murder, fire, theft, scandal, love—life.
7. March - "The Crosley March" .... Fillmore
8. National Anthem - "The Star Spangled Banner"
* * * * * * * * * * *
Happy Hour—8:15 P.M.
First six rows reserved for service men in uniform.
Admittance to the Auditorium will be from the Lounge entrance
Featuring—"The Honolulu Girls Glee Club"[3]

Selection Number 6 of that program was very prophetic. In just
three short months, we did hear the roar of the newspaper presses
as they ground out their headlines of war, murder, fire, theft, scandal, love—and death, and the *Arizona* band fulfilled its destiny.

Burdette wrote his parents the next day to tell them the concert
was a huge success. It lasted from seven-fifteen to eight o'clock. The
band played seven numbers altogether and ended up with the National Anthem. The first overture they played was particularly praised
by the many music critics who were attending the concert.

There were nearly a thousand people in the audience, all of whom
showered praises on the band after the concert was finished.

Arizona's bandsmen were especially pleased when Admiral Kidd
called after the concert to tell them it was the finest program he had
ever heard. The Admiral also told them that *Arizona*'s crew wanted
to hear the concert so badly that her sailors had practically demanded
the movies be cut out and the loud speakers turned on, so they could
hear their band play.

Kinney also received telephone calls from the highest officials in the Army and Marine Corps, praising his band for one of the finest programs they had ever heard. The Commanding Officer of the Army's music division telephoned Kinney to ask how many pieces he had in his band. He figured it must be a huge band to be able to put over such a well-known overture as Egmont, and to do it so well. When he was told it was a twenty-piece band, he could hardly believe what he had heard. The Army officer said it was the finest he had ever heard Egmont performed.[4]

After the bandsmen had worked so hard to perfect that concert, it was very gratifying for them to receive so many compliments.

That day, August 30, 1941, went far toward giving *Arizona*'s band the reputation they earned for being the best Navy band in the Pacific Fleet.

The concert was broadcast over the radio, but we did not receive it in Oklahoma. Burdette was going to try to obtain a recording of the concert and send it to his folks, but it never did arrive. He did, however, send his parents a copy of the band's photograph, which was taken during that concert. They would later share it with the other families.

On stationery which Clyde often used, with the letterhead of USS *Arizona* at the top, he wrote:

> *We had a lot of compliments, even from the Commanding Officer of the Army in Hawaii and from Rear Admiral I. C. Kidd of Battle Division One (Admiral of the* Arizona.)...
>
> *I have pictures of all the guys in the band but three and I'll send them as soon as they are printed. White, Hurley, and I made a trip around the Island with some soldiers who had a car and I got some fairly good pictures that I'll send later for you to put in my album, if you will. I might take some more later and I'll send them home.*
>
> *Tell Mate and Pate I'll write in a day or two.*
>
> *We're kept pretty busy playing for the crew, because they seem to enjoy the music very much, especially the dance music.*

I am sending twenty-five dollars to Pate in this letter, so give it to him please.

There isn't much to write about and there is a lot I can't write about, so I'll have to cut this one short.

Love and Kisses, Proke.

P.S. Take care of Dink.

CHAPTER 16

The Battle of Music 1941

In September, according to Hughes, *Arizona* was scheduled to return to San Pedro, where she would be put into dry dock for renovation.

That was followed by another big disappointment, however, when he wrote that a great British battleship, heavily damaged in action, was proceeding to San Pedro where it would go into *Arizona*'s dry dock space.[1]

Whether true or not, that story is an example of the rumors which constantly circulated and kept the boys on edge.

Arizona went back out to sea from September 4 to 10.[2]

While at sea, my brother wrote our parents, "There isn't much to tell you that I didn't write to Molly, but I'll try."

He had not yet seen Gordon McCulloch, a Marine Lieutenant who was the son of our family's close friends in Okmulgee. Gordon was stationed on the heavy cruiser *Astoria*, and had written his parents that he would look Clyde up when his ship went to Pearl Harbor.

My brother asked for the address of our cousin Newt Conway. After having been turned down for the service because of his poor eyesight, Newt had gone to California to attend the Anderson Airplane School and was now working at Lockheed Aircraft in Burbank. Clyde wanted to look him up when the *Arizona* returned to California.

Arizona was back in Pearl Harbor from September 10 to 15,[3] and her crew finally received its mail. Clyde wrote me:

> *I was beginning to think that the ol' home town had folded up. It's been a long time since I heard from you last. We are still here in Hawaii and have been since July 7th [sic].*

We move around quite often, so that is the reason that Gordon couldn't find me. I'll probably see him pretty soon, but Pearl Harbor is a big place.

It looks as though we are going to be here a long time, but we'll be back sometime.

We are going to play for a ship's dance tomorrow night and one the twenty-second. The crew seems to enjoy these dances, but there is usually a lack of girls at them. There are too many slant-eyes down here, anyway.

There are only seven guys in the band that aren't Musician Second Class now.

We haven't had to stand many watches lately, except in drills. That is only while we're at sea, though, and we can't practice too much then, anyway.

Well, this is sorta rambling, but there isn't anything to write about.

Give my love to Mate and Pate and everyone. Love, Proke

That was not the first time Clyde had mentioned "Japs" or "slant-eyes." Before the war, we were not bigoted against the Japanese in Okmulgee—we did not even know any. The boys were learning their fear of the Japanese from our Navy, which was expecting trouble from Japan.

The September 13 ship's dance which Clyde mentioned was, in reality, the beginning of the famous "Battle of Music 1941." Apparently Scruggs had received the word about the contest, as he wrote his family on September 13:

There is a contest tonight that our band is in. There are four dance bands and they pick the best one tonight then the best out of four next week [sic]. Later on the winners compete for a cup or something.

I don't know what we'll win as I've never heard these other bands and they could easily be a lot better than we are. It will be fun to try though.

By the fall of 1941, there were few families in the United States which had not been touched by the approaching war. Congress had passed the Selective Service Bill on September 14, providing for the registration of all men between the ages of twenty-one and thirty-five. That had caused an increase in the enlistments of boys into the armed services.

Consequently, swarms of new sailors descended upon Hawaii. They were being sent to the old ships in Pearl Harbor for training.

Contrary to the picture of hard-drinking sailors you always read about, the new "swabbies" were young, inexperienced boys, most of them fresh from small towns and farms. They soon threatened to outnumber the "old salts" of the Navy, much to their disgust. About all the "salts" could do was shake their heads and mutter to everyone about what a hell of a shape the Navy was in now.

Certainly there was nothing in Honolulu for the new gobs to do. With no money and no girls, most of them spent their free time on their ships. Since the boys could and did write back home, the Navy stepped up its entertainment program, hoping to improve the morale of its sailors.

Fleet Recreation had always tried to entertain the men stationed in Hawaii by promoting sporting competitions between the ships.

Contests were held in football, baseball, prizefights, wrestling matches, whaling boat races, and other competitions. Members of the crews of the various ships attended the contests and cheered wildly for their ships.

Most of the new sailors were barely out of high school and regarded those competitions the same way they had viewed their football teams back home.

Rivalry was intense between the ships and between sailors and Marines. Usually friendly rivalry, it could erupt at any moment into brawls, with the combatants being hauled back to their ships by the Shore Patrol.

The men who were present at Pearl Harbor at that time never forgot their pride in their ships and units. After more than fifty years, they still talk of their teams' victories.

That is how I heard that, once upon a time, the Marine Barracks beat *Arizona* in a baseball game.[4]

To provide additional entertainment for the sailors, the "Battle of Music 1941" was organized by Fleet Recreation.

The organizers of the contest had no way of knowing that the outcome of that "Battle of Music" would still be argued more than fifty years later.

There were seventeen Navy bands stationed at Pearl Harbor in the fall of 1941, either on ships or on shore, and the Marine Corps Barracks band made eighteen. All the bands were extremely competent.[5]

Most of the Navy bands had graduated from the U.S. Navy School of Music in Washington, and many of the musicians knew each other from their school days. The other Navy bands had been trained at the Fleet School in San Diego.

The Battle was organized along the lines of band contests everywhere. Beginning on September 13, a contest was held every other Saturday night at Bloch Arena. Four bands competed in three categories—Swing Numbers, Sweet Numbers, and Specialty Numbers. Using audience applause, points were given in each of the categories by the judges, and small cups were awarded the winners.

Last was the popular jitterbug contest. The four bands took turns playing their best jitterbug music while the competing couples danced to the music. At the end of each band's performance, some of the couples were eliminated, until finally, when the last band had finished playing, the winning dance team was chosen and was presented with a cup.

As a climax to the evening's entertainment, the best band was chosen from the four participating bands.

The program ended with an ensemble of all the bands, the awarding of the prizes, and the National Anthem, played by all the bands.[6]

With such extremely fine bands competing, it would be nearly impossible for the judges to pick a winner. Therefore, they sidestepped that painful task by choosing the two best bands by audience applause.[7]

The only drawback to that method was that it practically guaranteed that two bands from the big battleships would be declared the winners, simply because the battleships usually had more of their crews present. Fleet Recreation figured that the Battle was not a matter of life and death, anyway, and it served its purpose. The sailors had someplace to go on Saturday nights where they could hear music which reminded them of home and of their best girls. And they could spend the evening cheering wildly for their ships, convincing themselves that they were having a great time.

As an added bonus, the "Battle of Music" programs were broadcast by radio to the ships anchored at Pearl Harbor. Thus the crew members who had drawn the duty could also hear the music and dream of home as they worked.[8]

The first and second place bands chosen by the audience were awarded gold cups, and would play later in the semifinal contests. The other two bands were eliminated.[9]

There was bound to be some conflict between the people choosing the contestants for the next music contest and the people planning the next war maneuvers. Often, by the time the program was printed for the "Battle of Music," one of the competing bands had gone to sea with its ship. Therefore, it was not always the bands listed on the program which actually played in the contest that night.

On September 13, the first night of the Battle, the four bands listed on the program were the bands from the *Arizona*, *West Virginia*, *California*, and *Dobbin*.[10]

In actual fact, the band from the Submarine Base (SUBSCOFOR) played that night instead of the band from the *Dobbin*.

The *Arizona* band won first place in that first Battle of Music contest and was awarded a gold cup. The *California* band was awarded second place and was also presented a gold cup. Both bands were eligible to play in the semifinals scheduled to begin the last of November.

J. L. "Kid" Reed, the student from the School of Music whom I had dated in Washington, was now in Pearl Harbor in the band of the *West Virginia*. He wrote me on September 27:

...We just came in from a few days at sea...Haven't been doing much lately. There is some 'dope' going about that we are going back to the States within the next six or eight weeks, so I've been saving my money for when we go to the States, we will get leave and I'm going to go home...

A couple of weeks ago I saw your brother over at the Recreation Center. I suppose that you have heard by now that the Arizona *band won the battle of bands a couple of weeks ago. They really have a fine band.*

Gee, they played swell...

I forgot to mention that our band, the California *band and another band were in the contest. It was really quite an affair.*

There is going to be another battle of bands tonight and I'm going over to see how it is to be an onlooker and not a participant. I don't know what four bands are playing—but it should be good.[11]

Although he did not mention it, "Kid" Reed was very good on the trombone and had helped the *West Virginia* band win a small cup that night with its Specialty Number.[12]

Scruggs wrote, "We won the contest Saturday night and got the cup—a gold one."

Arizona had bent a propeller shaft on her last cruise and had to return to Pearl Harbor.

Scruggs wrote on Monday, September 15, "We are in dry dock now for about four or five days. They are going to fix it here, so there's no chance of us going to Bremerton to have it done."

My brother wrote on September 20:

There's not much to write about, but I'll make a stab at it.

We are playing for an officers' dance tonight and a crew's dance Monday night.

We are going to get orchestra uniforms before long to use at dances. We don't play for as many dances here as we will in the States.

The way things look now, I don't know when we will get back there.

I'm sorry I didn't get to see Gordon while he was here, but I may still be here when he comes back, and I'll get to see him then.

I am sending Pate a M. O. for twenty-five dollars in this letter. I don't know if I can send any next month, because I had to buy a trumpet. My old cornet was shot. It was even out of tune with itself and broken loose in one spot. I got a French make Selmer and it is a very fine horn. I got it for practically nothing.

Tell Molly "Hello" and ask Reginald if he is sure that I didn't write the last letter.

Sorry this is short, but there is nothing to write about.

Love, Proke

Again moored at Pearl Harbor from September 19 to 24, *Arizona* went to sea again from September 24 to October 2.[13]

Therefore, her band was at sea when the second "Battle of Music" was held on September 27.

About this time, six of *Arizona's* musicians reached their nineteenth birthdays—Brabbzson in July, Cox and Moorhouse in August, Williams in September, and Hughes and Shaw in October. For each occasion, they all went over to Honolulu to celebrate before they went back to sea.[14]

Arizona was again moored at Pearl Harbor from October 2 to 7.[15]

Kinney was known as a real showman, which was one of the reasons his band was so outstanding. In a move toward procuring new uniforms for his dance orchestra, he asked for a new allowance list for ship bands.

In a letter dated October 2, 1941, Captain Van Valkenburgh requested that the Chief of the Bureau of Ships forward a new Allowance List for Band Instruments for a twenty-one-piece unit band. The Captain wrote that the list which had been furnished to *Arizona* was for equipage and supplies for a seventeen-piece band, and was not suitable for the larger band now serving on *Arizona*.[16]

Certainly the allowance for the band would not be needed for new instruments, since Kinney had insisted that all his boys ship out with the very best instruments. Therefore, he planned to use the band allowance for dance band uniforms.

Clyde wrote me a letter postmarked USS *Arizona*—Air Mail, dated October 4:

> *I was beginning to think that you had lost my address. I finally got a letter from you and one from Mate and Pate.*
>
> *I have Dick Lucas's address now, thanks to Mate, and I'll start writing him again. Tell Reg. that I'll write to him soon, and that I thought he owed me a letter.*
>
> *I'm glad that you got your raise, and if you want to get into Civil Service, I hope you make it. If you are going to try to get a job in California, try to get it in Los Angeles instead of San Diego. When we go back to the States, we go to Long Beach, and that's only a little ways from L. A. You are always better off in your own backyard, though.*
>
> *I got the cake yesterday, and it was all in one piece. All the icing and the lettering were still on it, and it is really good. It was nice of you three to send it to me and* **we** *all enjoyed it. Thanks a million for it and I want another one when I come home.*
>
> *Nothing else to write and chow is ready, so I'll close until I get some more time. Love, Proke*
>
> *P.S. Write soon and take care of Dink. Tell Mate and Pate "Hello"*

The cake which he received on October 3 was his birthday cake which we had sent him in September. Evidently he had to wait until the ship came back into port to receive the package. That angel food cake had been on its way for so long that I am sure it was dry and the icing was cracking off, but he politely assured us that it was fine.

While still in port, Clyde wrote our parents on October 5:

Yes, I am still in Pearl Harbor and will be for some time. Of course, we have to go out to sea sometimes to keep from getting rusty. Until you get a letter from Long Beach, Ca., you will know that I am still in Hawaii, the land of sunshine and beautiful flowers.

We are going to play a band concert this afternoon at four o'clock in some park. This morning we played for church, as usual.

I think I told you that we won a dance band contest quite a while ago. We won a cup and later we are going into the finals for a bigger cup.

That trumpet I bought is a $180.00 horn and one of the best. It was in good condition when I bought it and if I get it dented or the lacquer comes off, the ship will fix it up. I'll have it paid for after next payday or the next.

How much money have I got at home now? I don't keep track of it, but I'm not worried about it.

I'll be going up for First Class Musician in about nine months and that will be seventy-two dollars a month.

Don't do anything I wouldn't and take care of Dink. Love, Proke.

P.S. I got the cake and it was really good. Thanks a lot. It was nice of all of you to remember my birthday.

One of the things for which I was always grateful during the horrible mess we went through after December 7 was that my brother did not ever know just how the Navy honored that guarantee on his new trumpet. Better he remained a happy, kind, trusting boy until the very end.

While still in school in Washington, Radford and Harbin had often gone down to Harbin's basement to shoot at targets with automatic pistols. Radford was glad to have that practice, because musicians had to qualify with a .45 before they could get their Musician First Class rate.

My brother sent me a copy of a classic poem, written by the usual anonymous poet.

SAILOR'S HYMN

Some poets sing of any ol' thing
And some sing of kings and queens,
And some sing of love and the skies above,
But I sing only of beans.

As the hands of the clock crawl together at twelve,
To the witching hour when we eat,
My pulses pound and my head spins around,
At the thought of the coming treat.

And the meal which awaits at the mens' hall
One of life's most stirring scenes;
I simply can't wait 'till I tackle my plate,
With its heaped-up mountain of beans.

Let those who wish stick to their lobster,
And others to their chicken and pork,
And others their greens, but it's lowly beans
Into which I will dig my fork.

And I know when I get to Valhalla
To first view the heavenly scenes,
To St. Pete I'll say, if he wants me to stay,
He's got to keep feeding me beans!

Most of *Arizona*'s crew would make their journey to Valhalla in six weeks.

Arizona went to sea again on October 7 and 8 and returned to Pearl Harbor from October 8 to 18.[17]

At the third "Battle of Music," held on October 11, *Arizona* was in Pearl Harbor, but our boys did not mention attending the Battle. The band from the *Argonne* won first place that night.[18]

All during that time, Tokyo and Washington were continuing their negotiations for an American-Japanese rapprochement. Both Japan and Germany were expressing pessimism over the outcome of those talks.[19]

On October 10, Japan began busily speeding up emergency preparations toward a complete wartime footing to meet an early crisis. On October 11, the U.S. State Department announced that American citizens wishing to leave Japan would be carried to the United States by three Japanese ships. Japan was sending the ships to the United States in order to repatriate Japanese nationals.[20]

Japan estimated there were about 300 nationals in San Francisco, another 300 in Los Angeles, some 200 in Seattle and Portland, and perhaps 1,000 in Honolulu.[21]

Our government was busy assuring us that all was well.

Arizona went to sea again from October 18 to 26 for short trips.[22] The weather was foggy and raining almost every day of the trip.

Consequently, on the night of October 22, *Arizona* and *Oklahoma* collided.

As Radford described it, *Oklahoma* rammed *Arizona* and tore a hole in *Arizona*'s hull "big enough to drive a hay rack through." Apparently *Oklahoma* got off course and *Arizona* did not see her until they were fifty yards apart. By that time, it was too late. Fortunately, no one was hurt.

Radford commented that people would soon be saying our Navy was as bad as the Japanese Navy. The boys had heard that Japanese ships were always running into each other when they were out on maneuvers.

Six weeks later, that same Japanese Navy which our boys held in such contempt would bring the airplanes to Pearl Harbor which would destroy *Arizona* and overturn *Oklahoma*.

With the Navy's paranoia about secrecy regarding her ships' activities, Clyde did not mention the collision, but he wrote the next day asking me to have his suit cleaned.

Scruggs wrote that they were again in dry dock for a checkup and possible repairs. He said they had a little accident out at sea, which he couldn't tell them about, of course. It might mean *Arizona* would have to go to Bremerton within the next couple of weeks. He earnestly hoped so.

In a letter dated October 23, Proke answered my complaint that he had not told us about the music contest which "Kid" Reed had written about earlier:

> *To start off with, I'm sure that if you would just read your back mail from me, you will find that I told you all about us winning the dance band contest. We beat the* West Virginia, California, *and the band from the Sub Base. The band got a cup and we play in the Semifinals about December.*
>
> *I hope you get a job in Civil Service, but try to get placed anywhere but in Hawaii. This place is fine for the first month, but after that, you'll wish you were back in the States. In the first place, a room here would cost you about two hundred dollars a month. Everything you do will cost you a week's pay.*
>
> *I still say that your best bet would be in Los Angeles.*
>
> *What is wrong with Okla[homa]? I'd give a lot to be there right now.*
>
> *I'd like to meet the new bandmaster of dear ol' O.H.S....*
>
> *In case you're interested, I won a dollar on Okmulgee's first football game. Hughes (trombone) and I bet on our home teams to win their first football game. His lost and Ok[mulgee] beat Tal[equah], I think, according to Mate's letter.*
>
> *I can't think of anything else that I can write about, so again, here's luck in your Civil Service exam. Love, Proke.*
>
> *P.S. How about getting my suit cleaned and pressed and lay it out for me, because when I get leave, it will be on a minute's notice.*

You can almost feel the delight and glee with which Clyde wrote that last sentence. Evidently the collision of the two ships and the damage inflicted on *Arizona* had raised their hopes again that they would be coming home. Surely *Arizona*, with that big hole in her side, would now have to go to Bremerton for repairs.

Again, it was not to be. The ship went into dry dock right there in Pearl Harbor, and the boys received yet another disappointment.

On October 24, Secretary of the Navy Frank Knox said he believed a collision between Japan and the United States was inevitable, and added, "The situation out in the Far East is extremely strained. We are satisfied in our own minds that the Japanese have no intention of giving up their plans for expansion."[23]

Arizona returned to Pearl Harbor on October 26.[24] Again, the boys missed the Battle of Music contest held on October 25. The bands from the *Pennsylvania, Tennessee, Maryland,* and *Honolulu* were scheduled to compete. *Pennsylvania* and *Tennessee* won first and second places.[25]

The program was much the same as the former contests, except now the singing of "God Bless America" had been added.[26]

October 27 was Navy Day, and the *Bremerton Sun* wrote a stirring tribute of thanks to our Navy, assuring everyone that "Now, when the call for 'battle stations' may ring through any ship of the fleet at any minute of the day or night," the Navy was ready.[27]

Radford wrote that the *Arizona* had gone into dry dock again on October 27 for the second time in a month. The workers at the Navy Yard were putting a big patch of steel over the hole in *Arizona*'s hull. The Yard workers were rushing their patch job, because they had to get *Arizona* out of dry dock by Saturday, November 1.

Arizona's crewmen were delighted. They would take that temporary patch and high-tail it to Bremerton for their long-awaited overhaul.

Radford thanked his family for giving him a subscription to the *Minden Courier,* a hometown weekly newspaper. He never failed to read the paper clear through, even reading all the store advertisements. He added that Williams, their skinny trumpet man from Oklahoma, also liked to read it.

Radford remarked that Williams especially got a kick out of the Navy propaganda printed in the paper, as they wrote of the fine recreation, travel, good chow, plenty of leave, etc. a boy would get if only he would join the Navy. In their situation, that never failed to give them a big laugh.

The bandsmen especially enjoyed the "travel" promotion, since they never did "travel" more than one hundred miles from Pearl

Harbor at any time. Radford said some of the guys had been in the
Navy for years and had never been any place except Long Beach,
San Francisco, Bremerton, and, of course, Pearl Harbor. He did not
believe you would ever hear any sailor brag about being trapped in
Pearl Harbor.

On the morning of October 29, *Arizona's* band drilled with over
1,000 Marines. It was one of Hawaii's hot days and the Marine drill
field, where the exercise was held, was wet and muddy from rain the
night before. When the musicians returned to the ship, their white
uniforms were a mess. Scruggs wrote that the drill was to practice
turns and marches which the kids in the band did not yet know, and
he added that it was "some fun."

The boys in *Arizona's* band had practiced marching at the school,
of course, but the musicians who had been at the school for only a
few months before they shipped out still needed some drilling.

When the N.Y.K. liner *Tatuta Maru* arrived in San Francisco from
Japan on October 31, she carried 350 American citizens, most of them
of Japanese blood. FBI and Naval Intelligence agents met the ship
and questioned the passengers extensively. One passenger from Tokyo
told them that the Japanese people believed they would eventually
engage in war with the United States.[28]

Now the musicians were becoming more and more bored with
their seven-day workweek. Scruggs told his family that if he didn't
seem to write much, it was only because the stuff which happened at
Pearl Harbor was just routine. He was afraid he would bore them if
he told them the same things over and over.

Radford noted that the sailors had never received that ten-buck
raise they were supposed to have.

It is everyone's God-given right to complain about his circumstances. Especially is that true for men in the armed services. But
there was something more now. From here until the end, we could
sense a growing uneasiness in the boys' letters.

As the world moved ever closer to man's ultimate stupidity, our
military men in Hawaii went about their daily duties.

And following orders from their superiors, as they had always
done, the bands played on.

CHAPTER 17

"We Won't Be Home for Christmas"

By November, *Arizona's* band had become very well known in Hawaii, and its musicians were steadily improving. Every member of Fred Kinney's band was outstanding, or they would not have been in his band.

White was recognized as an excellent snare drummer.[1] Moorhouse was said to play the best swing trumpet anyone had ever heard. And Bandy, although he had been a very quiet boy at the School of Music, had now developed into a great second trumpet player to Moorhouse in jazz music.[2]

Later, Ensign Thurmond was to say that Curt Haas played the "sweetest flute you will ever hear."[3]

The bands which had been trained at the School of Music each bore a number which had been assigned to the band when it was first formed at the school. From those numbers, one could ascertain how many bands the School of Music had graduated in its six years of existence.

The programs for the Battle of Music 1941 listed the leaders of the bands as "Bandmaster." That was merely an honorary title, since most of the leaders had not yet been promoted to the rank of "Bandmaster," but were, in fact, Musicians First Class.

For our purpose, however, the title of "Bandmaster" will be sufficient for the leaders of the bands.

The eighteen Navy ships or shore commands in Pearl Harbor late in 1941 to which a Navy band had been assigned, the bands' numbers, and the names of their Bandmasters were:

1) *Argonne*, (AG-31), Band No. 14, John Carey.
2) *Arizona*, Battleship (BB-39), Band No. 22, Frederick William Kinney.
3) *California*, Battleship (BB-44), Band No. 16, L. B. "Red" Luckenbach.
4) *Detroit*, Light Cruiser (CL-8), Band No. 5, J. A. Hardin.
5) *Dobbin*, Destroyer Tender (AD-3), Band No. 13, Bernard W. Park.
6) *Honolulu*, Light Cruiser (CL-48), Band No. 15, John Alexander Simpson.
7) *Indianapolis*, Heavy Cruiser, Band No. 18, M. V. Spencer.
8) *Lexington*, Aircraft Carrier (CV-2), A. G. Kazaa.
9) Marine Barracks Band, Eric Isaacson.
10) *Maryland*, Battleship (BB-46), A. Vinciguerra.
11) *Nevada*, Battleship (BB-36), Oden McMillan.
12) *Northampton*, Heavy Cruiser, J. R. Glover.
13) *Oglala*, Giant Minelayer (CM-4), Band No. 10, Robert Stancil Parks.
14) *Oklahoma*, Battleship (BB-37), J. B. Booe.
15) *Pennsylvania*, Battleship (BB-38), Band No. 8, Axel Anton Jensen.
16) Submarine Station, CINCPAC HQ., Band No. 12, L. R. Larson.
17) *Tennessee*, Battleship (BB-43), Band No. 21, James Lamar Smith.
18) *West Virginia*, Battleship (BB-48), Band No. 17, Thomas G. Carlin.

Although the battleship *Utah* (AG-16) was at Pearl Harbor in 1941, she was used as a target ship only. No longer an active battleship, there was no band assigned to her.

Arizona's deck logs for November and December 1941 went down with the ship.[4] But from the letters written by the members of *Arizona*'s band, we know how they spent their last five weeks.

The threat from the Navy Yard workers in dry dock that *Arizona*'s crew must get their "damned old ship out of here by Saturday," as reported by Radford on October 28, did not come to pass. *Arizona* was still in dry dock on November 4, when Radford commented that the "Kanacky" working on the ship made so much noise with their riveters, air hammers, etc. that the sailors on board could barely hear anything.

Now the base at Pearl Harbor was being built up so fast they would soon be able to put a battleship through her yard period in Pearl Harbor without the necessity of going back to Bremerton. To which Radford added, "Oh unhappy day!" The yard workers had already finished building one big dry dock and were working on two more.

According to Radford, the sailors in Pearl Harbor spoke of Bremerton as if it were heaven.

Late in October, Scruggs was summoned to the Admiral's stateroom and ordered to bring his accordion. One of the sailors owned a recorder and was also ordered to bring it to the Admiral's stateroom. Owning a recorder was certainly not so common then as it is now.

The Admiral had decided to make a recording of "Happy Birthday To You" and a "vocal letter" to send to his wife for her birthday on November 3. Scruggs played the introduction on the accordion, then accompanied Admiral Kidd as he sang the birthday song and read his letter to his wife. Before the sailors left, they listened to the recording, and Scruggs thought it all came out pretty good.

The Admiral's stateroom was very impressive. Scruggs said there was a fireplace, nice oak furniture, silver candlesticks, floor lamps, and rugs, "just like home."

Scruggs was most interested in the part of the Admiral's letter to his wife which said they should be leaving Pearl Harbor in a couple of weeks. Since the Admiral didn't say where they would be going, Scruggs guessed it might be Long Beach.

On November 5, the Naval Governor of Guam ordered the families of Naval personnel and American citizens who were living in Guam to return to the United States.[5]

And also on November 5, five Japanese men were held under bond by Federal authorities, charged with the misuse of identification cards in an attempt to enter the Pearl Harbor Navy Station.

The Federal agents declined to comment on the men's probable purpose in attempting entry to the Station.[6]

Tension was building among the boys stationed at Pearl Harbor. The musicians were more depressed than ever about their leave. They had been so sure that *Arizona*'s collision with *Oklahoma* would require her to go back to Bremerton for repairs. When Radford sent his mother the money for his horn payments, he told her it was late because he had planned to bring the money to her when he got leave. Now he guessed they would not get back for quite awhile.

And Scruggs wrote that, the way things looked, he probably would not get any leave when he got home. The *California* had just come back from Long Beach, and her sailors had reported that all they had been given was overnight liberty. Even then, they had to call the ship every night at ten o'clock to see if they could stay out for the rest of the night.

On November 4, Radford wrote that it was after lights out, but he had found a place down on the third deck where there was enough light to write his letter. The clipper was leaving on Wednesday, and he wanted to get his letter on it. They had just been paid, and he was sending another payment on his horn.

The boys heard that the *West Virginia* had pulled out on Tuesday, November 4, headed for Bremerton. They envied them, but they had heard the *West Virginia* had not been back to the mainland for over a year and a half. Don Harbin, Radford's friend from the School of Music, was on the *West Virginia*. The two friends met every week at the Recreation Center to have a glass of beer and visit.

Although in Hawaii sailors were given liberty nearly every afternoon, single men still had to be back on the ship by 1:00 A.M.

Radford repeated that few of the sailors went ashore in Pearl Harbor, but that most of them stayed aboard and saved their money. Then, when they got back to the States, they really tore loose. That, he said, was why sailors had such a reputation for being drunkards. The only time civilians ever saw sailors was when they had returned from a long monotonous cruise and were trying to make up for lost time.

Again Radford finished his letter by telling his mother he was going up to crawl into his lovely innerspring hammock.

In a letter dated November 4, my brother wrote:

> *I've waited until today to write because today was payday. I have my new horn all paid for and I can send twenty-five dollars home besides.*
>
> *Everything on board the ol'* Arizona *is still fine and I'm getting along OK.*
>
> *I've read in the papers out here that you have been having some floods in Oklahoma. Are there any of them near home? Don't let Dink get his feet wet.*
>
> *I talked to a fellow from the* Astoria *and he said that Gordon was stationed in San Diego. How much leave did he get? It has been quite some time since I last saw him. I doubt if I'll even recognize him.*
>
> *How is Molly coming along with her Civil Service deal? I hope she makes it but don't let her come out here to Hawaii, because everything out here is higher than a cat's back. If she is coming to the California coast, her best bet is in Los Angeles. That is our home port and we hit there maybe twice a year.*
>
> *I gotta go but I'll write later. Your loving son, Proke*

Apparently it was impossible for the band to rehearse while in dry dock, because of the noise the dock workers were making. On Wednesday, November 5, the musicians again went over to the Marine parade ground to practice marching.

That night they played for a dance held ashore, and on Friday night the band played for the boxing match.

The Fifth Elimination contest of the Battle of Music was held on November 8. Listed as contestants on the program were the bands of the Submarine Station, the *Lexington*, the *Oklahoma*, and the *Northampton*.[7]

None of the musicians on the *Arizona* mentioned attending that contest.

Clyde wrote me on November 12:

> *Here goes another letter with nothing to write about.*
>
> *It is still very warm out here, in fact most of the day the sun nearly burns you up.*
>
> *We had a steak fry Armistice Day for those on the ship that weren't on watch. We went swimming, saw a football game, had plenty to eat, and all hands (everybody) had a good time. We left at ten in the morning and came back at four. We have to be back on the ship every night at one o'clock midnight.*
>
> *How is the band doing this year? Who is playing first chair trumpet? Why don't you let me in on all the dope about the band?*
>
> *I'd love to see that new leader. I'll put our twenty-piece band against his on any type of number. We have a bunch of swell guys in our band and some of them are extra good. No kidding, the Navy is just full of good bands, concert and swing.*
>
> *It looks as though I won't be able to hear O.H.S. Band this year (I hope not).*
>
> *We got a batch of new numbers yesterday for the dance band. We don't need to buy any for the concert band because there was a big library aboard ship when we came on.*
>
> *I went over to the* Tennessee *quite awhile ago and saw Henry B. He is looking fine and I sure was glad to see him. We spent a long time talking about Okmulgee. I'm thinking about going over and visiting him again.*
>
> *I can't think of anything else to write about except keep your nose clean. Lots of Love from your bigger Brother, Proke*

Describing the Armistice Day party, Radford wrote that *Arizona*'s Gunnery Department threw a steak fry and beer drink over at the landing. *Arizona*'s football team played some Army team that afternoon, and *Arizona* lost 3-0.

Asa E. Streight, an Okmulgee boy stationed on the *Nevada*, saw Clyde at that Armistice Day picnic. Asa was walking around the Recreation Center and spotted Clyde swimming in the pool. The two boys had not seen each other for several years, but Asa said they knew each other immediately. They visited for quite awhile and made plans to get together with Henry Brown later. Asa thought Clyde seemed happy and looked good. That was the last time he ever saw him.[8]

Hurley, who was an expert swimmer and diver, entered the free-for-all swimming and diving contest at that Armistice Day party. In competition with contestants from seven battleships, Hurley won second place.[9]

That night, back on the ship, three boys in the band decided Scruggs needed a haircut. While two of them held him down, the other one got a big pair of shears and performed the service for him. Thanks to their efforts, Scruggs had to go to the ship's barbershop and have all his hair cut off very close to his head. He reported, "Now I look like a first-class moron!"

Scruggs had a receding hairline, and the guys promised they would massage his head every night to stimulate hair growth.

Arizona finally got out of dry dock on November 12 and went to sea again the next day. However, they did not go to Long Beach, as Scruggs had hoped, but just ran around in circles again on maneuvers, and then returned to Pearl Harbor. And another dream bit the dust!

While at sea, the boys heard that when the ship returned to Pearl Harbor, the Navy was planning to install cafeteria-style eating, instead of having their food brought to the table. Scruggs though they would like that better, since that was the way their food had been served at the School of Music.

Radford wrote his mother that they had returned to Pearl Harbor on Sunday, November 16, after having been out to sea for just four days. They fired the antiaircraft guns one day, the broadsides the next, and fired the main batteries (twenty) one night. Radford said it was quite a sight to see twelve projectiles go through the air all together. A person could follow them from the time they left the gun until they hit.

They were due to go out again on Tuesday to observe the *Pennsylvania* fire long-range. Later, in the same letter, Radford said they did not go out as they had heard they would. The constant rumors circulating about always kept them on edge.

They were upset to hear that *California*'s crew did not get even one day of leave while she was in Long Beach.

Radford now suggested that his parents drive out to Long Beach when the ship returned to the mainland. He had saved sixty dollars and he thought that would be enough to buy their gasoline for the trip. He said they had never been to California and that would be a good chance. He added that, of course, they were not sure they would even get back for awhile, but he wanted them to start thinking about it.

Radford's mother had asked if he knew a boy on the *Arizona* named Greenfield, who was from near their hometown. Radford did know him, and they often saw each other in the head when they were washing clothes. They both enjoyed talking about mutual friends back in Nebraska.

Greenfield was killed in action on December 7.

Radford asked his mother where they would be celebrating Thanksgiving that year. It was the second family Thanksgiving he had missed.

The bandsmen were razzing Radford unmercifully about the Nebraska football game. They often asked him about "Nebraska's Rose Bowl team," but Radford always told them to "wait 'till next year." He had already lost two bucks betting on that football team.

Clyde wrote on November 20:

> *I mailed a Money Order for twenty-five dollars on November 5th but I don't guess you got it when you wrote your last letter. It sure has been a long time since the letter before this one.*
>
> *I hope Molly gets a job with the Civil Service because I think that is her best bet. Don't feel so bad about being alone, because we will both be coming home at times if she gets a job away from home. You know yourself that there isn't much left in Okmulgee.*
>
> *We celebrated Armistice Day with an* Arizona *steak fry. We spent all day on the beach and had swimming, football game,*

and nearly everything. Everyone there had a good time.

After being in the Navy for a year away from home and a lot of time under war conditions, I can see how much Pate and the rest of the American Legion can celebrate the day their war ended. It will be a great day when these war scares are over.

I find that the guys in the Navy don't think that we will ever engage in a fighting war. If we do, though, you can feel safe because there isn't a Navy afloat that can get by ours. I know because I've watched them fire and they don't miss.

Tell everyone in Okmulgee "hello" for me and give Louise C[arter] my regards. Your Loving Son, Proke.

P.S. I enjoy every clipping that you send me and they all are appreciated.

It is obvious that the sailors at Pearl Harbor knew more about the approaching war than they were able to tell us.

After all the reading I have done about the December 7 attack, I am still puzzled at the complete confidence of the sailors stationed at Pearl Harbor then. Most of the men wrote home about how safe they felt on those big ships and how good our men were at shooting their guns.

On November 22, the first semifinal contest of the Battle of Music was held. There were now eight extremely proficient bands which had won first or second place in previous Battles. Now two semifinal play-offs would eliminate two bands each time, leaving four bands to compete in the final contest for the two top bands of the Pacific Fleet.

Competing in the first semifinal contest were the bands of the *Arizona*, the *California*, the Marine Barracks band, and a fourth unknown band. Much interest had been generated by the musical contests, and the arena was packed that night with servicemen.

With the judging done by audience applause, the result of the contest was foreordained. Although the sailors clapped and shouted for their favorites, their votes were split between the three Navy bands.

Every Marine in the audience, however, voted for the Marine Barracks Band. Consequently, the Marine Barracks Band won first place and *Arizona* won second place. They were both awarded gold cups and were scheduled to play in the finals later in December.

Former members of the Pearl Harbor bands still remember playing in those contests. To them, it was serious business.

James Clelland was a member of the Marine Barracks band who played that night. He still laughs as he tells how the men in charge at the Barracks ordered all the Marines out and marched them over to Bloch Arena to attend the Battle of Music. If a Marine did not choose to attend the contest that night, no matter. He went anyway.[10]

The judges must have had great difficulty choosing a winner from among the four outstanding bands which were playing that night.[11]

Even after all these years, many Pearl Harbor survivors who were there that night still maintain that *Arizona* was the hands-down winner.

Frank Worden, a musician in the Submarine Base band, said the *Oglala* band was very good and the *Arizona* band was well above average.[12]

Loren Bailey, who was stationed on the *Oglala*, was not a musician, but loved music and seldom missed the Battles. Loren said that, in his opinion, the *Arizona* and the *Oglala* bands were the best bands in the Fleet. He remembers that their big-band musical arrangements were outstanding.[13]

Hughes wrote that the *Arizona* band had won second place in the semifinals.[14] Scruggs wrote that their band played in the semifinals of the dance band contest on Saturday night, November 22, and that *Arizona*'s band won another gold cup, but for second place. He added that their band was still eligible for the final contest.

Scruggs explained, "They don't judge the bands by how they play, but by the number of guys there are from the ship to make noise for them. The Marines won last night because there were more Marines than sailors there."

There was no bitterness among the members of *Arizona*'s band over not winning first place in the contest. It was simply a fact of life in the contest business.

Tai Sing Loo was the official photographer for the Navy Yard at Pearl Harbor.[15] He went to Bloch Arena that night, November 22, and took the last photograph ever made of the *Arizona* band.

Since the photograph was of the smaller *Arizona* dance orchestra, five of the band members—Brabbzson, Burdette, Hurley, McCary, and Radford—do not appear in the picture.

Although he took a photograph of each band separately, the *California* band was seated so close to the *Arizona* band that part of *California*'s sign appears in the photograph of *Arizona*'s band.

Don Bright, a Marine at Pearl Harbor at that time, appears in the background of the photograph of *Arizona*'s band. Two Marines were sitting in the bleachers, and Bright is the Marine on the right.[16]

Arizona's band was playing even more often now.

They played Friday night, November 21, for the boxing matches at the Recreation Center and played Saturday night in the Battle of Music.

The week before, the daughter of *Arizona*'s Commander was married, and the band played for the wedding reception at the Commander's home. Scruggs was able to play the piano once again and thoroughly enjoyed it. I can imagine the delight of the members of the band as they sat for awhile in a real home.

Time magazine reported on November 24 that U.S. officials were "nine-to-ten" that Japan and the United States would go to war.[17]

On Monday night, November 24, the band played for another ship's dance at the Moana Hotel and George E. Fones, a member of *Arizona*'s crew, attended. He had written his mother in November that Honolulu was still dull, with nothing much to do. He would be twenty-one years old on November 25 and planned to go to the ship's dance to celebrate his birthday.

It was to be George Everett Fones' last birthday.[18]

After the ship's dance, the *Arizona* musicians were given special liberty and were taken to the "Y." There each boy was given a room all to himself, complete with a real bed.

They arose the next morning at nine-thirty, had breakfast, and went to Waikiki Beach to swim. They stayed at the beach all day, eating and swimming in front of the Royal Hawaiian Hotel. As Radford had done earlier, Scruggs complained about the coral and shells on the bottom of the ocean at Waikiki Beach.

Tuesday night, the bandsmen went to a movie in Honolulu, then returned to the ship.

They all enjoyed that small break from their routine. As Scruggs wrote, "It sure seemed good to get away from this tub, even for a day."

On the same day the musicians had such a nice day of relaxation, the Japanese carrier task force left its home waters, on its way to launch its attack on Pearl Harbor.[19]

A cartoon in the *Bremerton Sun* on November 26 showed a Japanese military officer offering his hand to the "Honorable Uncle Sam." One of the officer's hands was a clenched fist, covered with an armored glove. The other hand was open and covered with a velvet glove. The cartoon asked, "Which Hand?"[20]

The Territory of Hawaii observed Thanksgiving Day on November 27.[21] *Arizona* was at sea for the holiday, having left Pearl Harbor on Wednesday.

It was the last Thanksgiving Day *Arizona* and most of her crew ever celebrated.

Our musicians were becoming more and more uneasy. Before *Arizona* left Pearl Harbor on November 26, they hurried to write their families before mail call closed.

It is obvious they knew war was near.

Scruggs wrote that he wished they would soon get the awful war over.

Bandy wrote that rumors were flying that relations with Japan were getting tense and that war was a possibility. He told his girl back home that everything was uncertain and that they might be in war by the time she received his letter.[22]

My brother wrote for the last time on November 26. The envelope was postmarked USS *ARIZONA* Nov. 25, and was sent via Clipper.

Dear Molly, This won't be very long, because the mail closes in a few minutes.

About that insignia ring you mentioned, I don't want one of those rings very much, and if I decide to get one, I can get it from one of the guys I know on the ship here. He bought it and then hocked it before he had worn it very much. I could get one for half of what it would cost you.

I don't have any idea what I want for Christmas. Maybe subscription to some magazine or something like that.

If you have any idea what you, Mate, or Pate want, let me know. I'm really up a stump.

You ought to know now how you came out in your Civil Service exam.

If you go to D.C., keep your eyes and ears open. You'd be surprised at the kind of things that go on there. Whatever you do, don't let anybody pick you up.

Doesn't look like I'll be home for Christmas, much as I'd like to. We will most likely get back the first half of next year.

We played for a dance Monday night and got to stay over until midnight Tuesday. We stayed at the "Y" and spent all Tuesday at Waikiki Beach. That certainly is a fine place.

That's all the dope for now, so write soon and I'll have something else thought up, maybe. Love, Proke

Obviously uneasy, Clyde wrote in his last letter to Joan Watson that he had never seen so many Jap people.[23]

Jack Scruggs also hurried to finish his last letter. To the letter describing their trip to Waikiki, he added: "Well, we are going out today and the mail closes in a little while, so I'd better get this off. Well, hope to see you all soon but can't tell a thing. Hope we get there for the holidays, but right now I doubt it. Don't expect us till you see us."

Neal Radford wrote his last letter on November 25, wishing his mother a very happy birthday.

Bill Moorhouse wrote his last letter home on November 30, while the *Arizona* was at sea.[24]

Ernest Whitson, Jr. wrote home last on December 4. He told his parents to "keep your fingers crossed. I think I'll be home for Christmas!"[25]

Bobby Shaw's last letter home was postmarked five o'clock P.M. December 6. He was very homesick and was thrilled he was going to get home for Christmas.[26]

All the boys had been collecting photographs of their friends, but apparently only Wendell Hurley had a premonition. He hurriedly completed his album and mailed it to his home on November 29.[27] His father would later share the photos in Wendell's album with the other families of the musicians. For most of us, the only photos of our boys taken in Hawaii came from that album.

Hurley had begun his photograph album in Washington, D.C., in March 1941. As a budding photographer, he had photos of the Washington area, and of his trips to Lobien's home. In the back of his album was a section for autographs. He had begun the autograph section on May 20, as the musicians were graduating from the School of Music. Eighteen of the musicians at the school had signed his book, with the usual comments and insults.[28]

At various times in August, September, October, and November, Hurley took his album around the ship to have other friends autograph it. All the names in Hurley's autograph book which were signed after the May 20 date appear on the "Killed in Action" list for December 7.[29]

Most of the remarks in Hurley's album tear at your heart now, such as: "5/20/41—Dick Duryea, USS *Tennessee*—'See ya in Honolulu—New Years Eve.'"[30]

The comments written by the *Arizona* bandsmen in Hurley's album give us additional clues to their friendships:

May 20:
White—"To a swell shipmate who helps to drive away loneliness."
Floege—"To a swell guy and a constant menace to band 22."
Burdette—"Somewhat of a chowhound, but strictly 4.0."

September 19:

Hughes—"Yours for more good pictures."

September 25:

Moorhouse—"Best of everything to a fine guy who really likes his Grape Nuts."

Shaw—"To a 4.0 guy and shipmate with best wishes for a successful cruise."

Scruggs—"To a fine guy with the best of intentions that no one seemed to understand (Guess who?) Hope you have a 4.0 cruise."

Lynch—"To a shipmate of good character who tries hard, but doesn't, it seems to some, accomplish much. Keep plugging shipmate. You have the answer."

September 29:

Haas—"Good cruise fellow. Hope you can crack the profession you really like—photography. Keep at it."

October 2:

McCary—"Ich Vergisten Sil Nict."

Nadel—"Good luck and don't forget a Xmas card."

Williams—"Best Luck to the Casinova of Band 22."

Radford—"Good Luck and don't take any wooden nickels."

Diabbsoll—"Good luck, Lady Killer. Save a few ladies for me."

Whitson—"Hoping all your kids are Olympic champs."

November 28:

Sanderson—"To a real friend and a good egg I wish the best of luck."[31]

Newspapers in the United States reported on December 1 that Japan had reached the "put up or shut up" stage in the boiling Pacific crisis. They wrote that, unfortunately, Japan had worked herself into a situation from which there would be no graceful way to exit, and that the Japanese were growing weaker each day.[32]

They added that both the United States and Japan had grown pessimistic about the negotiations for peace in Washington.[33]

On December 4, three days away from their treachery, Japan stated there had been no progress by the United States and Japan in their peace talks.[34]

Since the Japanese Task Force was already on its way to blow up our ships at Pearl Harbor, that would seem to be an understatement on Japan's part.

During the first week of December, *Arizona*'s Officer of the Deck saw what he assumed to be the wake of the periscope of a submarine.[35]

American submarines were not operating in the waters anywhere near that spot, and news of the mystery raced throughout the ship.

Nevada was also out on maneuvers at that time. Her officers, too, thought they saw signs of submarines operating in the water, and *Nevada* began performing antisubmarine drills for the first time.[36]

When *Nevada* returned to Pearl Harbor on Friday afternoon, December 5, *Arizona* was already in her berth, with the repair ship *Vestal* tied up beside her. The next day, workers took off all *Nevada*'s old gunpowder and replaced it with new.[37]

West Virginia also returned to Pearl Harbor on Friday, December 5, and moored alongside *Tennessee*, in front of *Arizona* and behind *Oklahoma*.[38] Apparently my friend, J. L. "Kid" Reed of the *West Virginia* band, had spent his time at sea addressing Christmas cards. Long after the December 7 attack, I received a Christmas card from him, postmarked USS *West Virginia*, December 5, 1941.[39]

And so, one by one, our ships returned to Pearl Harbor on Friday or Saturday and took their places.

And for all of them, as well as all of us, time had run out.

CHAPTER 18

December 6, 1941

This book is the result of the search of many years by the families of the *Arizona* bandsmen, as we tried to find an answer to the question of what our boys did on December 6, their last full day of life.

Our wars were not conducted on television in 1941. There was a strict code of secrecy, promoted by President Roosevelt, and we were told very little by the Navy. Only gradually did we piece together the story of how our band boys spent their last twenty-four hours of life.

We did that by talking to men who had been at Pearl Harbor during the attack and who might tell us anything, and then passing that word on to the other families.

Some of the information given us was correct—some was not.

After following their usual morning routine, the bandsmen would have gone topside at seven forty-five, gathered near the quarterdeck, marched in formation back to the fantail, and lined up for colors.

With the big final contest of the Battle of Music set for December 20, Kinney would have wanted to hold his usual morning rehearsal from nine-thirty until eleven o'clock. Perhaps some of the rehearsal time would have been cancelled, due to the Saturday morning inspection.[1]

Also interfering with their rehearsal was the noise the workers from the *Vestal* were making that morning.

Vestal had been out on maneuvers all week and had participated with the fleet in exercises with dive bombers.[2] When the fleet returned to the harbor on Friday, she had tied up beside *Arizona*. *Vestal* was to make some repairs to *Arizona*, in preparation for her long-anticipated trip to the dry docks of Bremerton.[3]

One of the repairs *Vestal* was to make to *Arizona* was the rebricking of her boilers, and workers from *Vestal* spent Saturday removing the bricks from *Arizona*'s boilers.[4]

Also, men from the *Vestal* were inspecting the bottom of *Arizona* and other workers were preparing to repair *Arizona*'s generators.[5]

The "Lower Optical Ordinance Shop" on the *Vestal* was scheduled to send three of its gang over to *Arizona* at eight o'clock to change the liners on the main batteries. If the liners of the big guns were not changed often, they might crack when they were being fired.[6]

After the bandsmen ate their noon meal, they would have played their usual twelve-thirty concert for the crew. We know that sometime after their afternoon rehearsal, they were allowed to go ashore on liberty.

The musicians had three important things on their minds that day.

Of utmost importance was the rumor racing around the ship that the *Arizona* would leave for home in a week. According to Paul Stillwell in his book *Battleship Arizona*, when *Arizona* returned from sea on December 5, Admiral Kidd went over to the *Maryland* to confer with Rear Admiral Walter Stratton Anderson. Upon returning to *Arizona*, Admiral Kidd told Captain Van Valkenburgh that *Arizona* was scheduled to leave Saturday, December 13, for San Pedro.[7]

There are few places with more ears in the walls than that of a battleship, and it did not take long for that secret to travel far and fast. The crewmen had been fooled so many times that they hesitated to believe. But any scuttlebutt regarding going home was always accepted with no reservations!

Consequently, both Shaw and Whitson hurried to mail letters to their folks to tell them that they might be home for Christmas.[8]

The second important thing on the musicians' minds was mailing Christmas presents to their families. Although they hoped the ship might really be going home at last, they took no chances. They had just been paid, and they all rushed out on Friday and Saturday to purchase and send their Christmas gifts home.

Long after we knew that our boys were no longer living, those Christmas gifts from them began arriving at our homes.

White sent gifts to all the members of his family, marking on the package that it was not to be opened until Christmas Day.[9]

There was no danger of that.

Bandy sent gifts to his mother and to Ruth Cadwell, his girl back home. They arrived more than two months later.[10]

The other families also received their gifts much later. My brother sent our parents a set of drinking glasses, on which were decals of hula dancers. He left orders at the store for his gift to be sent to Okmulgee. The arrival of that package in February, with the "Japanese Bazaar" printed in bold letters all over the wrapping paper, was very heartbreaking for my parents.

Clyde sent his girl Joan a set of "Evening in Paris" perfume. She too received it long after his death.[11]

I had been begging my brother for a photograph of him in uniform. I am positive he had his photo made on December 5 or 6, but although I wrote many letters, I was never able to find it in Hawaii.

During the week ending December 6, the American Institute of Public Opinion conducted a nationwide survey, asking the question, "Do you think the U.S. will go to war against Japan some time in the near future?" Of those who were willing to express an opinion, approximately two-thirds said they thought war would break out soon.[12]

Certainly the musicians of the *Arizona* were apprehensive. They, along with most of the Pearl Harbor sailors, were sick to their very souls.

They were sick of Navy regulations.

They were sick of that romantic land of sunshine and beautiful flowers, which promised so much and delivered so little.

They were sick of sailors. Everywhere they went, they walked in a sea of sailors.

As a matter of fact, they were sick of men in general. They wanted to talk to a woman—just any female!

They were homesick. They were young and they had been away from home too long. The fact that they had volunteered for that duty did little to make them more content.

The third important thing on the boys' minds was the last semifinal contest of the Battle of Music 1941 being held at Bloch Arena that night. *Arizona*'s band did not have an engagement, for a change, so the boys were free to go listen to the four bands which were competing. They were intensely interested in the contest, since they and the Marine Barracks Band would compete with the first and second place winners in the final contest to be held in the Arena on December 20.

The families back home knew how much our *Arizona* band wanted to win that Battle of Music, and how very hard they had been working to take first place.[13]

Bandy had written his family that the band which won the "Battle of Music" would be awarded a one-year tour of the United States.[14] None of the other families heard that, but if it were true, all the competing bands would have sold their very souls to get back to the States for a week, much less a year!

The four bands scheduled to compete on the night of December 6 had been first or second place winners in earlier contests and had been awarded gold cups. They were the bands from the *Pennsylvania*, the *Tennessee*, the *Argonne*, and the *Detroit*.[15]

Although the *Detroit* band was listed on the program, it did not play that night. *Detroit*'s band had not been eliminated, but its bandmaster had pulled his band out to protest the nonprofessional way in which the Battles were being judged.[16]

Detroit's band was replaced by the band from the Submarine Base.[17]

All four of the competing bands had been trained at the United States Navy School of Music in Washington. The *Pennsylvania* Band Number 8, the *Argonne* Band Number 14, and the Submarine Base Band Number 12 were older bands, so the *Arizona* musicians did not know the musicians from those bands very well, if at all.

But *Arizona*'s Band Number 22 and *Tennessee*'s Band Number 21 had both graduated from the school in May and their musicians had been good friends at the school.

So, not only was the *Arizona* band eager to hear their competitors in the upcoming contest, they were eager to see their friends in the *Tennessee* band again.

Visiting friends on other ships was not an easy task for enlisted men. Our communication systems were very limited. There was no way a sailor from one ship could telephone over to a sailor on another ship, whether from ship to ship or from shore to ship. A personal visit involved taking a liberty launch from one's own ship over to the landing, then waiting for a liberty launch from his friend's ship to come in. After the sailor got to his friend's ship, he would have to search all over the ship for him. If his friend were on liberty, he was just out of luck.

Consequently, *Arizona's* musicians hurried through their shopping and went over to the Arena on the night of December 6, ready to enjoy the music and to check out the competition.

Kinney was also at the Arena that night. The bandmasters of the competing bands were all good friends, and Kinney visited with Axel Jensen of the *Pennsylvania* band, James Smith of the *Tennessee* band, John Carey of the *Argonne* band, and J. R. Larsen of the Submarine Base band.

By now there was keen interest in the outcome of the Battle of Music, and a huge crowd of military men was crowded into the Arena that night. Not only was it fun to hear the big-band sounds, but the reputation of a man's ship was at stake.

The contest was carried by radio to the ships in the harbor for the entertainment of the men who had the duty and could not attend,[18] and the men outside the Arena could also hear the music. Eugene Crawford of the U.S. Marine Corps was on guard duty at the gate of the Navy Yard that night. He could not see the bands, but he could hear them clearly.[19]

Because the men stationed on ships at Pearl Harbor had to be back on their ship by 1:00 A.M., Honolulu maintained strict "Blue Laws." No liquor was served after midnight, and the contest and the dance ended before midnight.[20]

Pennsylvania won first place and *Tennessee* won second place. Both bands would meet the Marine Barracks band and the *Arizona* band in the finals two weeks later.

When the contest was over, the *Arizona* musicians went down on the dance floor to visit with their friends while the bandsmen packed up their instruments.

It has been of special comfort to their families that our *Arizona* musicians were with so many friends at the Arena on that, their last night on earth, and that those friends all went to so much trouble to visit the families as soon as they returned to the States.

Luther Henry Brown, my brother's friend from Okmulgee and a member of the *Tennessee* band, told our parents later that, although the *Arizona* band did not play that night, its musicians had come over to listen to the competing bands. Clyde and Henry talked at length about the hometown folks.[21] They made plans to meet the next day and make another effort to find their Okmulgee friend, A. E. Streight, stationed on the *Nevada*.[22]

"Okmulgee" had always been a fascinating sound to the musicians at the School of Music, and the musicians from the *Arizona* band called my brother "Okmulgee." As they called out his nickname that evening, Leonard Orville Yandle, the bugler from the *Pennsylvania*, heard them and rushed over to meet Clyde. Yandle was from Henryetta, a short distance from Okmulgee, and the two boys had a wonderful time, visiting for nearly thirty minutes about mutual friends and recalling points of interest in their two hometowns.[23]

As a result of the semifinal contest which had just finished, the bands from the *Arizona* and the *Pennsylvania* would compete against each other on December 20. Yandle told Pate that Clyde laughingly remarked to him how strange it was that they, who had been such rivals in sports back in Oklahoma, would end up as rivals in Pearl Harbor.[24]

Both Henry Brown and Leonard Yandle told our parents later that Clyde looked good and that he seemed to be happy. We treasured that.

Roger Snyder, a member of the *Tennessee* band, also played that night. He told me the *Arizona* band boys had come over to Bloch Arena, not to play, but to listen to the music and to visit with their friends. Snyder knew several of the boys in *Arizona*'s band and talked with them for some time.[25]

Gerald E. Wentworth of the *Tennessee* band was glad that six or eight *Arizona* musicians came over while the *Tennessee* musicians were packing up. They all stood around renewing acquaintances and recalling school days.[26]

Not all the events of that evening were happy, however.

James Harvey Sanderson's mother had been trying all week to get word to Harvey that his father had just died. We did not have the facilities for emergency messages in those days that we do now. Her message was never delivered to Harvey, but was returned to her shortly after the attack. By that, she knew Harvey had not heard about his father's death before he, too, had died.[27]

However, a friend of Harvey's came to see her later and told her he had spent the evening before the *Arizona* was sunk with Harvey. They had gone to the band contest together, not as participants, but as spectators. He told her that Harvey heard of his father's death that night from another friend from Lindsay, California, who had received word from his own family. And so she knew that her son had spent his last night alive grieving for his father.[28]

Bloch Arena was a short walk from the fleet landing.[29] After the contest ended, *Arizona*'s musicians drifted down to the fleet landing in small groups. From all accounts, most of them were in good spirits.

James W. Montgomery of the *Tennessee* band said that, although *Arizona*'s band did not play that night, many of *Arizona*'s musicians were there to listen to the other bands and to check out the competition. Montgomery walked back to the landing with some of his good friends from the *Arizona* band, and they made plans for some of *Arizona*'s musicians to go over to *Tennessee* the next morning after colors to visit with each other.[30]

Gerald Wentworth said it was so good to visit with each other after so long a time that they let motor launch after motor launch go by while they talked until at last, only Wentworth and Chernucha remained on the dock. They had not known each other well at the School of Music, but they talked on and on about many things. They discussed political events, the likelihood of war, and how the war might start.[31]

Finally, each caught the launch to his ship, and Wentworth got back to the *Tennessee* at 1:00 A.M.[32]

That would mean that Chernucha was probably the last *Arizona* bandsman to get back to the ship that night.

John W. Crawford, a graduate of the School of Music and a member of the *Dobbin* band, walked back to the landing with four of the *Arizona* musicians—Floege, Haas, Lynch, and White. They stood on the landing and talked for about an hour until the liberty boats came to pick them up. John Crawford and Curt Haas decided to meet the next day at the "Y" to play over a collection of flute-clarinet duets which Crawford had with him on the ship.[33]

When Crawford boarded his launch, Lynch was still standing on the landing. Crawford thought that Lynch, as one of the older members of the *Arizona* band, had been detailed to watch out for the other musicians.[34]

Lamar S. Crawford, a Marine on the *Arizona*, said that if a man were single, he had to be back on the ship by 1:00 A.M. He added that when the last liberty launch left the dock, a sailor had better be on it or he would have to swim out to his ship.[35]

If he were late getting back to his ship, the Officer of the Deck took his liberty card away and turned it over to his Division Officer. The sailor would then have a meeting the next day with his Division Officer, and probably would be "written up." That would put the dreaded black mark on his record. Consequently, there were many fights on the dock over seats on the last liberty boat.[36]

Since the ship maintained "Lights Out" at ten o'clock, there would not have been much talking that night after they retired to their "innerspring hammocks." In spite of their discomfort, being young and tired, they would have fallen asleep right away.

Harvey Sanderson, however, no doubt lay awake all night, thinking of his father.

We can be sure their last thoughts as they fell asleep were whether or not they were finally going home on December 13.

And they would have wondered what would happen to the Battle of Music 1941 if *Arizona* really did leave before the final contest was held. Would that final contest, scheduled for December 20, be postponed until all the participating ships were back in Pearl Harbor?

I have long ceased to speculate about that. Since the Navy did not see fit to take *Arizona* out of Pearl Harbor before December 7, it does not seem very important to me now whether or not they were finally coming home.

Because eight hours later, *Arizona* and most of her crew would never be coming home again.

CHAPTER 19

December 7, 1941

Now it was time. The stage had been set. The preparations had been made.

It was the morning of December 7, 1941, at Pearl Harbor, Territory of Hawaii.

And our nation's most shameful military defeat was about to begin.

All up and down the chain of command, our U.S. military men and government officials had made their decisions. They had guarded our nations's secrets well—so well, in fact, that they had not even shared them with each other. Or with our military commanders in Hawaii.

Out at sea, the Japanese fleet had reached the point of no return. Japan's warmongers had won. Her peace seekers had lost, and Japan's most stupid military assault was underway.

People of all nations would pay for many, many years for that stupidity.

In Hawaii, our airplanes were parked wing-tip to wing-tip, and our ships were lined up in neat rows.

One of those ships was the USS *Arizona*.

It was a battleship which was not supposed to be sinkable, anchored in a harbor which was not supposed to be at risk. On board, there was a Navy band which was not supposed to be on that ship, composed of twenty-one musicians, most of whom were not supposed to be in that band.

Approaching was an enemy which was not supposed to be smart enough to be a threat to such a big, powerful nation as the United States of America.

It was a beautiful morning. The temperature was mild, the day was clear and bright, with only a few clouds floating around. It was a typical Hawaiian morning.

It was a good day to be alive. It was not a good day to die. And yet, 1,177 men serving on *Arizona* alone would die before nine-thirty that morning.

And many, many people—both American and Japanese, military and civilian—would die before the madness ended years later.

It was Sunday. In our country, we observed Sunday as a day of rest. We heeded the word of God and remembered to keep our Sabbath Day holy.

Arizona, too, was operating with a smaller crew than during the week. Most of her men were on board, since only married men who had wives in Hawaii were allowed to stay ashore all night. But most of them did not have to move quite so quickly on Sunday mornings. They were allowed to sleep half an hour later. They could linger a little over their breakfasts.

Most of her crew was not sleeping, as has been reported for so many years. *Arizona* was not just sitting dead in the water that morning. Certain duties must be performed twenty-four hours a day on a ship, and her men were up, shaving, washing, and dressing for their day's activities. If they had been lucky enough to obtain liberty, they were preparing to go ashore for the day.

Her band was one of the units on the ship for which it was just another day in the Navy, since the band worked seven days a week. The musicians would have been awakened at six o'clock by the master-at-arms. That departure from their customary five-thirty reveille was the Navy's gesture of respect for Sunday.[1]

If there was enough water that morning, they would have stood in line for a shower. If there was no water, or if they were too tired to stand in line, they would have washed and shaved with their half-bucket of water. By six-thirty, the musicians would have rolled up their "innerspring hammocks," stowed them away in the bins, and would have helped their mess cook lower the tables for breakfast.[2]

While they ate, the musicians would have discussed the scuttlebutt about returning to the States in one week.[3] They were afraid to believe yet another rumor, but oh how they hoped it was true this time!

Bill Moorhouse and Neal Radford would have talked about their plans to hitchhike to their homes together. My brother, who had become gun-shy about hitchhiking while he lived in Washington, would have told them he planned to wire home for money for train fare to Oklahoma. Wayne Bandy, Jerry Cox, Frank Floege, Curt Haas, Wendell Hurley, Bill McCary, Bobby Shaw, and Ernest Whitson would have agreed with my brother.

The boys would have discussed the probable cost of train tickets to their homes. Harvey Sanderson, Jack Scruggs, Charles White, and Fred Kinney lived the closest to Long Beach, with the Midwestern boys next. Oran Brabbzson, Ralph Burdette, Harry Chernucha, Bernard Hughes, and Alex Nadel had the farthest to go, as did Emmett Lynch, whose new wife lived in Washington, D.C.

Even with the new discount for servicemen on the railroads, they knew the price of the tickets would be high. But that was what they had been saving their money for all the time they had been in Hawaii—the means to get *Home*!

They would have tried to comfort their good friend Sanderson. Most of the boys had not experienced the loss of a parent, but Floege, Haas, Hurley, and Nadel knew that pain first hand.

The musicians would have talked about the upcoming Battle of Music and whether or not *Arizona* would still be in Pearl Harbor when that final contest was held.

They would have discussed the merits of the three bands they were to meet in the finals—the bands of the Marine Corps Barracks, the *Tennessee*, and the *Pennsylvania*.

The bandsmen would have talked about their plans for the day. They all wanted to go over to Honolulu to finish their Christmas shopping, but the band had been put on twenty-four hour guard duty.[4] That meant the musicians were on call if needed and could go no farther than the Navy Yard.[5]

Some of the boys would have told the others they had been invited over to the *Tennessee* after colors to visit their friends from the School of Music.[6] Since half the band would have to play for church, a few of the musicians would have tried to trade with someone else, so they could also go over to *Tennessee*. They would probably not have been successful.

My brother would have told them that he and Henry Brown planned to go on over to *Nevada* to look for A. E. Streight.

No doubt Radford was going over to *Tennessee*, since Montgomery was a good friend of both his and my brother's.[7]

Haas would have told them of his plans to meet John Crawford at the "Y" to practice together. Floege, White, and Lynch would also have discussed their visit with Crawford the night before.[8]

Sanderson would have been trying to figure how he could get leave, and how he could find the money to get back to California to be with his mother and sister.[9]

Chernucha would still have been talking about the chances of war, and what he and Wentworth had discussed.[10]

Hurley had just sent his photograph album home, and he would have been planning his next series of photographs.[11]

After breakfast, the bandsmen would have gone down one deck to the band room, located on the third deck, to warm up.

At 7:45 A.M., the band would have gone up to the quarterdeck, preparing to march to the fantail for colors.

On small ships, the call to colors was performed by the ship's boatswain, who piped his whistle. On larger ships, the ship's bugler played the call to colors, while on really large ships, the band always played for colors.[12]

The duties varied among the eighteen bands at Pearl Harbor, depending on the type of ship to which they had been assigned. On smaller ships, the band was usually excused from playing for colors on Sundays and holidays. Only the senior officer had the authority to call out the band on those days.[13]

That luxury was not extended to the battleship bands. For them, there was no relief. When the ship was in port, the battleship bands played for colors seven days a week.[14]

For the ship's band, the ceremony began when the band call was sounded at seven-fifty. The musicians immediately got into formation near the quarterdeck.[15]

The band for colors was the full band. No musician was ever excused. The band was dressed in full uniform, with no casual shorts nor skivvy shirts allowed.[16]

A crewman stood on the fantail and watched the tower at the Navy Yard through a telescope, called a long glass. When the "Preparation for Morning Colors" flag was raised on the tower at the Navy Yard at seven fifty-five, the crewman signaled the bugler.[17] Instantly, the bugler sounded first call for colors, the blue prep flag was raised on all the ships, and the band lined up on the fantail near the Marine color guard.[18]

At exactly eight o'clock, at a signal from the tower, the prep flag came down and the American flag was raised. At that instant, the band broke into the National Anthem.

No matter what a crewman was doing, if he were on topside, he was to stop, come to full attention and salute as our flag was raised.[19]

Church services on the Arizona were held every Sunday morning on the quarterdeck. The mess tables were moved out by the crew and benches were set up in the open air. A canvas cover, about thirty by thirty feet, was stretched over the area as a sunscreen. In inclement weather, church was held on the deck below the quarterdeck.[20]

The Chaplain serving on each battleship was either Catholic, Protestant, or Jewish. At eight o'clock, motor launches stood by at each ship to take the crew members to the church service of their own denomination.[21]

Motor launches also made trips to shore to pick up the ship's officers and married enlisted men who had spent the night in Hawaii, returning them to their ships for church.[22]

Seaman Jimmy Burcham of the Arizona watched her bandsmen gather on the quarterdeck that morning, carrying their band instruments. Burcham had eaten breakfast and had reported to the quarterdeck to help set up the benches for the eight-thirty church service. Burcham heard the first call for colors at seven fifty-five and watched the band march back to the fantail to line up for colors.[23]

Louis Conter, Quartermaster Third Class, was on the bridge of the Arizona that morning and also saw the band lined up in formation on the fantail.[24]

Gunner's Mate Third Class Harvey Milhorn of the *Arizona* was perched on a crane 157 feet above the aft deck of the fantail. He looked down and saw the band lined up in two rows on the fantail, ready to play for colors.[25]

On the *Vestal*, next to *Arizona*, Marine Private James Kennedy was standing topside. He had just stood the four to eight o'clock watch and had reported to the fantail for color guard duty. At seven fifty-five, he glanced over at *Arizona* and noticed she was being readied for church services. Her awnings had been spread and her band had assembled in formation on the fantail, ready to play for colors.[26]

Seaman Jack E. Rininger of the *Vestal* was standing topside. He also looked over at *Arizona* and saw her band on the fantail, lined up ready to play for colors.[27]

They came at seven fifty-five that Sunday morning—the first wave of Japanese airplanes, filled with machine guns, bombs, and grinning little yellow men. Painted on the underside of the wings were red circles—the famous "Rising Sun" of Japan. None of us has ever been able to look at that symbol since without a feeling of horror.

Not all the eighteen bands were present at Pearl Harbor that morning. The aircraft carrier *Lexington* and the heavy cruiser *Indianapolis* were parts of two task forces which had left Pearl Harbor a few days before. Their bands were, of course, with their ships.

Since the bands of the smaller ships were not required to play for colors on Sundays, their musicians were getting ready to go on liberty.

Musician Second Class John Crawford of the *Dobbin* band had arisen early and was dressed, preparing to go meet Curt Haas.[28]

Musician Second Class Frank Forgione of the *Oglala* band was also getting ready for liberty.[29]

But it was a different story for the members of the eight bands stationed on the battleships.

Only the *West Virginia* band had been excused from playing for colors that day—the other seven bands were all standing on the fantails of their respective ships and had front row seats for the beginning of hell.

The men who were in a position to observe the start of the disaster that morning and who lived to tell about it all speak of hearing the drone of planes, which they naturally assumed were ours. The planes flew in from the East, so anyone looking into the sun breaking through the clouds could not see them.

Various comments were made among the men about how somebody was going to catch hell for making so much noise on Sunday morning.

At seven fifty-five, just as the prep call was sounded by the ships' buglers, the first bombs fell on our airplanes lined up on Ford Island. One minute later, the Japanese airplanes began their attack on our battleships.

As the airplanes banked to fly low over Battleship Row, our men could see the Rising Sun on the wings and the grinning aviators, smiling and waving to our sailors as they dropped their bombs upon them.

All over, the cry went up, "It's the Japs! Japs! Japs!"

Directly ahead of *Arizona* were the battleships *Tennessee* and *West Virginia*, whose bands had graduated with *Arizona*'s band in May.

The men on the *Tennessee* thought the noise of the bombing of Ford Island must be an airplane crash or an accident on Ford Island and sounded the alarm for general quarters, followed immediately by air alert.[30]

Bandmaster James Lamar Smith was standing with his band on *Tennessee*'s fantail. Smith had served in China for several years, so when he saw the planes drop down from the clouds and saw the emblem on the wings, he shouted, "For Christ's sake, those are Jap planes! Everybody run!"[31]

Immediately his bandsmen ran to their battle stations down in the ammunition hold for turret number three, where their job was to put the gunpowder on the hoist.[32]

Musicians Second Class Richard Duryea and Paul Holdaway vividly recall being on the quarterdeck that morning. As soon as they realized the planes were not our own, they ran with their fellow bandsmen to their battle stations down in the ammunition hold.[33]

Musician Second Class James W. Montgomery was looking forward to seeing some of *Arizona*'s musicians later that morning. On hearing General Quarters sounded, he ran for his battle station. Both he and Musician Second Class Roger Snyder recall the airplanes strafing the musicians with machine-gun fire as they ran. They took their instruments with them, but Snyder threw the bass drum over the side as they ran, to get it out of the way.[34]

Tied beside *Tennessee* was the *West Virginia*. Bandmaster Thomas G. Carlin and his band had been excused from playing for colors that morning. Her bandsmen had finished eating breakfast when they heard the call for fire and rescue, followed almost immediately by general quarters.[35]

Musicians Second Class Howard G. Hare and William Harten ran to their battle stations. Musician Second Class Sol Blaine had put up his hammock and had finished breakfast when he heard the alarm. He also ran to his battle station.[36]

Musician Second Class R. J. Tippets remembered that all the hammocks had been taken down by six-thirty. Although *West Virginia*'s band had been excused from playing colors that morning, Tippets had the duty to play in the church band. After he had shaved, washed, and dressed, he set out to find a musician who would take his place in the church band that morning, so he could go ashore.[37]

Not finding a replacement, Tippets ate breakfast and went to the band compartment to write letters until time for church to begin. Just as he had settled down, the fire and rescue call came over the loud speaker. For that drill, the bandsmen's battle station was in the sick bay, so Tippets ran there. Suddenly the general quarters call sounded over the loud speaker, so he ran back down to the third deck, where his battle station for that call was located.[38]

Directly ahead of *Tennessee* and *West Virginia* were the battleships *Maryland* and *Oklahoma*. The bands of both those battleships had been trained at the Fleet School in San Diego, California.

Bandmaster A. Vinciguerra was standing with his band on the fantail of the *Maryland*. When general quarters sounded, the bandsmen ran to their battle stations in the forward magazine of the ship. Musician William W. Bucher remembers that, as they ran, they threw their instruments into a compartment on the deck near the quarter-deck, where they were always kept.[39]

On the *Oklahoma*, Bandmaster J. B. Booe and his bandsmen were also standing on the fantail. Since *Oklahoma*'s Chaplain was Catholic, Coxswain Ray Bowden was waiting beside his motor launch to take the Protestant and Jewish sailors to church services on other ships. As he waited for colors, Bowden watched the ship's band and the Marine color guard assemble on the fantail.[40]

Marine Private Charles Risher also saw the *Oklahoma* band topside that morning. Risher had been on the four to eight o'clock watch and had fallen in for color guard at the end of his watch. He remembers there were probably ten Marines lined up with the band that morning.[41]

Directly ahead of *Maryland* and *Oklahoma* was the battleship *California*, sitting alone. Her band, directed by Bandmaster L. B. "Red" Luchenbach, had graduated in May with *Arizona*'s band.

According to Musician Second Class Warren G. Harding, the *California* band had gone back to the fantail to begin forming at seven forty-five. The Prep flag had just gone up when the attack began.[42]

Musician Second Class Larry Conley, Brabbzson's friend at the School of Music, was not on the *California* that morning. He was recovering from an appendectomy and was still on the hospital ship *Solace* when the attack began.[43]

Musician Second Class Mike Palchefsky was sitting on the rail of the *California*, blowing into his trumpet to warm it up. They were not playing, as it was not yet time. They all heard the drone of many airplanes, but could not see the planes through the clouds. Streams of sunlight sifted through the clouds, and one plane suddenly dropped through a cloud and skimmed over Ford Island. Palchefsky saw the bomb drop from the plane onto Ford Island. When he saw the "Rising Sun," he ran to his battle station on the third deck. As he ran, he carried his trumpet with him and tucked it between a mattress and a pillow on someone's bunk for safety. It would be several weeks before he saw that trumpet again.[44]

The *Pennsylvania* was sitting in dry dock on the morning of December 7, having repairs made to the ship. Her band had trained at the U.S. Navy School of Music but had graduated long before *Arizona*'s band. The bandmaster was Axel Anton Jensen.

On the morning of December 7, *Pennsylvania*'s bandsmen were still talking about the "Battle of Music" contest which they had won the night before. They were in formation on the fantail, waiting to play, when they saw a group of airplanes dropping down. They assumed they were our planes and that it was just another drill until they saw flames shoot out of a large hangar on Ford Island.[45]

As the Officer of the Deck screamed for all hands to man their air defense stations, Bandmaster Jensen immediately marched his band on the double from the fantail. They ran to the band room, threw their instruments into their cases, and ran to their battle stations on the second deck, where they were to serve as stretcher bearers.[46]

Directly behind *Arizona* was the *Nevada*. Her band had been trained at the Fleet Music School in San Diego and was led by Bandmaster Oden McMillan. *Nevada*'s band was standing on the fantail, ready to play for colors. Fireman Second Class James W. Henry was also standing topside on the *Nevada*, watching the band members milling around tuning up their instruments.[47]

Nevada's band was the only band which actually played the National Anthem that morning. Bandmaster McMillan had begun the National Anthem slightly ahead of schedule, and because of the music coming from his band, did not hear the general quarters signal. As he was directing his band, he was astonished to see Japanese planes dive down on them, strafing them with machine-gun fire. McMillan faltered once and stopped directing and his band stopped playing. But all his years of training took over—one simply did not quit playing our National Anthem until it was finished.[48]

Musicians Second Class Dean R. Kreek and Clyde S. Griffin remember that *Nevada*'s bandsmen carried on, playing the National Anthem to the very last note, all the time under machine-gun fire. Finally, at the end of the song, they broke and ran for their battle stations, carrying their musical instruments with them.[49]

As he ran, Musician William E. Clemons threw the big bass horn over the side, so it would not plug up the hatch.[50]

Over on *Arizona*, her band and her Marine color guard would also have heard the drone of the airplanes and would have tried to see through the clouds and sunshine beams. They, too, would have seen the planes come down toward Ford Island and the bombs dropping. They would have seen the hangar blow up. As the airplanes turned toward our battleships, they would have seen that red ball on the underside of the wing —the dreaded "Rising Sun."

They would have known that this was it—the war they had all been expecting.

Immediately, the cry went up on *Arizona*—"Japs!" The cry was repeated up and down the ship by all the men who were topside. Instantly, air alert was sounded on *Arizona*, followed by general quarters.[51]

Bandmaster Fred Kinney had been in the Navy for fifteen years. He was responsible for his twenty musicians and he took that responsibility very seriously.[52] He had served on the battleship *Idaho* and in shore bands. He would have known that those were Japanese planes and that it was not just another drill.

The second he saw the planes and heard air alert, meaning "All Hands Below the Armored Deck," Kinney would have shouted, "To your battle stations—on the double!"

Arizona's band ran to the door (or hatch) located at Frame 88, near the quarterdeck, and disappeared through the door.[53]

Altogether, the musicians had been topside that morning for no more than six or seven minutes.

On the *Vestal*, Signalman John H. Birmingham was holding the Prep flag on the fantail of the *Vestal* when he was alerted by *Arizona*'s sounding general quarters. At first, Birmingham was impressed that *Arizona* would conduct a drill so early on Sunday morning, but when he looked closely, he could see her men running to their battle stations. As soon as he saw that the planes were Japanese, he slid down the ladder to the pilot house and sounded general quarters for *Vestal*.[54]

As the men on *Arizona* and *Vestal* ran to their battle stations, they heard our National Anthem ringing out above the noise of the bombs and machine guns. Seaman First Class Jimmie Burcham thought *Arizona*'s band was playing, since he had just seen it standing on the fantail a minute or two before.[55]

Seaman First Class Jack E. Rininger on the *Vestal* also thought the music was coming from *Arizona*'s band, since he had just seen it lined up ready to play for colors. However, he soon remembered that he had seen *Arizona*'s musicians scatter when general quarters was sounded.[56]

The music was, in fact, coming from *Nevada*'s band.

Marine Private First Class Lamar S. Crawford was with the Executive Officer of the *Arizona* that morning. They were standing by the hatch when general quarters sounded, and Crawford saw the band boys run past him, carrying their band instruments.[57]

After the bombs began to hit, Captain Jim Dick Miller came down to the deck from *Arizona*'s turret number three. He noticed that all the men on the deck, including the bandsmen, had already scattered.[58]

In case of an air attack, *Arizona*'s band had been assigned to the third deck to man the ammunition hoists for turret number two. As the musicians ran down to the ammunition hold, they were carrying their band instruments with them. Some of the boys were still making payments on their instruments, while others had only recently made their final payment. They would have hung on tightly to those instruments, since they had no way of knowing they would never need them again.

As they ran past the band room, they would have thrown their instruments into that compartment.

Their duties were to close all the watertight doors and hatches and to turn off all the air pumps, in case of a gas attack. They were then to take their places by the hoists.[59]

The hoists going up to the big guns in the turret were operated by electricity. Powder bags about fourteen inches in diameter were placed on the hoists down below by seamen. The bandsmen's duty was to stand in rows on each side of the hoists to make sure the powder bags did not become jammed or snagged as the bags rode up the hoists. If the powder were to spill out, it would become extremely dangerous and could not be put into the guns in the turret above.[60]

The bags were made of cloth and were filled with gunpowder. Black powder was sewn into the ends with silk thread.[61] The powder was more like pellets than actual powder. The pellets were about twice the size of a pencil lead and about three-fourths of an inch long. Each powder bag weighed seventy-five pounds.[62]

Arizona's bandsmen had just reached the ammunition hold and had begun sending the bags of powder up to the big guns, when that Japanese aviator dropped his bomb on *Arizona*. The bomb drove through the armored plate on her deck, starting a fire. In seconds, the powder magazines for the two forward turrets, Numbers One and Two, blew up with a mighty roar.

And at that moment—eight-ten on Sunday morning, December 7, 1941—*Arizona*, along with most of her crew, died.

And the last United States Navy band ever to serve aboard the USS *Arizona* disappeared forever.

Part II

THE FAMILIES

MY FRIEND

O' Mighty Mystic Deep,

...O' thou who hast stolen away my friend.

O' thou in whose bosom sleep the bones that once were men,

And the broken hulks that once were ships.

And yet I hear thy whisper, as if from a thousand unseen lips.

And in your whisper, and your roar, your breakers and your waves

You seem to say that he, my friend, died not in vain,

But for a thing much greater than man.

And you tell me that though he rests beneath your mighty waves,

A part of him is somewhere else,

That part of heaven made for men who give their lives,

That others might live in peace and happiness.

You are there, my friend,

Well have you earned your rest,

And now I follow in your footsteps...

God grant that I may sometime find that place where you have gone.

Fred Watson
Okmulgee, Oklahoma
December 1941

Written in memory of his friend, Clyde R. Williams,
who was a member of *Arizona*'s Last Band.

CHAPTER 20

We Hear

Thanksgiving Day, 1941, was difficult for the families of *Arizona*'s bandsmen. For most of us, it was our first Thanksgiving without our boys.

Most of the country celebrated Thanksgiving that year on the fourth Thursday of November. President Roosevelt had been moving Thanksgiving Day to the third Thursday in November for several years, trying to boost Christmas sales for the department stores. We called his attempt to counter the depression "Franksgiving Day."[1]

In 1941, the president allowed the various states to set the date for their Thanksgiving celebration, and most of them chose the fourth Thursday. Congress would officially set the date for the fourth Thursday in 1942.[2]

As people across our nation gathered to give thanks that year, many were saddened because an important family member was missing from the celebration.

It was soon to get worse.

It is fortunate none of us knew how our simple lives were about to change forever, for that was the last holiday the United States was to celebrate in a normal way for a long, long time.

My brother's last letter to us was written on the day before Thanksgiving. No doubt he was thinking about our annual Thanksgiving Day family reunion and how very much he would have liked to be there.

As usual, our family went to Henryetta to spend Thanksgiving with our Grandparents Williams.

Our cousin, Carl W. Phillips, had joined the Army Air Force but was home on leave. After dinner he, his sister Mary Louise, and I walked downtown, and we discussed how we would like to send Clyde a telegram, telling him how much we missed him. We walked over to the Western Union office and checked on the price of a telegram to Hawaii. All the way back to our grandparents' home, we tried to figure how we could raise that much money. Finally, knowing that all our relatives were on a tight budget, we let the matter drop.

How I have wished since then that we could have found that money—it would have meant so much to me to have told Clyde, just ten days before he died, that his family loved and missed him.

That dinner in 1941 was the last Thanksgiving our family ever celebrated together in our grandparents' home.

After Thanksgiving, we all settled down again to our routine. Although Okmulgee seemed pretty dull to me, my brother had recently written that he would give anything to be back there.

He was right to be so uneasy.

Japanese envoys had been in Washington for weeks, discussing plans for peace between our two nations. But even as Japanese dignitaries sat and talked peace, their war ships were on their way to Hawaii to begin hostilities.

It is clear we had absolutely no clue as to the type of enemy we were facing, and we still refused to believe that war was imminent.

On the morning of December 7, some newspapers pointed out how Japan's pleading for peace and understanding showed her fear of the United States. They added that the Philippines had been put on alert and guessed that, in the face of that, Japan had softened and had asked for more negotiations in Washington.[3]

Even while people were reading that in their Sunday newspapers, they were hearing on their radios that Japan had just attacked our Naval base in Pearl Harbor.

On that Sunday morning, I was sitting in my friend's living room, waiting for her to finish eating dinner so we could go to the movies. The radio was tuned to the symphony orchestra, and I was enjoying the beautiful music, when suddenly the announcer broke in to inform us of the attack on Pearl Harbor. I blurted out, "My brother is there" and ran out of the house.

As I ran home, about a mile away, I remember the deathly quiet all around me. No cars went by, nor was there any sound. Even the dogs had ceased barking. It was as if all the world had stopped, and there was total void.

Our telephone rang all afternoon. One of the calls was from my friend Vincent Barger. Vinny and I had dated for several months, but some time before, he had been transferred to another town in Oklahoma and now came home only on weekends.

When I answered the telephone, Vinny asked me abruptly where my brother was stationed, and then asked me to go out with him that night.

Vinny and I and another couple went to one of our honky-tonks, but we did not go in. None of us felt like dancing. We drove around town, and again I remember the total quiet. Our town of seventeen thousand was not too lively anyway on Sunday evenings, and now it was like a ghost town.

We discussed the shocking news and our anger at Japan. We tried to figure what would happen next. We suspected, even then, that our lives would never be the same. The boys knew they were now on their way to some branch of the armed forces.

If I had any premonition of Clyde's death, I buried it deep inside my soul. We were just waiting for him to call or write to tell us he was fine.

We waited—and we waited.

On Monday, December 8, I bought a spiral notebook and started a journal. I thought it would be great fun to let Clyde read it when he came home on leave, and he and I could have a good laugh over all the worry he had caused us.

> ***Sunday, December 7, 1941***—*I stayed all Saturday night with Kay and Margaret Mary. They got up early and went to Tulsa. I got up later and went home. Everyone was in the best of spirits.*
>
> *I was at Mary's when the announcement came that Japan was bombing Pearl Harbor and Manilla. My brother is in the Harbor, in the U.S. Navy on board the USS* Arizona. *When I*

heard the announcement, I grabbed my coat and ran all the way home.

All afternoon we stayed by the radio. We had a radio in the front room, kitchen, and bedroom, each on a different station. We heard the USS West Virginia *was sunk, and I know two sailors on that ship.*

Japan had attacked us with no warning, and later in the afternoon she declared war on the U.S. The president will meet with the House and Senate tomorrow.

I had a date tonight with Vinny, but no one felt much like having fun. We all feel nothing but hatred for Japan. Everyone is worried about his or her son.

People have been very nice to us, calling to see if we have heard anything about Clyde. All we know is that Pearl Harbor is greatly damaged and Hickam Field (an Army air field in Hawaii) reports 350 boys killed in one barracks.

All we can do is wait.

***Monday, December 8, 1941**—So many false reports are coming through that we are beginning to believe only official reports. The president asked Congress to declare war, and a few hours later, both House and Senate declared war on Japan. Only one vote was cast against war, by Jeanette Rankin of Montana, in the House. Public opinion is very marked against her, because our nation is certainly not going to stand by and let Japan or any country do such a dirty trick to us!*

Germany will probably declare war on us, but we expected that.

The nations are all lining up. They predict that all nations will be in before long.

We still have no word from Clyde. Mother heard that all families have been notified if their sons were killed, so she feels a little better.

That last statement shows the emotional roller coaster which the families of the men stationed at Pearl Harbor were subjected to during the next few weeks. The false hopes held out to us, when we were at our wits end, were nothing short of torture. We were neither eating nor sleeping and spent our time listening to the radio. Each radio report we heard told us something different, until we were completely worn out.

Our nation's reaction, after our shock and disbelief of such treachery, was fury—total, unadulterated fury! As one of Japan's statesmen expressed it, Japan had truly awakened a sleeping giant!

All our information about the attack was coming from Germany and Tokyo, with our Government denying all their reports.

Thus, on December 8, the Berlin radio broadcast a Tokyo announcement that the battleship *West Virginia* had been sunk and that the battleship *Oklahoma* had been set afire. They added that, altogether, three U.S. ships were hit, with the third ship not named.[4]

It was the name of that third ship which we were straining to hear.

> *Tuesday, December 9, 1941—Still no word about Clyde. They tell us that "no news is good news," so we try to keep cheerful. Some families are acting so silly! They try to call, cable, or wire their sons, but no messages are being put through. My goodness, if everyone did that, the official messages couldn't get through.*
>
> *New York City had an air raid practice today, and California had one last night. They prepared to black out the White House today.*
>
> *Had a date with J. B. tonight, and we listened to the president's speech in the kitchen of a honky-tonk. He said he feels the great concern of the families of the boys, and we will be notified as soon as possible.*
>
> *There is still no report of the USS* West Virginia.
>
> *Mother spent all day Sunday and Monday crying and Daddy spent it cussing!*

On Tuesday morning (we did not receive a paper on Mondays), Clyde's photograph was on the front page of our newspaper, with the story that he was on the USS *Arizona* at Pearl Harbor.[5] There would be many photographs and news releases about Clyde during the next weeks, as we all waited for word from him.

Also on Tuesday, newspapers began listing the Pearl Harbor casualties of the Air Corps, Army and Marine Corps.[6]

But still the families of the Navy men waited.

I have always remembered how people would stop me as I walked back and forth to work to ask if we had heard from Clyde. We were so grateful for the concern the townspeople showed us, but it did get mighty tiresome repeating the same story over and over—"No, we have not heard anything from him." Invariably, they left me with the phrase, "Well, no news is good news." I learned then that no news is *not* good news, and I have never used that expression since.

It is apparent how naive we still were, staying off the wires to give our government officials freedom to send their messages. We did not know then that our officials did not send many messages to Hawaii, whether the wires were busy or not! Our top military brass in Hawaii were apparently on their own when it came to information from our government.

The White House was indeed blacked out. I saw that later when I went to Washington to work for the Army Signal Corps in January 1942. During the war, we were not allowed to walk on the side of the street next to the White House.

Reading of President Roosevelt's great concern for the families of the victims of the attack rings a little hollow now. It has been said that he was the one who was so paranoid about secrecy and would not allow Secretary of the Navy Frank Knox to notify the next of kin until long after our government knew that our boys were dead.

> **Wednesday, December 10, 1941**—*The Japs claimed today to have sunk the USS* Enterprise. *Two of our Okmulgee boys are on it. The report on it and on the* West Virginia *are still unofficial.*
>
> *We still haven't heard from Clyde.*
>
> *All the cities on the West Coast are blacked out tonight. A Japanese air raid is expected in twelve hours. Enemy planes*

are hovering near the coastline.
These are awful times for all of us.

Our whole nation was living under extreme tension as we waited for Japan to come over and attack our country. Rumors and lies were circulating in our newspapers and on our radios, and the silence the government maintained only fed the flames of those rumors. Obviously, that imminent air raid was another rumor. Japan did not attack California.

On December 10, Washington revealed that Rear Admiral Isaac Campbell Kidd had been killed during the attack on Pearl Harbor. For security reasons, the ship on which he was serving was not identified.[7]

But the families of *Arizona's* bandsmen knew on which ship Admiral Kidd had been serving. We knew that he was our boys' beloved Admiral, the man who had always enjoyed their music so much.

And we waited.

Thursday, December 11, 1941—Germany and Italy declared war on us today, and we returned the compliment. Still no news from Clyde.

It seems that all the dopes don't live in Japan, Germany and Italy. One woman from Tulsa called the newspaper office Sunday night, the day Japan attacked us for the first time, and asked the newspaper if they could tell her how the war between Japan and the U.S. came out. We'll be in it a long, long time, I'm afraid.

I took the Civil Service Exam one month ago today. I'm just dying to go somewhere to do my small part for Uncle Sam.

I only wish I could go to Pearl Harbor and fight the dirty rats myself!

Reality was just sinking in for us, as we contemplated the huge task we faced in fighting so many countries on so many oceans. We were beginning to see that it was not going to be an overnight skirmish.

Friday, December 12, 1941—Still no news from Clyde! I think if I could break down and cry for about an hour, and have hysterics and scream, I'd feel better. I haven't cried yet. After all, I have faith in God and I know he will bring Clyde safely through.

A little boy about ten years old went into the recruiting office somewhere today, and told the officer he wanted to enlist. The officer asked him if he thought he could whip the Japs. The boy said, "No, you have enough big guys to do that. But those Japs have little boys, and I can whip all the little Japs."

That shows how we Americans feel!

The Japs have only eleven battleships, and today we sank one battleship and badly crippled another. They have no material or money to build new ones, so—! And we haven't even started yet!

The Axis powers will soon find out they have bitten off a lot more than they can chew!

Just as I started to get ready for bed, it was announced over the radio that Secretary of Navy Frank Knox, who is in Pearl Harbor investigating the Sunday attack, would speak from the Harbor at midnight. I stayed up to listen, but atmospheric conditions made it impossible to get Hawaii.

Certainly, we were now whistling in the dark about the war, as we realized more and more what was before us. We talked that way to each other to bolster ourselves up, because we were all so very frightened, both about Clyde and about the war.

Our family was being told a lot of nonsense now about putting our faith in God. I was told that, if I only had enough faith, Clyde would come out safely. That was a pretty large load to put on a twenty-year-old girl.

Saturday, December 13, 1941—Daddy goes to work every morning at five o'clock, and at five-thirty Mother woke me up crying and practically having hysterics! I rushed into her bedroom, and they had just announced that the Japs claim to have sunk the Arizona, the ship Clyde is on. They kept saying that the report was not confirmed at Washington, so I finally convinced her that it was probably just a scheme to find out where the Arizona was, as it is the flagship of the fleet [sic].

We were pretty worried, but when we got back to work after supper, one of the ladies told us that the radio had announced that the Arizona definitely was not sunk. We felt a lot better then.

Had a date with J. B., and we double-dated with Catherine, my best friend. Had a good time 'cause I was so relieved. Stayed all night with Catherine.

I can still picture me standing in the hall listening to my mother scream! There were cold shivers passing all through my body from shock, until I nearly fainted. After I returned to bed, I shivered for a long time. Our nerves were strung as tight as they could possibly go.

Sunday, December 14, 1941—*Went to church and then came home. Pate told me the radio had announced that the War Department had neither confirmed or denied that the Arizona had sunk. I'm sure it didn't, though, 'cause I wouldn't believe anything the Japs say!*

Had a date all day with Vinny. He works at Bartlesville now. Had dinner at his folks home, then went to the Lake with Mr. Barger, Jack, and Lois. We took pictures at Barger's cabin. We went to the show and dancing that night. Had a good time.

Monday, December 15, 1941—*The first half of today was very peaceful. We heard that Sec. Knox had arrived in Washington this morning. Then—! Aunt Sarah called from Tulsa to say that Knox had released his report and the Arizona and four destroyers were sunk. There were 2,684 killed, ninety-one officers killed, and 678 wounded.*

We still haven't heard from Clyde.

There are nearly fifty missing. Of course, if they are dead, the parents have probably been notified, so we are sure he is alive. But there is no way of knowing if he is wounded. He must be, 'cause he hasn't written us. This has been the longest day I ever lived through!

Our relatives have been so kind, to say nothing of our friends. Our aunts and uncles have telegramed [sic], called long-distance, and written to see if we have heard anything. The phone has been hot all evening!

I'm afraid we won't have a very Merry Christmas this year.

That report released by Secretary Knox was by way of preparing our nation for the bad news about our losses at Pearl Harbor. It has been said that President Roosevelt still would not let Secretary Knox tell the full extent of our losses, so the torture for the families continued.

In reply to friends and relatives who telephoned continually, we could only report to them what we had heard from the Navy, which was nothing.

On December 16, Clyde's picture was published again in the newspaper, along with that of two local boys also stationed in Hawaii.[8] Both boys survived the attack, but it was a long time before their families heard they were all right.

Tuesday, December 16, 1941—Still no news from Clyde. People have been calling all day to encourage us. This book helps a lot to unburden myself.

I have to keep my spirits up for Mate and Pate.

The full meaning is just beginning to dawn on me. If Toke (our pet name for him) got out okay, which I'm sure he did, just think of the things he lost. He had just bought a new cornet, which probably was sunk. And the boys get paid on the fifth and the attack was on the seventh, so I imagine everyone is pretty broke.

Frank Gross told me today that I have more spunk than he would have. I have to, or go nuts!

If we could only hear something!

From shock and total rejection of the possibility of Clyde's death, I had now moved to considering the consequences of his being hurt and losing all his possessions. None of us could take in the whole story at a single time, and had to adjust to it one small fact at a time.

> ***Wednesday, December 17, 1941***—*Now I know how it feels to have a broken heart! Pate told me tonight that I had better prepare for the worst. He said he gave up yesterday and fully expects to get bad news tonight or tomorrow. The ship went so fast that there is no way that we can see for any of them to get off.*
>
> *The Nesbitt boy's parents received word today that their son is missing.*
>
> *I don't think I can* ***stand*** *this!*

> ***Thursday, December 18, 1941***—*We still haven't heard, so our hopes are getting up a little. We figure the government would have let us know by now.*
>
> *This suspense is terrible! If I didn't think so much of him, it would be different.*

> ***Friday, December 19, 1941***—*Still no word! The rumor about the Nesbitt boy is false—he is okay.*

Then, finally, we heard.

It was Saturday, December 20. Again, we were working at A.P. Brown's. Pate took Mate and I home for supper at 5:00, and we returned to work at 6:00. Still firmly convinced that we would soon receive the telegram, he went back home to wait.

Fearing Mate would receive word while she was alone, Pate had asked the Western Union office not to deliver the telegram to our home, but to find him and give it to him personally. He always kept them advised where he would be at all times.

Now he notified Western Union that he would be home for the next several hours, and it was not long before they called him.

Pate picked up the telegram from Western Union, then walked over to the newspaper office to notify them, as he had promised. They had everything ready—Clyde's photograph and his statistics—and were just waiting, as was the whole town.

Then Pate went to the store to take Mate and I home. At 9:00, Pate came up to me where I was working at the big cash register and asked me to hurry to my office to get my coat and purse. He also told me I must help him with Mate.

He did not tell me what was wrong—he did not need to.

Somehow we all got to our car. Pate drove home in stony silence, while I sat in the back seat crying. Mate was puzzled that we did not stop at the ice cream shop on the way home, as we had planned. She decided that Pate and I were having an argument and were not speaking to each other. So she also rode along in silence.

Even when we reached home and she saw all the people standing in our front yard, she still did not allow herself to admit that our waiting was now over.

We drove down the long driveway to our garage at the back of the house. Pate shut off the motor and turned to Mate. He said brokenly: "Jane, I would rather cut off my arm than to have to tell you this. Our Clyde is gone."

Mate went into the primitive, hopeless keening which had filled me with such horror the week before. I bolted from the car and ran to our front door, and somehow my parents staggered into our home.

> *Saturday, December 20, 1941—Pate got the telegram at eight-thirty, and told us at nine o'clock.*
> *Clyde is dead!*
> *The telegram lists him as missing, because he went down with the ship and his body was not recovered.*
> *I don't think I can stand it!*

The telegram:
KM108 71 GOVT=WASHINGTON DC 20 651P
[The date of receipt, 1941 Dec 20 PM 7 23, was stamped in the upper right hand corner.]
RICHARD B WILLIAMS JR=
1006 GRIFFIN ST

THE NAVY DEPARTMENT DEEPLY REGRETS TO INFORM YOU
THAT YOUR SON CLYDE RICHARD WILLIAMS MUSICIAN SEC-
OND CLASS US NAVY IS MISSING FOLLOWING ACTION IN THE
PERFORMANCE OF HIS DUTY AND IN THE SERVICE OF HIS
COUNTY [sic]X THE DEPARTMENT APPRECIATES YOUR GREAT
ANXIETY AND WILL FURNISH YOU FURTHER INFORMATION
PROMPTLY WHEN RECEIVED X TO PREVENT POSSIBLE AID TO
OUR ENEMIES PLEASE DO NOT DIVULGE THE NAME OF HIS
SHIP OR STATION=

REAR ADMIRAL RANDALL JACOBS CHIEF OF
THE BUREAU OF NAVIGATION

> *The house was full of friends until midnight, and Aunt
> Lola, Uncle Sylvester, Grandma and Grandpa, and Aunt Ha-
> zel are on their way [from Texas].*
> *We never will get over this!*

That sentence about keeping my brother's ship a secret has always rankled me. Had not the families given enough? Was not Japan telling us which ships they had sunk? Were not spies in Hawaii
telling Japan all of our damage?

Perhaps there was a reason for that secrecy—I sincerely hope so.

In our case, the whole town of Okmulgee had known since May
on which ship my brother was serving, so the warning did not mean
much.

> ***Sunday, December 21, 1941**—Relatives, friends, flow-
> ers, candy, and sympathy have been coming in all day. Every-
> one is surely swell to us. The neighbors fixed dinner for us.*
> *[After they all left,] Kay and I went to the show to get away
> from it all, and I had to sit through thirty minutes of news
> reels about Pearl Harbor.*
> *All the relatives wanted us to go back to Texas with them,
> but we figure we would be better off here.*
> *He was a swell brother while he lasted.*

On that Sunday, December 21, two weeks after Clyde's death, our relatives from Texas came, ate dinner with us, then went right back to Texas. They had driven all night after we called them, and must now drive all night to open their drugstore on Monday morning.

When a person dies as my brother did, there is no funeral to arrange. There is no body to tell good-bye. There is no burial.

> ***Monday, December 22, 1941**—Pate and I went to work today. We feel we will be better off working.*

> ***Tuesday, December 23, 1941**—The Pony Girls sent us out a whole ham today. Everyone is just swell!*

At that time, there was a tremendous outpouring of emotion being expressed in our country. We were not ashamed of our patriotism, nor were we ashamed to express our feelings.

And we were angry!

The next day, Pate wrote the following letter to the newspaper, expressing our feelings:

> *Mr. Joe Croom, Editor*
> *The Okmulgee Times*
> *Dear Mr. Croom:*
>
> *We received a message last Saturday night, Dec. 20, from the United States Navy, stating that our son and brother, Clyde Richard Williams, is missing following action in the performance of his duty and in the service of his country.*
>
> *That can mean only one thing in this particular case— Clyde went down with his ship and his body was not recovered.*
>
> *To us that was a terrific blow—a blow from which we will never completely recover—a blow that has us, for the moment, floored.*
>
> *But, with the help of God and the hundreds of friends here in Okmulgee, we will not stay down for the count. We can't*

stay down because we, like every other citizen of Okmulgee, have a job to do.

One very important thing for all of us here in Okmulgee is to have courage. If we do not have courage, how can we expect our servicemen to have courage? And without courage a serviceman is worthless. Yes, above all, we must have courage and faith.

Another job we have to do is to help our government furnish our servicemen with arms, ammunition, clothing, and food, without which they can never win the war. This we will do by buying all the defense stamps and bonds we can. We know that if Clyde could speak to all of his friends today, he would say, "This do in remembrance of me."

So let us all put our shoulder to the wheel and push a little harder, and win this war so Clyde's death will not have been in vain.

To our many friends who are standing by, ready and willing to assist us in any way we may need assistance, we are indeed grateful.

Sincerely, JANE, DICK, AND RUTH MAE WILLIAMS[9]

Published in the same issue of the newspaper was the following poem, composed by our friend, D. E. Handy:

IN MEMORY OF CLYDE

Among the lists of missing lads, another name appeared,
And to another mother came the sacrifice she feared;
She didn't dread that parting hour, when her boy marched
     away,
She loved him and the flag too much to ask him home to stay.

Okmulgee has a hero now, a cheerful, smiling lad,
In truth we have four heroes, his Mother, Sis, and Dad.
Clyde Richard Williams missing, another sailor true,
Our Clyde has merely traveled on, as many more must do.

More sailors just like Clyde will mothers have to give,
To keep our great flag flying, that liberty may live.
This be my thought, this be my prayer, as I lay down the pen,
That God may make us worthy to glorify such men.[10]

Wednesday, December 24, 1941—We took our tree down yesterday and threw it away. We unwrapped our gifts and sat them around like we had had them all our lives. We can't stand to have a Christmas ceremony.

Got some defense stamps, underclothes, pajamas, and my boss gave me five dollars. Aunt Hazel gave me a robe, but I already had one, so she gave me five dollars. Kay gave me stationery.

Went to midnight mass with Kay, and then went to Ann's for breakfast. She gave me some creme sachet.

Thursday, December 25, 1941—Spent Christmas with the Bargers. Vinny gave me a beautiful locket and his family gave me some cologne. It was a nice Christmas, though, of course, our hearts weren't in it.

Mate and Pate spent it at McCullochs. Aunt Gertie, who is staying with us for awhile, went to Henryetta.

It was impossible for us to stay in our home for Christmas. We had planned to postpone our Christmas anyway until our Toke came home to join us, so we just decided not even to have one.

It was so kind of the Bargers to take me into their home for Christmas. They were depressed and uneasy because their two sons would soon have to go into the service, and this would probably be their last Christmas together for awhile.

And it was so good of the McCulloughs, who were always such good friends of our family, to have Mate and Pate come over to their home for the day. They were the parents of Gordon McCullough, the Marine Lieutenant who had been looking for Clyde in Pearl Harbor in September.

Friday, December 26, 1941
*Mrs. Homer White, who works at the store, wrote this poem
for Clyde:*

TO CLYDE

The awakening sun's first lonely gleam
Had scarcely called to you
Across the harbor, misty green,
Oh laddie, brave and true.

You may not ever sounded there
Your stirring reveille,
But you sent to us awaiting here
A vision we can see.

The pearly waters of your grave
Shall ever hallowed be.
May they baptize and for us save
A world again set free.

Though sacrificed to hate and greed
Your glorious youthful prime
Your just reward—your country freed
From tyranny and crime.

Our answer to your reveille
With blood and tears and pain
Forever graven on our hearts
You have not died in vain.

Your call, though from eternity
In our memory shall not lapse.
To us, the call to reveille,
Though you have answered "Taps."[11]

Also printed in the newspaper was the poem, "My Friend," written in memory of Clyde by Fred Watson, his high school friend.[12]

We received many expressions of sympathy—flowers, food, cards, telegrams, telephone calls, visits and letters. We heard from Clyde's former teachers and from his friends, telling us how much they had loved him.

Earlier in the month, we had received a Christmas card from our friend, Marine Lieutenant Gordon McCulloch, which he had mailed on December 6, the day before the attack.

One year later, Gordon was dead—caught in the horror that was Guadalcanal.

The Carter cousins, Reginald and Vernon, sent flowers "In memory of our good pal."

Four years later, on December 17, 1944, Clyde's best friend, Reginald Carter, was dead.

As an infantryman in the Army, Reginald suffered from the cold rain, snow, and sleet of the Battle of the Bulge in Germany. He was wounded and captured by the Germans on December 13, and died four days later in a German prison camp.

We received a sympathy card from Clyde's good friends, Billy and Norma Bess Wingate.

Billy died a few years later on board his ship.

We heard from our friends, the Dishmans.

Their son Garland died five months later in an airplane crash while training at Luke Field in Phoenix, Arizona.

And so Pearl Harbor was just the beginning. Our nation now faced four years of horror—four years of sorrow—four years of terror.

CHAPTER 21

We Search

When the attack on Pearl Harbor began, a tight censorship was immediately clamped down on all news coming from Hawaii.[1]

Secrecy was the name of the game now. We knew there was much about our bandsmen's Pearl Harbor days they had been unable to tell us, because they had all hinted of it in their letters.

In a day when we watch our wars unfolding battle by battle on television, it is hard to explain how very secretive we were then. The moment the bombs began falling on Pearl Harbor, our government began admonishing us not to talk about ship movements, lest we cause our servicemen to die.

Six weeks later, when I went to Washington, D.C., to work for the Personnel Department of the Army Signal Corps, we were put into a "Secret Room" and warned again and again not to discuss our work with anyone.

Our servicemen were ordered not to divulge any information in their letters home which might help the enemy. Any hint of where they were or what their ship was doing was cut out of their letters by the censors, until many times their letters were so full of holes that not much remained but the salutation and the man's signature.

We all heeded that plea for secrecy. We hated the enemy so much that we would never do anything to help them.

As we moved into January 1942, the families of *Arizona*'s last band knew nothing of our bandsmen's last few hours of life.

All we knew was that we had turned our musician sons or brothers over to the Navy. The Navy had tersely told us on December 20 that it had now lost our boys, and had asked us not to tell anyone from which ship they had disappeared.

And we knew that, for some reason, the Navy had withheld notifying us for weeks. Although the Army had published its first list of casualties on December 9, and on that same date, Admiral Husband W. Kimmel, Commander of the Pacific Fleet, had announced that a list of Navy casualties had been sent to the Navy Department in Washington,[2] we still had to wait for word about our musicians.

The December 20 "Missing" telegram left us with many, many unanswered questions. There was so much we wanted to know. First, of course, was whether there was some chance any of our band boys were still alive.

After our bleak Christmas, one of the mothers set out to find some answers.

Bonnie and Harold Moorhouse, Bill's parents, had both served in the military in World War I—Harold as a Marine and Bonnie as a Navy nurse. She, more than any of us, knew what we were facing in trying to find out what had happened to our boys. As a former nurse, she also knew that our boys might well have suffered horribly before they died.

She determined to find out.

Since we had met the wives of Fred Kinney and Emmett Lynch in Washington, my parents and I were the only family who had met any of the other families of the bandsmen. And because our boys had called their friends the "guys" most of the time, we did not even know most of the musicians' last names.

But Bonnie Moorhouse had a clue.

At the time the band went aboard the *Arizona* in Long Beach, California, Bill Moorhouse and others had mailed their families a copy of the July 1941 issue of *Arizona*'s newspaper, *At 'Em Arizona*. An article in that newspaper welcomed her new band aboard and listed the names and hometowns of her new bandsmen.[3]

Beginning with that meager information, Bonnie was able to bring all the families of the *Arizona* band together into a strong support group. And gradually, by pooling all our information, we were able to piece together the story of our band's last days.

It is fortunate for us that she did that, because for many years the Navy's records were marked "Secret." After they were removed from the "Secret" category, they were protected by the "Privacy Act." Under such restrictions, families and historians find it difficult to gather information for research.

Bonnie began on January 7, 1942, when she simply sat down and wrote twenty letters, using the hometowns which were listed in *Arizona*'s newspaper. Our envelope read: "To the Parents or Next of Kin of Clyde Richard Williams, Okmulgee, Oklahoma."

We lived in a small town and our dad worked for the post office, so there was no problem with the delivery of our letter. But the post office in those days made a great effort to deliver every piece of mail they received, so even the families who lived in large towns received their letter from Bonnie Moorhouse.

It helped, of course, that all the boys had just been featured on the front pages of their hometown newspapers as one of the first local boys to have been killed in the war.

At that time, Bonnie did not know just how many of the musicians were missing. So she wrote:

> *To the Relatives of Clyde R. Williams, Okmulgee, Oklahoma*
> *We are trying to establish contact with any possible survivor of the twenty-piece band stationed on the Battleship* Arizona. *Our son, "Bill" (William Starks Moorhouse), first trumpet in this band, is reported "Missing Following Action," and since receipt of the formal notice from the State Department [sic] we have had no other word.*
>
> *We feel that it would be a source of real comfort to hear from any survivor, or from any of the parents or relatives of other band members.*
>
> *If you have any information whatever, will you please write us? Any information will be so appreciated.*
>
> *Thanking you very kindly for whatever aid you may give us, we are,*
>
> *Gratefully yours, Mr. and Mrs. H. M. Moorhouse.*[4]

On January 14, June Brabbzson, Oran's sister, obtained the names and addresses of the *Arizona* band members from the School of Music and wrote a letter to each of the families in much the same vein.[5]

On February 25, Ralph Burdette's mother Mabel wrote my parents, asking for the addresses of the families which Bonnie had sent them.[6]

From that beginning, the families of *Arizona*'s bandsmen found each other and exchanged letters and personal visits for many years. That network of information became invaluable as we struggled to find out just what had happened to our boys. Each time someone in the network talked to anyone who had been present at Pearl Harbor that day, he passed the word on to the others. Therefore, although never through official channels, we have known almost from the start about our bandsmen's last days of life.

In answer to Bonnie's question about the "Missing" telegram, all except the family of Gerald Cox answered in the affirmative. They wrote that their telegram had stated Gerald had been "Killed in Action."[7]

That caused great distress among the families. They had pictured the band all together, and each family had taken much comfort from the thought that its boy had died among friends. Now, hearing that one body was not with the rest of the band caused them great sadness.

The body of Gerald Cox was the first of three bodies of the *Arizona* bandsmen to be recovered. Gerald was listed from the beginning as "Killed in Action," because his body had been blown into the ocean and was found several days later.

Don Bright, a Marine stationed at Pearl Harbor, found Gerald's body a few days after the attack while out on body patrol. The body was floating under an oil dock, far from the *Arizona*. They had to get a boat to pull it out.[8]

Bright found Gerald's name stenciled on the underside of his skivvy shorts. That explained how Gerald Cox's body was identified so quickly and listed from the beginning as "Killed in Action."[9]

Don Bright said that Gerald's body was in good shape, with no wounds or marks. It appeared to them that he had died from concussion or by drowning.[10] The official "List of Dead" of the U.S. Navy shows the cause of death of Gerald C. Cox, grave number 473, as "Probably drowned."[11]

Gerald was later buried in Punchbowl, the National Cemetery in Honolulu.[12]

Although Bobby Shaw was listed as "Missing Following Action" on both telegrams his family received, his body had, in fact, been recovered.

His family first learned that almost eight months later when, late in July 1942, they received Bobby's high school ring by registered mail from the Navy. It was in an envelope marked with Bobby's name and body number 410. His parents were glad to receive his ring, because Bobby had always been so very proud of it.[13]

Thus, seven months later, we all knew that Bobby Shaw had also been blown off the *Arizona* when she exploded.

The Navy's "List of Dead for Pearl Harbor as of December 7, 1941," gave the cause of death for R. K. Shaw, body number 410, ship unknown, as "Third degree burns and drowning."[14]

Robert K. Shaw was eventually buried in Nuuanu Cemetery in Honolulu.[15]

It says a lot about the type of men who were trying to clean up the mess at Pearl Harbor that Bobby's ring was safely restored to the Shaw family.

By the time the Shaws received Bobby's ring, I was working in Washington, D.C. Pate promptly asked me to try to get my brother's class ring back from the Navy. It took many coffee breaks at work and many telephone calls to find the correct office for information of that sort. The Navy officer kept telling me it would not be possible to find Clyde's ring, but after I persisted, he finally told me that the ring would no longer exist, because it would have melted in that extreme heat.

I sat and cried in that telephone booth for a long time after he told me that.

After believing that their son Jack was buried in the *Arizona* with the rest of the band, the Scruggs family received word from the government in 1949 that Jack's body had now been identified. It was a terrible shock to them, since they did not even know that his body had been recovered.[16]

As soon as the war was over, our government began moving the Pearl Harbor victims' bodies from the temporary cemetery in Hawaii to permanent graves. Jack's body had been identified by his dental records, and the government was holding his body above ground, waiting for his family to designate disposition.[17]

The Scruggs family chose to have Jack's body brought back to Long Beach for burial. He was buried on January 7, 1950, at Sunnyside Memorial Park in Long Beach, California.[18]

And so Jack Scruggs became the only member of *Arizona*'s band to go home, although certainly not in the way he had pictured for so long.

His mother, Mae Scruggs, immediately wrote the other families about that development, so they could prepare themselves for such news about their own sons.[19] There were, however, no more *Arizona* band boys' bodies ever identified.

Jack's burial, eight years after his death, was very hard for the Scruggs family. After a period of healing and after they had resolved Jack's manner of death, they must again face the question: Where was he when he died, and did he suffer?

It again raised our doubts that the bandsmen had been together when they died. We finally came to understand the band's duty in the ammunition hold, as sailors told us how our boys would have been lined up along the hoists, not gathered together in a bunch. We also finally understood the terrible force of that explosion, and how they could very well have been blown off the ship.

As we interviewed everyone we could find who was present that day in Pearl Harbor, we learned early on that one must be very skeptical of eye-witness accounts of anything so totally horrifying as the sneak attack on Pearl Harbor. As with any disaster, the men who were there that day knew only what was happening in their small area—nobody saw the whole picture. For more than fifty years, we have listened, but not always have we believed.

It required many letters over the years among the families to arrive at the truth. Gradually we came to understand why the Navy did not tell us anything about the manner of our boys' deaths. It was not only the secrecy under which we all operated during the war—it was that the Navy just did not know.

In an atmosphere of secrecy, rumors ran wild and largely unchecked. As early as February 1, 1942, the Navy found it necessary to issue a statement denying the "rumor of the bodies."

Shortly after Pearl Harbor, the story began circulating that ships filled with bodies of persons killed in the attack were drifting around in the ocean. According to "people who knew," those ships had come into New York but could not be unloaded because no workmen would take the job.

The Navy tried at first to ignore the ridiculous rumor, but finally had to issue a statement to the press that no such ships existed and that the story was fantastic.[20]

Such rumors were almost unbearable for the families of the Pearl Harbor victims. We were out in limbo, with our loved ones "missing." We could not lay them to rest, since we had no body to bury. We could not bear the thought that their bodies were not being honored.

Shortly after we received the "missing" telegram, a woman told my mother that we should not believe the telegram. She had heard there were many, many sailors in California hospitals, burned so badly that they could not be recognized. She was positive one of those boys was our Clyde, and that someday he would be identified.

That story was, in fact, true, but just how that woman thought it would be of comfort to us has never been clear to me. As horrible as Clyde's death was, and as unspeakable as was the manner in which he died, it was at least final. The picture of him lying in a hospital bed, burned and suffering horribly, and eventually dying with none of his family present, was unbearable.

Many families had to endure that horror, but the families of *Arizona*'s band did not.

Bonnie Moorhouse, as a former Navy nurse, lay awake many long nights thinking about that. She knew, more than we did, how horrible can be the suffering from wounds in war.

We did not fully comprehend the Navy's problem with identifying bodies until some of our musicians' friends came home on leave.

It was of great comfort to us to talk to people who had known and loved our boys.

In January, Betty Kinney, now living in Bremerton with her parents, obtained the names and addresses of the next of kin of Fred's band from the School of Music and wrote each family a letter of sympathy. She too had received her telegram on December 20, but had not been able to write sooner. She guessed that, although the telegram said "missing," that was about all they could say of most of the boys on the *Arizona*.[21]

Betty told us she had talked to some of the band members of the *Tennessee*. The *Tennessee* had not sustained as much damage as the other battleships and was able to leave soon after the attack for Bremerton to undergo extensive repairs, arriving on New Year's Eve, 1942.[22] As soon as the ship arrived, James Smith, *Tennessee*'s bandmaster, went to offer his condolences to his friend's widow.[23]

Smith told her that *Tennessee*'s band had been gathered on the fantail to play for colors when the attack began, and that he was sure *Arizona*'s band had been doing the same thing.[24]

Betty asked if there was any chance any of *Arizona*'s musicians had survived, and he said to be truthful, he did not think so. *Tennessee* had to go right past *Arizona* to get away and to keep from catching fire, forcing the boys in the *Tennessee* band to witness the horrible fire which was all that remained of *Arizona* and to know their good friends were down in that inferno somewhere.[25]

Bandmaster Smith also told Betty he was sure none of our boys suffered, because it had all happened so suddenly.[26]

That statement, "none of the boys knew what hit them," has been repeated to us over and over during the years, and we have clung desperately to that thought.

Betty Kinney also talked with some of the *Tennessee* band members, and it was then she realized how terrible it must have been for them all. She wrote us that Bandmaster Smith and most of his musicians were nervous wrecks, as they never had time to sleep anymore.[27]

We were sorry for the boys in the *Tennessee* band, but we were very, very thankful they had survived.

When Henry Brown, my brother's friend in the *Tennessee* band, came home on leave, he told my parents about seeing Clyde on the night of December 6 and how they planned to visit the Nevada the next day. He added that Clyde seemed happy and cheerful that night, enjoying the music and visiting with his friends.[28]

A year later, Mate received a Mother's Day greeting from H. C. Kane, a Pharmacist's Mate from Pennsylvania. I had met Kane at a dance in Washington, but never saw him again, as he soon shipped out. Kane was so touched about our loss of Clyde that he wrote my parents for many years.

Then stationed in Hawaii, Kane wrote that he had visited Henry Brown aboard the *Tennessee* and had heard the band play the "Star Spangled Banner" as they lowered the flag at dusk. Brownie told him he and Clyde were together on December 6, and had planned to go out the next day together, but as Kane wrote, "This never came about as the yellow rats came in before the boys could carry out their plans."[29]

On April 2, 1942, the Navy released an article regarding the *Arizona* band, and the article was picked up by newspapers all over the country.

After asking what becomes of the boys in the band when the guns begin to roar, the article told how, when the battle at Pearl Harbor began, the musicians in the *Arizona* band went to their battle stations down below. There they began passing ammunition to the guns above. The entire band was killed when the battleship's magazines exploded.

We fervently hoped that article meant our boys did not suffer.

On April 4, Catherine White, Charles' mother, wrote that one of her sons had been able to talk to Radioman First Class John Edward Nichols, who was visiting in Salt Lake City. Nichols, a member of *Arizona*'s crew, had been standing on the dock at the time the ship was destroyed and saw it blow up. He was sure the band and the other men did not know what had happened. He said we should be glad the boys went so quickly and weren't suffering, as were so many who had been so badly burned and wounded in the attack.[30].

It was not always possible for us to talk to the *Arizona* survivors. In Washington, friends of mine obtained the telephone number of one of *Arizona*'s Pharmacist's Mates, who was visiting in Washington. I called him, but he told me emphatically that he could not and would not talk about the attack. He said he had lost all his best friends that day and was just not able to discuss it. He did tell me that yes, he knew my brother, and had been treating Clyde for athlete's foot. Whether true or not, we never did know.

Many of the survivors of the attack did not discuss that day for many years. They knew, as we did, that people just could not understand what we were going through.

Mabel Burdette wrote on April 22:

> *Two young men who were on another ship at Pearl Harbor have just been home in our town on a furlough, but I couldn't bring myself to talk with them—I couldn't have asked the questions I most wanted to know.*
>
> *The mother of one of them talked to me and she said her son was so shocked that he hadn't mentioned it once since he had been home and they hadn't said a word to him in regard to it.*[31]

Late in April, Bonnie Moorhouse read in the paper that one of *Arizona*'s Marines was in Wichita, Kansas, visiting his mother. Bonnie wrote down his telephone number, but decided not to call him after all. She was afraid she would learn some horrible thing about the band that she did not want to know. As we all did, Bonnie preferred to think that our boys went quickly, with no pain.[32]

On August 2, Edna Shaw, Bobby's mother, wrote the parents that she and her husband Therel had heard of an *Arizona* survivor who was visiting in Pasadena, Texas. Therel finally found him at the USO in Houston and went to talk to him, but Therel was so very sorry he had done so. The survivor could not talk about the attack without crying. He had been on shore when the Japs attacked, was wounded, and had spent time in the hospital. He did not know their son Bobby.[33]

In September, Ralph Burdette's mother Mabel went to visit relatives in Kansas City. One day she read in the newspaper that L. P. "Spud" Murphy was a delegate from Hawaii to the American Legion Convention and had brought souvenirs from the *Arizona*.[34]

The souvenirs were on display at one of the local department stores, and Mabel went down to see them. She wrote:

> *There is the flag—all soiled and torn on edge, of course, from the fire, and the uniform of a petty officer who escaped, some coins from a locker of someone, a gun, shrapnel, and bullets taken from wounded and dead on the ship....*
>
> *You don't know what a feeling it gave me to see the flag that our boys had always played for the rising and had been on their ship.*

Mabel went to the hotel where Murphy was staying, and he came down to the lobby to talk to her.

Murphy repeated what we had always heard—that our boys didn't know what had happened, and that *very* few got off the ship. Mabel added: "Of course, he couldn't say the exact number—that isn't permissible, but not very many. I guess that report that Mrs. Kinney heard of 140 is about right."[35]

In reality, the Navy did not know the total number of *Arizona*'s survivors for many years. The number of survivors now given is 337, including all the men who were attached to the ship but were elsewhere on the morning of the attack.[36]

After she was stronger, Bonnie Moorhouse wrote in September:

> *Through a good friend, I contacted a woman near here whose son was a survivor of the* Arizona. *I went to see her one Sunday and had a long talk. I will try to tell you the highlights of the talk.*
>
> *First, she said her son told her they didn't even believe it was the Japs when they were attacked. Her son graduated from Annapolis and was at the time Secretary to the Captain. He was on the second deck and shaving when the attack started.*

He escaped through the hatch. The large heavy cover over the hatch had been blown off from the explosion, otherwise he wouldn't have been able to escape in that manner.

He said the ship was in total darkness from the first and the monoxide gas was terrible. The entire attack lasted only fifteen minutes from the start to finish. He said the men below hadn't a chance in the world.[37]

Bonnie was so thankful the Navy officer had been saved, as his mother was a widow.

Ralph Burdette's parents visited the School of Music in January 1949 and talked with Warrant Officer John Carey, who had been stationed at Pearl Harbor during the attack. Carey was the band-master of the *Argonne* and told her he was in charge of all the bands in the Pacific Fleet. Carey told Mabel Burdette that he doubted very much that *Arizona* was preparing to leave for home on December 7, as *Arizona*'s band had been put on guard duty for the whole day of December 7 and until the next morning. He felt that would not have been done if *Arizona* had been ready to sail.

Carey saw the *Arizona* blow up, and he felt that none of them knew what had struck them. He told her the *Arizona* band was ready to play for colors at the time of the attack and that, of course, all the musicians rushed to their battle stations.[38]

And so we built up our knowledge of our band's last hours. We were always so grateful for the survivors who took the trouble to tell us what they knew.

Most of the information we received was nearly unbearable. The stories of how parts of the bodies of *Arizona*'s crew rained down on the surrounding ships were very difficult for us to hear. We could imagine the horror of those young boys as they saw body parts falling all around them, knowing they belonged to their fellow servicemen.

One of my parents' visitors early in 1942 was an Okmulgee boy who had gone to high school with Clyde. He was a Marine who had been stationed in Pearl Harbor during the attack and had been a member of several body patrols.

Their visitor told my parents that body patrols went out in boats day after day, searching for bodies which kept bobbing up long after the attack. Taking hold of those bodies was a horrible job for our men, most of whom were still young boys.

The boys who had to go out on body patrols did not ever forget it. Several men I interviewed told me that the sights, sounds, and smells of those days still haunt them after all these years.

We were, therefore, not the only ones who struggled for many years with our horror.

Their visitor told my parents that the bodies were placed on the beach in long lines. After listing all identifying marks, the bodies were buried in temporary graves. The Navy encouraged our service-men to walk down those lines of bodies each day, trying to help with the identification.

And their visitor told my parents he had seen Clyde's body lying in that line of unidentified victims.

By then, we had received the second telegram from the Navy, telling us that, after exhaustive search, they had not been able to locate Clyde and had officially declared he had lost his life in the service of his country.

We did not know what to believe.

Fortunately for us all, Ernest Whitson's father left immediately after the attack to work in the Navy ship yards at Pearl Harbor, and eighteen months later, his wife was able to join him. They did much research for all the families of *Arizona*'s band while they were living there.

As soon as Elizabeth Whitson arrived in Pearl Harbor, Mate asked her to contact the Navy about the story of Clyde's body. Ernest, Sr. went to the officials at Pearl Harbor in November 1943 and asked for a check of bodies. He was told he could submit no more than three names and should come back in two days to learn the results.

He submitted the names of his son, Ernest Whitson, Jr., Gerald Cox, and Clyde Williams. When he returned, he was told the Navy had no record of any of the three boys having been found, and that they were all still on the *Arizona*.[39]

Since we all knew that Gerald Cox's body had been found right away, we could see we were on our own as far as obtaining any official information about our boys.

In February 1942, we did not have a photograph of the entire *Arizona* band. After Bonnie Moorhouse established that there had been no survivors of the band, she set out to correct that.

Bill Moorhouse had sent a copy of *The Washington Post* to his parents in May 1941. The newspaper carried a story of the U.S. Navy School of Music and featured a photograph of Fred Kinney's band.

Bonnie wrote the editor of *The Washington Post*, explaining our situation, and asked if he could have twenty-one copies of that photograph made and permit each family to purchase one. Of course I, as the Washington representative of all the families, was sent down to the newspaper to plead our cause.

As another example of the kindness extended to us by total strangers, the Managing Editor of *The Washington Post* had a copy of the photograph sent to each family at no charge. Under the letterhead of *The Washington Post*, dated March 10, 1942, he wrote:

> *My dear Mrs. Williams:*
> *We are very happy to be able to send you the picture of the boys in the band of the Navy School of Music, printed by* The Post *on May fourth.*
> *Under the circumstances, this picture may be very helpful at this time.*
> *Cordially yours,*
> *Alexander F. Jones, Managing Editor*[40]

He was correct—the picture of the band was indeed very helpful to us.

It is strange that one and only one band was photographed at the school that day in May. And that seven months later, one and only one band was wiped out at Pearl Harbor that day in December.

Then began a flurry of correspondence as each family tried to identify its son. To their dismay, not all the members of the band appeared in the picture. Mr. Burruss took the photograph at the

School of Music early in May. Since Kinney was still changing his musicians all during the month of May, the last members to be taken into his band do not appear in the photograph.

The boys' families were very disappointed that their musician was missing from the photograph. They were even more upset when they realized how close their boy had come to being spared.

The boys not shown in *The Washington Post* photograph are Bandy, Cox, Hughes, Hurley, Lynch, Nadel, Radford, and White.

Over the years, the myth of the famous "Last Photograph of the *Arizona* Band" has grown so much that almost every book on the *Arizona* features the photograph with the caption that it was taken on the last night of the band's life. That is one of the things which makes good copy in a book or newspaper article. The only problem is—it is just not true.

The Navy released the photograph of the *Arizona* band, along with the following press release, to the newspapers a few months after the band's death:

> *Navy Band That Was Silenced:*
> *On December 7 the entire membership of the band of the USS* Arizona *was lost when the battleship was attacked by the Japanese. This photograph of the band orchestra, prob ably the last taken of it entire, has just been released for publication by the Navy. The band was one of the best in the 14th Naval District and often gave much pleasure to music-lovers. It is shown with a background of sailors at Pearl Harbor. The contest trophy won by the* Arizona *in the "Battle of the Bands" not long before December 7 was post-humously [sic] awarded to the members by vote of all the competing orchestras.*[41]

As soon as that photograph was published, my parents requested a copy from the Navy.

The appearance of the sign from the *California* band next to *Arizona*'s band proves the photograph was taken at the "Battle of Music 1941" on November 22, since neither the *California* band nor the *Arizona* band played on the night of December 6.

The presence of the string bass and guitars in the photograph and the absence of the heavy brass shows it was *Arizona*'s dance orchestra and not her entire concert band. Therefore, five members of the band are not shown in the picture—Brabbzson and Burdette on French horn; Hurley on clarinet; McCary on bass; and Radford on baritone.

From the beginning, the families searched for photographs of their boys. Of great help to all of us was the Hurley family, who shared the photographs from Wendell's album.

With the exception of that album, it is now almost impossible to state which musician actually snapped the pictures we have collected over the years. Each picture has been sent to so many families that, in most cases, we have lost track of the originator.

In addition to the photographs, the mothers began scrapbooks and exchanged newspaper articles about their sons.

I was always convinced that my brother had his photograph made for me for Christmas, since I had asked him so often to do so. We did not know anyone in Honolulu then, but we knew *Arizona*'s band had played for a ship's dance on November 24 at the Moana Hotel. From that faint clue, we wrote the manager of the Moana Hotel to ask for the names of any Honolulu photographers we might contact.

Mrs. M. Tragella graciously questioned all the photographers she could find, but discovered that most of them had packed up their photos and gone to war. She added: "May I take this opportunity of expressing my sympathy to you in the loss of your son. While I did not know him personally, I saw the orchestra the night they played here, and thought them a very, very fine lot of young men."[42]

I also wrote the Chamber of Commerce in Honolulu. They ran my story in the newspaper and Don Senick, who owned his own studio in Honolulu, responded. In another act of extreme kindness, Mr. Senick sent us some photographs he had taken earlier of Clyde Williams. He said Clyde had already picked up his photos, but no doubt they had been destroyed with his ship.[43]

There were several very good photographs in the packet Mr. Senick sent, but unfortunately, they were not of our Clyde. Over the years, we have tried to find the other Clyde Williams to send the photographs to his family, but have not been successful.

Our only clue to the snapshots which Clyde took in Hawaii was a receipt from the "Grass Shack" for rolls of film Clyde had left there for developing. The receipt was included in the contents of Clyde's locker on shore, which the Navy sent to us long after the attack.

Later, when Ernest Whitson's parents went to Hawaii to work, they tried very hard to find the "Grass Shack." It had moved, but they persisted, spending their days off searching for the shop. They were not successful in finding it.[44]

And so, little by little and with the kindness of many people we did not even know, the families gradually gathered their collections of photographs of the *Arizona* band and of its musicians.

The "story of the bugle" is one puzzle I was never able to solve.

When Mate attended a Navy Mothers Convention in Dallas, Texas, in March 1944, a Navy Mother told her in the restroom that her son had a trumpet from the *Arizona*. Mate immediately told her that it was her son's trumpet!

Of course, Mate had no way of knowing that. There were four cornet players in *Arizona*'s band, plus the buglers, so that instrument could have belonged to any of them.

But we have wondered all these years, "What if it really was Clyde's cornet?"

After I began researching this book in 1993, I accidently found a few clues about the "bugle story." They did not solve it completely, but did seem to add up.

In 1994, former Coxswain James Leamon Forbis told me an interesting story. Forbis, a survivor of the *Arizona*, saw one of the buglers on *Arizona* drop his bugle as he ran to his battle station on the morning of December 7.[45]

Later, I read an account of Edward A. Teats of the U.S. Navy, who had been stationed on Ford Island. On the morning of December 7, as he was running to his battle station, the *Arizona* suddenly blew up and a bugle from the ship landed about twenty feet from him. He picked it up and ran on to his station.[46]

That bugle is now in the Navy Historical Museum in Washington, D.C.[47]

The same bugle? I will probably never know.

It would indeed be strange if any of the band's instruments had
been blown from the ship. The band room was right across from the
ammunition hold for turret two. The instruments would more likely
have melted together into a mass. But stranger things than that
happened in *Arizona*'s blast that morning.

My favorite "sea story" happened in December 1942 to Ralph's
parents, Mabel and Harry Burdette. They had gone to Atlantic City
to attend a Grange Convention. They were startled to see signs of
war everywhere in Atlantic City. Most of the hotels had been taken
over by the military and our troops drilled on the boardwalks and
down all the streets.

After their evening meeting, the Burdettes returned to the lobby
of their hotel to find it filled with servicemen. Several men were standing in a group, singing old songs.

During the war, most of us were far away from home. Often, when
groups of servicemen and civilians were thrown together, someone
would begin singing and all would join in. Music, the common language, was our way of relieving tension and of remembering home
for awhile.

Mabel Burdette was an accomplished pianist and had often played
accompaniment for Ralph when he was living at home. She immediately moved to the piano and played for the singing until 2:00 A.M.

After the songfest broke up, everyone began drifting up the stairs
to their rooms. As Mabel climbed the stairs, she looked back and saw
a Navy boy sitting alone in the lobby. The sailor appeared to be so
sad that she had an overpowering urge to go back down and speak to
him.

Mabel introduced herself and told the sailor about her Navy son
and what had happened to him. He replied that his two brothers
also went down on the *Arizona*, and that they, too, were passing
ammunition. Mabel was very moved to think that his brothers were
with our boys at the end.

She immediately wrote all the families about the sailor, and we all took much comfort from that story.[48]

We did not know enough about the ship then to realize that there was more than one ammunition hold, so we clung to the idea that our boys were surrounded by friends at the end. It was always very important to us that they had not died alone.

We have treasured that story for fifty years. Unfortunately, I cannot find those brothers' names on any of the crew lists for the *Arizona*.

And another favorite story was laid to rest.

We did not have to wait long after the attack to begin hearing the negative gossip about our servicemen in Hawaii that we were to hear all our lives. Right away, we realized that the most learned and expert authorities on the Pearl Harbor attack were those people who were not even there that morning.

Thus, the minister of our church in Okmulgee arose in his pulpit on Sunday, December 14, just a week after the attack, and thundered that all our servicemen were taken by surprise by the Japanese because they were all lying around on the beach drunk, after carousing all night in Honolulu. Just how that minister could possibly know that, living as he did in Oklahoma and having never been to Hawaii, is one of the mysteries we often encountered.

Fortunately for him, we were not present in his church that morning, but we heard about his sermon from many irate friends.

Newspapers were also repeating that nonsense, and the survivors of the attack have been denying the rumor ever since.

The truth is that the servicemen at Pearl Harbor were the same as citizens of any city—some of them drank a lot of liquor, some of them drank a little liquor, and some of them did not drink at all.

Over the years, we have been told that our servicemen in Hawaii were drunk, disorderly, not on duty, in bed asleep, panicky, untrained, hung over, cowardly, privileged, pampered, and many more epitaphs.

The only problem for all those gossipmongers is that there are men who served at Pearl Harbor that day who know differently.

And the boys who lost their lives in the attack had friends. And their friends took the trouble to look us up and to tell us the truth.

In that manner, piece by piece, we finally solved the puzzle of our boys' last hours. Much of what we learned was very painful to hear, but it was better than not knowing.

And all that we learned filled us with pride.

CHAPTER 22

We Grieve

There has never been such a shock to this nation, neither before nor after, which would ever compare to the Japanese attack on Pearl Harbor.

On a national level, the publicity concerning the attack did not ever subside. For those of us who were living in 1941, that horror and rage were never forgotten. Even after fifty years, many of us cannot talk about the treachery of Japan without crying.

And oh, the many times we were to see the picture of the *Arizona* blowing up, both in our newspapers and in our newsreels at the movies. It simply tore out our hearts every time we saw it—and we were to see it over and over for more than fifty years.

When you love someone deeply, he or she becomes a permanent part of your very soul. Therefore, it is not possible to recover completely from the loss of a vital part of your being.

It is even harder to recover from the senseless murder of your child.

The families of the musicians on the *Arizona* went through all the classic stages of grief for many, many years.

There was no end to the shocks we received for so long after Pearl Harbor.

First, of course, was the attack itself, catching us all by surprise, and the endless wait for some word of our loved one. By the time the telegram finally came, most of the families were prepared for the worst. But how does one prepare for such an unspeakable horror?

The Whitsons received their son's last letter on the morning of December 20. In it, he told them to cross their fingers, because he might be coming home for Christmas. A few hours later, his "Missing" telegram was delivered to their home.[1]

Because Elizabeth Haas had never officially adopted her stepson, his "Missing" telegram was delivered to Curt's relative in another town. Notice that he was missing appeared in the *Kansas City Times* on Christmas Eve, but Elizabeth's family withheld that information from her until after Christmas dinner the next day. Immediately upon hearing the news, Elizabeth went to a hotel in Kansas City and stayed there alone for several days.[2]

With shock came numbness. Unable to comprehend such horror, our minds darted from one thought to another.

We concentrated on getting out of bed and getting to work. We told ourselves we could do that—just walk, putting one foot in front of the other—left—right—left—right. That was all we could manage for awhile.

On February 3, 1942, the Navy released the official photograph of the *Arizona* as she now looked.[3] We were heartbroken. The beautiful *Arizona*, of which our boys had been so proud, lying in the water, broken and dead. We could picture our boys also lying in the water, broken and dead.

So when, on February 6, we received the last telegram from the Navy, it was no shock to us—we already knew it was all over. We had seen the picture of our boys' beloved Admiral and had read that he was dead. We had heard Japan bragging to one and all that they had sunk the *Arizona*.

The Navy stated that: "After exhaustive search, it has been found impossible to locate your son...and he has therefore been officially declared to have lost his life in the service of his country as of December Seventh Nineteen Forty One. The Department expresses to you its sincerest sympathy."

It was then we realized we had no body to bury and no funeral to arrange. We could not even tell our boys good-bye.

After that came the constant stream of letters and Christmas packages which our boys had sent us before they died. Seeing their handwriting, when we knew they would never write again, was very painful.

Equally painful was the receipt of all the letters and Christmas packages we had sent them. For a long time those items were returned to us with "Dead—Return to Sender" stamped on the outside.

The Navy sent the contents of my brother's locker, which he had rented on shore. Included in the box was his camera, which he had not been allowed to take onto the ship, and a receipt for the film he had left at the "Grass Shack." We were never able to find those invaluable pictures.

Our main emotion in the beginning was denial—this could not be happening to us, and it certainly could not be happening to our boys. We were, after all, good people—we were living in a good country. God would not let something this bad happen to His good people.

For a long time, we denied the horror with all our beings. If we stood firm, it would all go away.

We suffered from the "Maybes." Maybe our loved one had been ashore that morning and was safe—maybe the *Arizona* had gone to sea—maybe he was only injured—maybe he was all right.

Even after we received the "Missing" telegram, we hoped against hope. We had not yet comprehended the total destruction that was now *Arizona*. We told ourselves that if the Navy had not been able to find their bodies, there was still a chance they could have survived. Our boys were excellent swimmers—maybe they had been able to swim out of danger.

With no bodies to finalize their deaths, we always had the feeling that they were somewhere, wandering around with amnesia, and that we must go find them. I looked for my brother for many years, staring intently into the faces of anyone who even faintly reminded me of him.

We spent many sleepless nights, picturing them lying in a hospital in great pain, horribly burned and unrecognizable, but still alive.

And we were so angry! From the first radio broadcast we heard of the Pearl Harbor attack, our entire nation rose up in fury.

Everyone looked for some way to get even with Japan. Our only thought was to "Beat the Japs" and to "knock off a few of those yellow dogs." We took comfort from the boys who wrote how many Japs they had taken out.

Most of the brothers and sisters of the *Arizona* bandsmen left home to join the service or to accept a defense job in another city.

Their mothers wondered how long it would be before they saw them again, if ever. We all had the feeling that, if it could happen to us once, it could happen to us many times.

Pate tried to enlist in the Army, but was rejected. Ernest Whitson's father signed up for duty in the Pearl Harbor Navy Yard, and worked there for several years.[4]

After I began working in Washington, I tried to transfer to Pearl Harbor, but was turned down. At that time, only wives of men already working there were allowed to live in Hawaii.

Most of us became very resentful. We resented the dangerous duty the Navy had assigned our boys, as if musicians were expendable.

As the government opened its veil of secrecy little by little, we learned that it was not the men on our ships who were asleep that morning, as we had been told. It was our government and military leaders who were asleep, and we became very disillusioned.

The Pearl Harbor attack ended the era of peace in our country forever. We were never the same after that—not the same country, not the same people, not the same way of life. Our Age of Innocence was over—an Age when we thought we could trust our government to do the best for us.

The War of Red Tape began almost immediately after the attack, and lasted for more than seven years. While the parents of the victims were still numb with grief, they began receiving official government forms to be filled out in triplicate and returned to the respective offices. The forms were to ascertain their qualifications for various benefits stemming from their sons' deaths.

Most of the parents were rejected for benefits because of their lack of financial dependency on their sons, and, in some cases, even payment of the boys' life insurance was denied. None of the parents were reimbursed for their son's clothing or musical instruments.

Of most concern to the parents was the controversy over the granting of six months' pay to the next of kin of the Pearl Harbor victims. In the beginning, Congress stated that the six months' gratuity would be awarded only to persons who were dependent on the victim.

However, when some families were granted the six months' gratuity and some were not, the families became very resentful. Pate vented his feelings to the Secretary of the Navy Frank Knox and to his Congressmen on June 17, 1942. In his letter, Pate reviewed his son's service record with the Navy, and stated: "I am very proud of my son's record with the U.S. Navy. I wonder if Clyde would be proud as he was when he was living of the Navy if he knew what the Navy did to him after he died."

After reviewing his efforts to fill out all the application forms, only to be told he was not a dependent of Clyde's, Pate told Secretary Knox that he agreed with most of the Navy's decisions on his application. However, he strongly objected to its decision to pay the six months' gratuity only to the dependents of the deceased. He wrote:

> *I procured a copy of the law covering such cases and was very much surprised to find that our Congress had passed such a discriminatory act. It is not only discriminatory, it is rotten as hell to give a $5,000.00 life insurance policy to one boy who was killed in action at Pearl Harbor and give nothing to another boy who was killed at the same place and at the same time. It cannot be said that the dependent parents need the insurance or the six months pay to buy beans or biscuits. The pension takes care of their daily needs.*
>
> *I am not saying that the Navy owes me anything, but I take it as an insult to my son for the Navy to say to some of the boys killed at Pearl Harbor, "We are going to give your parents $5,000.00 and an amount equal to six months of your pay" and to my son who was also killed in action at Pearl Harbor, "We are not going to give your parents anything."*
>
> *I think, with the exception of the pension, if the Navy is going to give anything to one parent, they should give it to all parents, and if they can't give it to all parents, they shouldn't give it to any. Dependency should not enter into anything except the pension. So I guess the Navy and I are about square now unless they send me a bill for my son's board and room while he was stationed on the battleship. If I am supposed to*

> *pay for his board and room, because I didn't prove dependency,*
> *I would appreciate it if you will arrange it for me to take care*
> *of it in monthly payments, as I have what little surplus cash I*
> *have on hand tied up in War Bonds.*[5]

Whether or not Frank Knox ever read that letter, I do not know. But certainly the public outrage was heard by Congress. Because by now, some reports were filtering out to the public about the inefficiency and mistakes of our high government and military officials. Our citizens took up the cause of the "six months' pay" for all the victims of the Pearl Harbor fiasco, and clamored for justice for their parents.

In November 1942, the parents were notified by the Navy that, by a recent decision of the Comptroller General and by directive of the Secretary of the Navy, the six months' death gratuity would be paid to the parents of all the boys who were killed at Pearl Harbor that day.[6]

So finally, on November 19, 1942, almost a year after their sons had been killed, the parents of *Arizona*'s musicians were sent a check for $448.80, representing their sons' last six months' pay.[7]

Each parent was in different circumstances, and they wrote each other for many years, struggling to understand all that red tape. Several families finally retained an attorney to help them.

We resented the complaints we heard from civilians about shortages of sugar, coffee, butter, meat, silk hose, and gasoline. Compared to our loss, such matters seemed trivial to us.

As one mother wrote, "When they have to give up a loved one, then they'll realize something about what war means."

Grief is a lonely path to follow. It was not long after our "Missing" telegrams finally arrived that the families of the *Arizona* bandsmen realized it would be better if we did not discuss our grief with outsiders. Any attempt to describe our inner feeling invariably led to the usual "Buck Up" pep talks.

We had not heard of support groups then, nor did we know anything about the stages of grief. But we sorely needed someone to whom we could bare our souls—someone who would not think we were just rolling in self-pity.

That need was met by the families of the other boys, and the mothers wrote each other for years, describing their innermost feelings.

As one mother remarked: "It seems sort of comforting to me to hear from them all, and have some idea of the different boys in the band, for they were all so closely associated together. The terrible loss, at least to me, makes me feel as though we were one big family—drawn together through the loss of our boys."

Reading their letters, which expressed such raw grief, is much like reading a very private diary. At first, the mothers wrote of complete and total despair. They were so broken up it seemed they would never get over it. The remaining years stretched endlessly before them, but they knew they would have to go on living until it was their time.

The war news was so bleak that our whole nation was depressed. The mothers of the *Arizona* bandsmen knew what was in store for the families who would soon face the same tragedy with which we were struggling, and they prayed those mothers would be given strength. As one mother put it, "I wish I could help all these mothers who have lost their sons, but I guess they will just do as we did and suffer as we did also."

They prayed for the end of the war, and wondered how the world had gotten into such a mess. They hoped our boys had not given their lives in vain, but that their sacrifice would end wars forever.

Music was especially hard for us. We had listened for so many years to our boys as they practiced their musical instruments in our homes, and now all music reminded us of our loss.

For a long time, we tortured ourselves with the "What-If" game. "What if" our musicians had not joined the Navy, or "what if" they had failed their physical or musical tests, or "what if" we had not signed the consent for them to enlist? We blamed the Navy for not having given them the two years in the School of Music they had been promised.

And most of all, "what if" the *Arizona* and the *Tennessee* bands had not been switched at the last minute?

We soon realized we must not play the "What-If" game anymore, because at the end of that road lay severe depression and illness.

Over the years, we have been plagued with many regrets.

The parents' biggest regret was that they did not see their sons before they shipped out. Money was so very tight then, but they were always sorry they did not find some way to go visit them.

And we never forgave the Navy for not allowing our boys to have that last leave before they shipped out.

We regret not knowing our boys after they became men and not being able to meet their wives and children.

We regret that they had so little time and were cheated out of their lives.

We regret that they were not able to finish their song.

We regret that they were forced to give their lives for people who were not worthy of such sacrifice.

We regret that their deaths did not end all wars, as we had hoped.

We regret that people are rewriting the history of our war, with little regard to the true facts.

We were never the same people after the Pearl Harbor attack. It takes good health to stand up under so much grief, and it was inevitable that our grief led to physical problems. The doctors could do little for us, except tell us that our nerves had been weakened by the shock.

We often said that our boys were the light of our lives, the light had gone out, and now there was nothing left but darkness.

With time, most of us finally conquered those negative emotions and returned to the light.

As we accepted the unspeakable thing which had happened to us, we finally put aside our grief for the sake of the other members of our families.

We learned to cling to the good memories we had of our boys and to be grateful for the few years we had with them. We found that if we did not take time to think, we could get through the day much better.

We taught ourselves to think of our boys as being away on a long journey and we pictured them playing in another band somewhere. But the truth was, of course, that our boys were not just away on a long journey—their journey took just a few seconds and ended instantly in a blinding flash.

Rather, it was their families who took the long journey—a journey which lasted for the rest of our lives.

We kept busy and tried to help others. Most of the parents joined local volunteer groups and formed the first service clubs in their areas. They served in the Gold Star Mothers clubs, the Navy Mothers clubs, and worked at the USO clubs, mothering the servicemen who visited there.

My parents, as representatives of the Red Cross, went to call on all the local families shortly after they received their telegrams. In order to save gasoline ration coupons for that service, Pate rode his bicycle to work every day.

Oran Brabbzson's mother took a nurse's training course and helped deliver her neighbor's baby.

It was a long time before we knew the whole story of the unspeakable horror that began with Pearl Harbor. As we learned more and more of the facts of the surprise attack, and as we heard what was happening to our soldiers in the Philippines, we began to realize that perhaps our boys had been fortunate. If they had to die, better they died right away in a quick flash, rather than go through what our American boys were enduring in other parts of the world.

As we read how the Japanese were torturing our boys in the Pacific and about the death march in Bataan, we began to comprehend the type of enemy we were facing. And we understood at last that sometimes there are worse things than death.

The mothers told each other that we would not have to worry now about our boys falling into the hands of the Japanese or the Nazis. They shuddered to think of our boys as prisoners of such fiends as we were hearing about. They wondered if they could have endured having our boys missing, with no chance ever to know if they were dead or alive.

And they told each other that our boys had perhaps missed a lot of grief and suffering, and that they were doing what they loved up to the very last minute.

It was always the dream of the families of the *Arizona* bandsmen to have a reunion and meet all the friends who had helped them so much. They planned to gather somewhere in the Midwest, to make it convenient for the families who lived on both coasts.

During the war, with the shortage of gasoline and the uncertainty of commercial travel, their reunion did not seem feasible.

Later, although many of the families did visit each other for many years, the reunion of all the families did not ever materialize.

An important step toward healing from such a shock as was the Pearl Harbor attack is understanding. None of the parents of the boys on the *Arizona* ever mastered that step.

We did not ever understand why Pearl Harbor was allowed to happen, nor why our boys had to be sacrificed.

Our boys had told us what a powerful Navy we had, and that we must not worry about them, because they were so very safe. After all, they said, was not our country the strongest in the world?

It would seem not, judging from the news coming out of Pearl Harbor.

We waited and prayed for the war to end. One mother expressed it for us all: "Maybe this mess will be over soon and won't it be wonderful? But so sad too. When we think of our broken homes that will never be the same. Maybe someday we can understand why."

But we never did.

PHOTOGRAPHS FROM THE COLLECTIONS OF
AUTHOR AND OF HER PARENTS,
DICK AND JANE WILLIAMS, DECEASED

Clyde R. Williams, Okmulgee,
Oklahoma, January 10, 1941.
Photo taken the day before he left
home for the last time.
(Photographer: Author)

Dinky, Okmulgee, Oklahoma,
January 10, 1941. Author's
brother ended every letter to his
family with "Take care of Dink."
Dinky died in 1944.
(Photographer: Author)

From left to right, William S. Moorhouse, his dog Bruno, his mother Bonnie, and his brother Robert W. Moorhouse, Erie, Pennsylvania, 1940. (Courtesy Moorhouse family)

From left to right, Jane Williams, her son Clyde, and her daughter Molly Williams, Okmulgee, Oklahoma, January 10, 1941. (Photographer: Dick Williams)

Ralph W. Burdette and his dogs, Plainfield, New Jersey, 1941.
(Courtesy Burdette family)

From left to right, Oran Milton Brabbzson,
Violet Brabbzson, and their son Oran
Merrill Brabbzson, East Meadow, Long
Island, New York, 1940. (Courtesy
Brabbzson family)

Frank W. Floege, 1940.
(*Chicago Times*, April 2, 1941.
Courtesy Warren O. H. Floege)

William M. McCary, 1941. (*The Birmingham News*, February 1, 1941)

Gerald C. Cox, April 1941.
(*Moline [Illinois] Daily Dispatch*, April 11, 1942.
Courtesy Cox family)

Jack L. Scruggs, 1941. (Courtesy Pauline Scruggs Ellis)

Wendell R. Hurley, 1941. (Courtesy Hurley family)

Fred W. Kinney's band at the U.S. Navy School of Music, Washington, D.C., in early April 1941. Eight musicians pictured here were replaced before the band graduated May 27, 1941. (Photographer: Mr. Burrus of *The Washington Post*. ©1941, Washington Post Writers Group. Reprinted with permission.)

Arizona band members appearing in *The Washington Post* photograph: (1) Floege, (2) Sanderson, (3) Kinney, (4) McCary, (5) Whitson, (6) Chernucha, (7) Haas, (8) Burdette, (9) Brabbzson, (10) Moorhouse, (11) Scruggs, (12) Shaw, (13) Williams. Musicians not appearing, but added to Kinney's *Arizona* band before graduation were: Bandy, Cox, Hughes, Hurley, Lynch, Nadel, Radford, and White.

One hundred sixty musicians, including the new *Arizona* band, and eight new bandmasters at their graduation exercises, May 23, 1941. This was the largest graduating class in the history of the U.S. Navy School of Music at that time, and reflects the prewar speed-up of our armed forces. Seated on the front row, from left to right, are the graduating bandmasters: F. B. Donovan, 1st Musician; T. G. Carlin, 1st Musician; J. A. Simpson, 1st Musician; Bandmaster L. B. Luckenbach; Bandmaster M. V. Spencer; F. W. Kinney, 1st Musician; H. J. Beauregard, 1st Musician; L. J. Breaux, 1st Musician. Standing: Lieutenant Charles Benter; Commander R. A. Dyer. (Official U.S. Navy Photo. *Our Navy*, July 1941. Courtesy John Crawford and Dr. Walter Wenner)

U.S. Navy School of Music barracks at the Navy Yard, Washington, D.C., March 1941. (Photographer: Wendell R. Hurley. Courtesy Hurley family)

Clyde R. Williams,
Annapolis, Maryland,
May 24, 1941.
(Photogragher: Author)

Author (lower right) and students from the U.S.
Navy School of Music at Mother Steed's Soldiers,
Sailors, and Marines Club, Washington, D.C., May
25, 1941. (Photographer: J. L. Reed)

Wayne L. Bandy on deck of *District of Columbia* as the *Arizona* band began its transfer from Washington, D.C., to the USS *Arizona*, May 26, 1941. (Photographer: Jack L. Scruggs. Courtesy Scruggs and Bandy families)

Ernest H. Whitson, Jr., Long Beach, California, June 1941. (Photographer: Wendell R. Hurley. Courtesy Hurley family)

Charles W. White, Long Beach, California, June 1941. (Photographer: Wendell R. Hurley. Courtesy Hurley family)

Harry G. Chernucha, Long Beach, California, June 1941. (Photographer: Wendell R. Hurley. Courtesy Hurley family)

From left to right, Emmett I. Lynch, James H. Sanderson, Curtis J. Haas, Long Beach, California, June 1941. (Courtesy Scruggs family)

From left to right, Curtis J. Haas, Jack L. Scruggs, Wayne L. Bandy, Long Beach, California, June 1941. (Courtesy Scruggs family and Ruth Cadwell Sanders)

From left to right, Jack L. Scruggs, Alexander J. Nadel, James H. Sanderson, Hawaii, July 1941. (Courtesy Scruggs family)

USS *Arizona* (BB 39). (Official U.S. Navy Photo)

Front row, unidentified boy. From left to right, back row, James H. Sanderson, Jack L. Scruggs, Clyde R. Williams, Hawaii, July 1941. (Photographer: Wendell R. Hurley. Courtesy Hurley family)

Royal Hawaiian and Moana Hotels, July 1941. (Photographer: Wendell R. Hurley. Courtesy Hurley family)

Neal J. Radford, Hawaii, July
1941. (Photographer: Wendell R.
Hurley. Courtesy Hurley family)

From left to right, Oran M. Brabbzson, Jack L. Scruggs, James H.
Sanderson, Bernard T. Hughes, Gerald C. Cox, Clyde R. Williams, Neal J.
Radford, Alexander J. Nadel, Hawaii, July 1941. (Photographer: Wendell R.
Hurley. Courtesy Hurley family)

Alexander J. Nadel, Hawaii,
July 1941. (Photographer:
Wendell R. Hurley. Courtesy
Hurley family)

From left to right, Alexander J. Nadel, Jack L. Scruggs, Clyde R.
Williams, Wendell R. Hurley. Far right, unidentified boy, Hawaii,
July 1941. (Courtesy Hurley family)

Robert K. Shaw, Hawaii, July 1941. (Courtesy Scruggs family)

From left to right, front row, Harry G. Chernucha, Bernard T. Hughes, Emmett I. Lynch, Curtis J. Haas. Back row, James H. Sanderson, Jack L. Scruggs, Ernest H. Whitson, Robert K. Shaw, Hawaii, July 1941. (Courtesy Scruggs family)

Emmett I. Lynch, Hawaii, August 1941. (Courtesy Scruggs family)

From left to right, front row, unidentified coxswain from *Arizona*, Robert K. Shaw. Back row, Ernest H. Whitson, Jr., unidentified boy, Clyde R. Williams, Jack L. Scruggs, William S. Moorhouse, Hawaii, August 1941. (Courtesy Shaw family)

Arizona band loading bus in Hawaii, August 1941. (Photographer: Jack L. Scruggs. Courtesy Scruggs family and Ruth Cadwell Sanders)

Arizona band holding jam session on bus in Hawaii, August 1941. (Courtesy Scruggs family and Ruth Cadwell Sanders)

Arizona band practicing on beach in Hawaii, August
1941. (Photographer: Jack L. Scruggs. Courtesy
Scruggs family)

Arizona band in concert, Fred W. Kinney, bandmaster. Army and Navy
YMCA, Honolulu, 30 August 1941. (Official U.S. Navy Photo)

Arizona dance band, Bloch Arena, Pearl Harbor, during Battle of Music 1941 semifinal contest, November 22, 1941. The *Arizona* band won second place in that contest and was scheduled to compete with the bands from the USS *Tennessee*, the Marine Barracks, and the USS *Pennsylvania* in the final Battle of Music on December 20, 1941. That final contest was never held, due to the Japanese attack on Pearl Harbor on December 7, 1941. (Photographer: Tai Sing Loo. Official U.S. Navy Photo)

Members of the *Arizona* dance band appearing in its last photograph are: (1) Haas, (2) Cox, (3) Whitson, (4) Floege, (5) Williams, (6) Hughes, (7) Nadel, (8) White, (9) Shaw, (10) Chernucha, (11) Moorhouse, (12) Lynch, (13) Bandy, (14) Scruggs, (15) Sanderson, (16) Kinney. *Arizona* band members not shown in the photograph are: Brabbzson, Burdette, Radford, McCary, and Hurley.

Arizona Band Trophy, 1941. (Official U.S. Navy Photo)

Painting of *Arizona* Band Trophy by Alfred Dupont, 1942.
(Official U.S. Navy Photo)

USS *Arizona*'s powder magazines exploding during the Japanese attack on Pearl Harbor, T.H., December 7, 1941. At this exact moment, the lives of *Arizona* and most of her crew, including the twenty-one members of her U.S. Navy Band Number 22, ended forever. (Official U.S. Navy Photo)

Honor Roll, U.S. Navy School of Music, 1942. (Courtesy Boatswain's Mate James M. Thurmond)

Part III

REQUIEM FOR THE BAND

TRANQUILLO

I lay upon a grassy plain
Below the clouds in merry mood.
The sun made bright the sky and air,
And grass blades thru my fingers stood.

Soon shattered was my solitude,
The sky was wont to pitch and moan.
Blood has stained the blades of grass
And I see I'm not alone.

I sit up now and look about
The plain — a battlefield.
My solitude is drowned in shouts,
The grass by sod is sealed.

Wake not O heroes—sleep ye on
The earth is barren now and chilled,
Beauty that was once a song
Died in the earth's throat—unfulfilled.

Come—let's start the song again.
The blood will fade—the noise will cease,
The sun and grass will come again
And I can lie back down in peace.

Jack Leo Scruggs, Apprentice Seaman,
who was a member of *ARIZONA*'s Last Band.
Written while he was a student at the
U.S. Navy School of Music,
March 13, 1941

CHAPTER 23

Obituaries

The United States Navy Band Number 22 graduated from the U.S. Navy School of Music in Washington, D.C., on May 23, 1941. Its musicians reported on board the *Arizona* on June 17, 1941, and served on her until December 7, 1941. All twenty-one members of the band were killed at Pearl Harbor, Territory of Hawaii, during the sneak attack by the Japanese upon our military installations.

Their names are engraved on the marble wall of the Shrine Room of the USS *Arizona* Memorial at Pearl Harbor, Hawaii.

FREDERICK WILLLIAM KINNEY, Musician First Class, USN, was from Ashland, Kentucky. He was bandmaster of the *Arizona* band and was an accomplished baritone player.

He was born in 1910 in Ashland, the son of George and Mary (John) Kinney of Ashland. He graduated in May 1926 from high school in Ashland, where he was a member of the band and orchestra.

He joined the U.S. Navy in 1926. He served in the bands of the *Idaho*, the *Argonne*, and at the Puget Sound Navy Yard.

Fred married Elizabeth (Betty) Marie Von Babo of Bremerton, Washington, on June 10, 1938, in San Pedro, California. She was the daughter of Alexander F. and Mary (Redding) Von Babo of Bremerton.

In 1940, he was transferred to the U.S. Navy School of Music for bandmaster training. His wife Betty was with him in Washington, D.C., while he attended the School of Music.

He held the rate of Musician First Class when his new band graduated from the U.S. Navy School of Music.

Frederick William Kinney was thirty-one years old when he died. His body was never recovered.[1]

WAYNE LYNN BANDY, Musician Second Class, USN, was from Waynesville, Missouri. He played cornet in the *Arizona* band and orchestra and was one of the singers in the band.

He was born October 14, 1920, in Broken Bow, Oklahoma, the son of the Reverend John Livingston and Mattie Mae (Davis) Bandy. At the time of Wayne's death, his father was minister of the Baptist Church in Waynesville.

Wayne attended schools in Walters, Maude, and Skiatook, Oklahoma, and in Waynesville.

He graduated in May 1939 from Waynesville High School. He was a member of the high school bands and orchestras in Skiatook and in Waynesville. He won several first place awards in high school competitions with his cornet solos, both in Oklahoma and Missouri.

In addition to music, Wayne excelled in swimming, tennis, and softball.

After trying unsuccessfully to find work in Oklahoma City and in Waynesville, Wayne enlisted in the U.S. Navy in September 1940. He attended boot camp at the Naval Training Station in Great Lakes, Illinois, and reported to the U.S. Navy School of Music in October. He was granted a fifteen-day leave on December 29, 1940, and went home for the last time.

He held the rate of Seaman Second Class when he graduated from the U.S. Navy School of Music.

A memorial service was held for Wayne early in 1942 at the Baptist Church in Waynesville.

In addition to his parents, Wayne was survived by his brothers, Kenneth Paul Bandy, John Merle Bandy, Glenn Reed Bandy, and James Houston Bandy, and by a sister, Onita Ruth (Bandy) Till.

Wayne Lynn Bandy was twenty-one years old when he died. His body was never recovered.[2]

ORAN MERRILL BRABBZSON, Musician Second Class, USN, was from East Meadow, Long Island, New York. He played French horn in the *Arizona* band.

He was born July 14, 1922, the son of Oran Milton and Violet Brabbzson, and was raised in East Meadow. His father was a veteran of World War I, a member of the Disabled American Veterans, and was a former commander of the American Legion post in East Meadow. At the time of Oran's death, his mother was president of the American Legion Auxiliary.

Oran graduated in May 1940 from Hempstead High School in Long Island, where he was a member of the high school band and orchestra. He also played in the college band and the Nassau Military Band. He was Captain of the Sons of Legion.

Oran was also on the high school football team and excelled in boxing, wrestling, and tennis.

He enlisted in the U.S. Navy on September 5, 1940, and attended boot camp at the Naval Training Station in Norfolk, Virginia. He was granted leave in December 1940 and lived close enough that he could go home often.

His sister June visited him in Washington, D.C., while he was a student at the School of Music.

He held the rate of Musician Second Class when he graduated from the School of Music.

A memorial service was held for Oran on Palm Sunday, March 29, 1942, at the Hempstead High School by the American Legion, the Sons of the Legion, the Disabled American Veterans, and other organizations. Sailors from the Brooklyn Navy Yard were in attendance.

In addition to his parents, Oran was survived by three sisters, June, Carolyn, and Gladys Brabbzson, all of East Meadow.

Oran Merrill Brabbzson was nineteen years old when he died. His body was never recovered.[3]

RALPH WARREN BURDETTE, Musician Second Class, USN, was from Plainfield, New Jersey. He played French horn in the *Arizona* band and was also proficient on the cornet.

He was born March 11, 1921, in Plainfield, the son of Harry S. and Mabel Burdette. Harry Burdette was a paperhanger and Mabel was an accomplished piano player.

He graduated in May 1940 from the Plainfield High School, where he was the solo cornetist for the band and orchestra.

Ralph enlisted in the U.S. Navy on February 3, 1941, and attended boot camp at the Naval Training Station in Norfolk, Virginia.

He reported to the U.S. Navy School of Music in March 1941.

He was not granted leave, but was able to go home often, since his parents lived nearby.

He held the rate of Apprentice Seaman when he graduated from the School of Music.

A memorial service was held for Ralph on February 19, 1942. His high school band played a concert in his honor. The bandmaster, Mr. Andrews, who had been Ralph's cornet instructor for six years, played "Taps" at the end of the concert. On May 27, 1943, the high school unveiled a tablet in Ralph's memory.

In addition to his parents, Ralph was survived by three brothers, Bernie, Louis, and Paul Burdette.

Ralph Warren Burdette was twenty years old when he was killed. His body was never recovered.[4]

HARRY GREGORY CHERNUCHA, Musician Second Class, USN, was from North Merrick, Long Island, New York. He played clarinet and saxophone in the *Arizona* band and orchestra.

He was born in 1922, the only child of Mr. and Mrs. H. H. Chernucha. His parents were of Russian descent.

He graduated in May 1940 from the Mepham High School in North Merrick, where he was a member of the band and orchestra.

Harry, who weighed 130 pounds, was an outstanding wrestler, winning the 1940 title for his weight in the State of New York.

He enlisted in the U.S. Navy in January 1941 and attended boot camp at the Naval Training Station in Norfolk, Virginia. He entered the U.S. Navy School of Music in February 1941. His parents lived close to Washington, D.C., and he was able to go home often.

He held the rate of Seaman Second Class when he graduated from the School of Music.

Harry Gregory Chernucha was nineteen years old when he was killed. His body was never recovered.[5]

GERALD CLINTON COX, Musician Second Class, USN, was from East Moline, Illinois. He played clarinet, saxophone, electric Hawaiian guitar, and Spanish guitar in the *Arizona* band and orchestra. He also played the violin.

He was born August 17, 1922, the son of Nat and Amy Cox. At the time of Gerald's death, Nat Cox was a welder at the Arsenal Plant in East Moline. Gerald's father was also an accomplished musician, and his grandmother was still playing the violin at the age of eighty-three.

Gerald graduated in May 1940 from the East Moline High School, where he was a member of the high school band and orchestra.

He enlisted in the U.S. Navy on February 25, 1941, and attended boot camp at the Naval Training Station in Great Lakes, Illinois. He entered the U.S. Navy School of Music in March 1941. He was granted leave in April and went home for the last time.

He held the rate of Apprentice Seaman when he graduated from the School of Music.

His family held a memorial service for Gerald early in 1942. Later, on April 10, 1942, the East Moline High School band dedicated its annual concert to the memory of Gerald. The band concluded its concert by playing "Remember Pearl Harbor."

In addition to his parents, Gerald was survived by a younger sister.

Gerald Clinton Cox was nineteen years old when he was killed. He was the only member of the *Arizona* band whose first telegram stated he had been "Killed in Action." He was buried in the National Memorial Cemetery at Punchbowl, Honolulu.[6]

FRANK NORMAN FLOEGE, Musician Second Class, USN, was from Harvey, Illinois. He played clarinet and saxophone in the *Arizona* band and orchestra.

He was born November 20, 1921. Both his parents died when he was still quite young, and Frank and his brother lived in various orphanages in the Chicago area or were boarded out to private homes, sometimes together and sometimes in separate homes.

Frank graduated in May 1939 from high school in Harvey, where he was a member of the band and orchestra.

He enlisted in the U.S. Navy on March 28, 1941, and attended boot camp at the Naval Training Station in Great Lakes, Illinois. He entered the U.S. Navy School of Music in April 1941. He did not receive any leave.

He held the rate of Apprentice Seaman when he graduated from the School of Music.

Frank was survived by his brother, Warren O. H. Floege of Zion, Illinois, who was two years younger.

Frank Norman Floege was twenty years old when he was killed. His body was never recovered.[7]

CURTIS JUNIOR HAAS, Musician Second Class, USN, was from North Kansas City, Missouri. He played clarinet, saxophone, and flute in the *Arizona* band and orchestra, was one of the singers, and one of the band's music arrangers. He was the assistant director of the band.

He was born March 26, 1919, in North Kansas City, the only child of Curtis Haas, Jr. and Mary Haas. His parents were divorced in 1921, and his father and Curt lived with Curt's grandparents until Curt's father married Elizabeth Barr in 1930.

Curt's father was an accomplished musician and singer, and encouraged Curt to develop his musical talents. Curt's father was a department head at the Unity School of Christianity in Lee's Summit, Missouri, and his stepmother was on the editorial staff of the same college. Curt's father died in April 1937 at the age of thirty-seven.

Curt graduated from the North Kansas City High School in May 1937, where he was a member of the band, orchestra, and chorus. He received a rating of "Excellent" on the flute at the national instrumental contest for both the years of 1935 and 1936. Among other clubs, he was a member of the glee club, the mixed chorus, the Hi Y, the National Forensic League, the Honor Club, the Collectors Club, the Lyre Club, and was the Humor Editor for the school yearbook.

After graduating from high school, he attended business college in Kansas City in 1937-1938. In 1939, he formed his own dance band and toured the country in a bus. After an emergency appendectomy in Pierre, South Dakota, Curt enlisted in the U.S. Navy on November 2, 1940, in Pierre. He attended boot camp at the Naval Training Station in Norfolk, Virginia. He entered the U.S. Navy School of Music in December 1940. He was not granted leave and he did not return home after his enlistment.

He held the rate of Seaman Second Class when he graduated from the School of Music.

He was survived by his stepmother, Elizabeth Barr Haas, of North Kansas City.

Curtis Junior Haas was twenty-one years old when he was killed. His body was never recovered.[8]

BERNARD THOMAS HUGHES, Musician Second Class, USN, was from Athens, Pennsylvania. He played trombone in the *Arizona* band and orchestra.

He was born October 1, 1922, the son of Thomas and Gertrude Hughes.

Bernard graduated in May 1940 from the local high school, where he was a member of the high school band and orchestra. His deepest ambition was to learn to play the trombone well enough to get a job in Glenn Miller's dance band.

To that end, he enlisted in the U.S. Navy in February 1941 and attended boot camp at the Naval Training Station in Norfolk, Virginia. He entered the U.S. Navy School of Music in March 1941. He was not granted leave, but he lived close enough to his home that he could go visit his family.

He held the rate of Apprentice Seaman when he graduated from the School of Music.

In addition to his parents, he was survived by a sister, Alene Hughes.

Bernard Thomas Hughes was nineteen years old when he was killed. His body was never recovered.[9]

WENDELL RAY HURLEY, Musician Second Class, USN, was from Marion, Indiana. He played clarinet, saxophone, and Hawaiian guitar in the *Arizona* band and orchestra. He also was an expert baton twirler, and performed many times with the band.

He was born September 12, 1919, in Marion, the son of Raymond and Edna Hazel Hurley. Wendell's mother died in 1936 and his father married Evelyn in 1938.

Wendell graduated in May 1936 from Marion High School, where he was a member of the high school band and orchestra. He took top honors in high school music competitions in baton twirling. He performed twirling exhibitions at basketball games in surrounding counties.

His main interest, after music, was photography, and he spent many hours perfecting that art. He was also a champion diver.

After graduation, Wendell taught baton twirling for several years in high schools in Indiana, Michigan, and Illinois.

He enlisted in the U.S. Navy in November 1940 and attended boot camp at the Naval Training Station in Norfolk, Virginia. He entered the U.S. Navy School of Music in December 1940 and went home on a fifteen-day leave on December 28. He taught baton twirling at the Navy School of Music.

He held the rate of Seaman Second Class when he graduated from the School of Music.

A memorial service was held for Wendell at the Second Friends Church in Marion on February 1, 1942.

In addition to his father and stepmother, Wendell was survived by his brother, Donald Lee Hurley, and by his half-brother, Robert Delmar Hurley.

Wendell Ray Hurley was twenty-two years old when he was killed. His body was never recovered.[10]

EMMETT ISAAC LYNCH, Musician Second Class, USN, was from Louisville, Kentucky. He played drums in the *Arizona* band and orchestra. He also played piano.

He was born in 1916.

He graduated in May 1933 from the local high school, where he was a member of the band and orchestra.

He enlisted in the U.S. Navy on April 29, 1940, and attended boot camp at the Naval Training Station in Norfolk, Virginia. He entered the U.S. Navy School of Music in May 1940.

Emmett was married to Lorraine Lee Sisk of Washington, D.C., on February 8, 1941, in Hyattsville, Maryland.

He held the rate of Musician Second Class when he graduated from the School of Music.

Emmett Isaac Lynch was twenty-five years old when he was killed. His body was never recovered.[11]

WILLIAM MOORE McCARY, Musician Second Class, USN, was from Shades Mountain, Alabama, near Birmingham. He played the tuba in the *Arizona* band. He also played cornet, along with nearly every musical instrument.

He was born July 23, 1924, the only child of William N. and Nelle M. McCary. At the time of Billie's death, his father was secretary of a local real estate and insurance company. Billie's father was a veteran of World War I and was a member of the American Legion.

Billie graduated in May 1939 from South Highland High School, where he was a member of the band and orchestra.

He was a member of the Birmingham Concert Orchestra and was the drum major for the Sons of American Legion band and for many other musical organizations.

He attended the Georgia Military College Preparatory Department for one year, where he served as substitute director of the college band.

Billie had been an avid deep-sea diver since childhood, and had always loved the Navy and the sea.

He enlisted in the U.S. Navy September 12, 1940, at the age of sixteen. Too young to enter the U.S. Navy School of Music, he remained at the Naval Training Station in Norfolk, Virginia, until January 1941, at which time he was allowed to enter the School of Music. He did not go home on leave after he joined the Navy.

He held the rate of Seaman Second Class when he graduated from the School of Music.

A memorial concert was presented in his honor on January 21, 1942, at the Birmingham Y.M.H.A. by the Birmingham Concert Orchestra. A tribute was given by his former school principal and friend, Robert C. Johnston. The musical selections chosen by Carl F. McCool, the conductor of the orchestra, were special favorites of Billie's.

William Moore McCary was seventeen years old when he was killed. His body was never recovered.[12]

WILLIAM STARKS MOORHOUSE, Musician Second Class, USN, was from Erie, Pennsylvania, and from Wichita, Kansas. He played cornet in the *Arizona* band and orchestra.

He was born August 14, 1922, in Wichita, the son of Harold M. and Bonnie Moorhouse. His father was a Marine and his mother was a Navy nurse during World War I. His father was the head of the Packard automobile agency in Erie. At the time of Bill's death, his father was floorman at a department store in Wichita.

Bill was raised in Erie and graduated in May 1939 from Strong Vincent's High School in Erie. While in high school, he was a member of the band and the orchestra and was on the golf team at his high school.

He attended the Conservatory of Music in Erie.

During Bill's last three years of high school, he and his brother formed the Mac Moor Orchestra in Erie. His band was much in demand for playing for local dances.

Bill returned to Wichita with his family in August 1940 and enlisted in the U.S. Navy on September 18, one month later. He attended boot camp at the Naval Training Station in Norfolk, Virginia, and entered the U.S. Navy School of Music in October. He did not return home on leave.

He held the rate of Musician Second Class when he graduated from the School of Music.

In addition to his parents, Bill was survived by his brother, Robert Wallace Moorhouse.

William Starks Moorhouse was nineteen years old when he was killed. His body was never recovered.[13]

ALEXANDER JOSEPH NADEL, Musician Second Class, USN, was from Astoria, Long Island, New York. He played cornet in the *Arizona* band and orchestra and was one of the music arrangers for the band.

He was born April 14, 1921. At the time of Alex's death, his father had died. Alex was the only son of Mrs. Amelia Nadel.

Alex graduated from the local high school in May 1939, where he was a member of the band and orchestra. He often played with the New York Symphony on radio broadcasts. He also played in orchestras which played accompaniment for operettas in New York.

He attended the Juilliard Conservatory of Music in New York, where he studied cornet and musical arranging.

He enlisted in the U.S. Navy in April 1941 and attended boot camp at the Naval Training Station in Norfolk, Virginia. He entered the U.S. Navy School of Music in May 1941. He was able to go home often, since his mother lived close to Washington, D.C.

He held the rate of Apprentice Seaman when he graduated from the School of Music.

In addition to his mother, he was survived by one married sister.

Alexander Joseph Nadel was twenty years old when he was killed. His body was never recovered.[14]

NEAL JASON RADFORD, Musician Second Class, USN, was from Newark, Nebraska. He played baritone in the *Arizona* band. In addition, he played tuba.

He was born February 16, 1915, in Nebraska, the son of Boyd and Edna Radford. His father was a farmer and stock raiser in south central Nebraska.

Neal graduated in May 1932 from the local high school, where he was a member of the high school band and orchestra. In addition, he was active in sports and was an avid football fan.

After graduating from high school, Neal worked on his parent's farm.

He enlisted in the U.S. Navy in October 1940 and attended boot camp in Norfolk, Virginia. He entered the U.S. Navy School of Music in November. He was granted a fifteen-day leave and went home for the last time on December 28, 1940.

He held the rate of Seaman Second Class when he graduated from the School of Music.

In addition to his parents, Neal was survived by four brothers: Dallas, Harold, Robert, and Rex, and by five sisters: Doris, Ethel, Alice, Marian, and Norma. Dallas and Doris were twins.

Neal Jason Radford was twenty-six years old when he was killed. His body was never recovered.[15]

JAMES HARVEY SANDERSON, Musician Second Class, USN, was from Lindsay, California. He played clarinet and saxophone in the *Arizona* band and orchestra.

He was born in 1920, the son of James A. and Anna Sanderson. His father died on December 2, 1941, just a few days before Harvey's death.

Harvey graduated in May 1938 from the local high school, where he was a member of the band and orchestra.

He enlisted in the U.S. Navy in October 1940 and attended boot camp at the Naval Training Station in Norfolk, Virginia. He entered the U.S. Navy School of Music in November 1940. He was not granted leave after he entered the Navy.

He held the rate of Seaman Second Class when he graduated from the School of Music.

A lily plant was placed in Harvey's church in memory of him and his father on Easter Sunday, April 5, 1942.

In addition to his mother, Harvey was survived by one sister.

James Harvey Sanderson was twenty-one years old when he was killed. His body was never recovered. His mother had Harvey's name engraved on his father's cemetery stone.[16]

JACK LEO SCRUGGS, Musician Second Class, USN, was from Long Beach, California. He played trombone and accordion in the *Arizona* band and orchestra, was one of the singers, and wrote musical arrangements for the band. He also played piano and had his baritone horn with him on the ship.

He was born March 9, 1919, in Hanford, California, the son of H. Paul and Mae Scruggs. He moved with his family to Long Beach in 1932.

Jack graduated from Franklin Junior High School in Long Beach and graduated in May 1937 from Wilson High School in Long Beach, where he played in the school band and orchestra. He also played in the band and orchestra of the Grace Methodist Church in Long Beach.

He attended Long Beach City College, where he was a member of the band and orchestra.

He wrote poetry for a hobby.

He enlisted in the U.S. Navy late in December 1940 and attended boot camp at the Naval Training Station in Norfolk, Virginia. He entered the U.S. Navy School of Music on February 6, 1941. He was not granted leave, but was able to go home when the *Arizona* was in Long Beach in June 1941.

He held the rate of Seaman Second Class when he graduated from the School of Music.

For eight years, Jack was buried as Unknown Number X-35 in the Halawa Naval Cemetery at Oahu.

His body was finally identified in 1949 and was returned to his family for burial in 1950. Memorial services were held for Jack on January 7, 1950.

In addition to his parents, Jack was survived by one sister, Pauline.

Jack Leo Scruggs was twenty-two years old when he was killed. He was buried in Sunnyside Memorial Park, Long Beach, California.[17]

ROBERT KAR SHAW, Musician Second Class, USN, was from Pasadena, Texas. He played trombone in the *Arizona* band and orchestra.

He was born October 3, 1922, in Fort Worth, Texas, the son of Therel T. and Edna Shaw. Bobby moved with his family to Pasadena in 1930, where his father was employed by an oil refinery.

He graduated in May 1940 from Pasadena High School and was a member of the high school band and orchestra. He won many honors at the annual state competition at Huntsville, Texas, for his trombone solos. He was invited by the Alvin School Band to attend the World's Fair at New York in the summer of 1940. That special band visited seventeen states and Canada on its trip around the country.

He enlisted in the U.S. Navy on November 29, 1940, and attended boot camp at the Naval Training Station in Norfolk, Virginia. He entered the U.S. Navy School of Music in January 1941. He was not granted leave and did not return home after he enlisted.

He held the rate of Seaman Second Class when he graduated from the School of Music.

Bobby's oldest sister visited him in Long Beach, California, when *Arizona* was there.

In addition to his parents, Bobby was survived by three brothers: Theo, Howard, and Billy, and by three sisters: Frances, Connie, and Betty Ann.

Robert Kar Shaw was nineteen years old when he was killed. His parents first learned that his body had been recovered when they were sent his high school class ring by the Navy in July 1942. The package was marked with his Body Number 410. He was buried in the Nuuanu Cemetery in Honolulu, Hawaii.[18]

CHARLES WILLIAM WHITE, Musician Second Class, USN, was from Bountiful, Utah. He played drums in the *Arizona* band and orchestra. He also played piano.

He was born April 11, 1920, in Salt Lake City, Utah, the son of Arthur E. and Catherine White. His family moved to Bountiful when he was young.

He graduated in May 1938 from the Davis County High School, where he was a member of the high school band and orchestra. He attended the Brigham Young University at Provo, Utah, majoring in music.

Charles enlisted in the U.S. Navy on March 13, 1941, and attended boot camp at the Naval Training Station in Norfolk, Virginia. He entered the U.S. Navy School of Music in April. He was not granted leave and did not return to his home after enlistment. His mother visited him in June 1941 when the *Arizona* was in Long Beach, California.

He held the rate of Apprentice Seaman when he graduated from the School of Music.

In addition to his parents, Charles was survived by two brothers, Douglas D. White of Bountiful and Arthur S. White of Salt Lake City.

Charles William White was twenty-one years old when he was killed. His body was never recovered.[19]

ERNEST HUBERT WHITSON, JR., Musician Second Class, USN, was from Cincinnati, Ohio. He played the bass horn and the string bass in the *Arizona* band and orchestra.

He was born in 1918 in Cincinnati, the son of Ernest Hubert Whitson, Sr. and his wife Elizabeth. His father was a veteran of World War I and was working at a local delicatessen when Ernest died. His mother was a nurse.

Ernest graduated in May 1936 from Withrow High School, where he was a member of the high school band and orchestra. He attended the Cincinnati Conservatory of Music for two years, and was a salesman for the Baldwin Piano Company.

He enlisted in the U.S. Navy in March 1941 and attended boot camp at the Naval Training Station in Norfolk, Virginia. He entered the U.S. Navy School of Music in April 1941. He was granted an emergency leave in May to visit his mother, who was seriously ill.

He held the rate of Apprentice Seaman when he graduated from the School of Music.

In addition to his parents, Ernest was survived by one brother, Fred A. Whitson of Cincinnati.

Ernest Hubert Whitson, Jr. was twenty-three years old when he was killed. His body was never recovered.[20]

CLYDE RICHARD WILLIAMS, Musician Second Class, USN, was from Okmulgee, Oklahoma. He played cornet in the *Arizona* band and orchestra. He also played French horn, baritone, and violin, and studied clarinet at the School of Music.

He was born September 25, 1922, in Henryetta, Oklahoma, the son of Richard B. Williams, Jr. and his wife, Martha Jane (Fretwell) Williams. Clyde's father was a veteran of World War I and was a member of the American Legion and of the Veterans of Foreign Wars. At the time of his son's death, he was employed at the local post office.

Clyde's family moved to Wetumka, Oklahoma, in 1925 and to Okmulgee in 1930.

He graduated in May 1940 from Okmulgee High School, where he played in the high school band and orchestra. He was baton twirler for the band in 1938-39 and was the head drum major for the band in 1939-40. He played with the Okmulgee Junior College orchestra for two years, performing on many local radio programs. He also played with several other local bands and orchestras.

Clyde won many awards in high school competitions with his cornet and violin solos, as well as with brass ensembles.

He excelled in swimming, diving, and tennis. His hobbies were drawing and wood burning. He was a member of the Sons of the American Legion.

Clyde enlisted in the U.S. Navy on November 27, 1940, and attended boot camp at the Naval Training Station in Norfolk, Virginia. He entered the U.S. Navy School of Music on December 24, 1940. He was granted a fifteen-day leave on December 28 and went home for the last time.

He held the rate of Seaman Second Class when he graduated from the School of Music.

In May 1941, while he was still at the School of Music in Washington, D.C., he was visited by his parents and sister.

In January 1942, a memorial trophy was presented to the Williams' family by Clyde's friends in the Okmulgee High School Band.

On December 7, 1944, a memorial service was held in honor of Clyde by the White-Williams Post of the American Legion in Okmulgee. The name of that organization had been changed to honor Clyde.

In addition to his parents, Clyde was survived by one sister, Ruth Mae (Molly) Williams of Okmulgee.

Clyde Richard Williams was nineteen years old when he was killed. His body was never recovered.[21]

CHAPTER 24

Honors

As members of their high school bands and orchestras, the musicians of the *Arizona* band had been in the public eyes of their hometowns for years and were well-known to the townspeople.

Far from being "just another sailor," as they had been to the citizens of Washington, D.C., and of Hawaii, they were highly respected local boys. As such, they were honored for many years by their hometowns, and were featured often in newspaper articles. In an outpouring of sorrow, friends wrote poems in their honor, and memorial concerts were given by their former high school bands.

There were many memorial plaques and trophies unveiled in their honor.

For many years, Okmulgee continued to heap honors on Clyde, as the first boy from our town to be killed in action in World War II. A memorial was presented to our family by the members of my brother's high school band. We were especially touched by their gesture, since we knew it expressed the sincere grief of so many of Clyde's musical friends in Okmulgee.

The idea of the memorial was conceived by Frank Gross, who had been the head drum major when Clyde was the baton twirler. Pate had remarked to Frank one day: "Clyde's death will hurt me most on Memorial Day when people go decorate their loved ones' graves. I won't have a grave. I don't even have a body."

A committee of band members voted to accept donations toward a memorial plaque to honor their former drum major, and it was presented to us on January 8, 1942.

The trophy was made of walnut with a brass lyre on top. On the bronze plate was inscribed: "In memory of Clyde R. Williams, Pearl Harbor, presented by his O.H.S. band friends 1942"

In the first entry I had made in my journal since December 26, I wrote:

> ***January 8, 1942***—*Thursday—A committee of band members from the Okmulgee High School brought the memorial plaque out tonight. It is beautiful.*
>
> *Everyone in town thought a lot of Clyde—it's hard to get used to not writing him letters and planning his next box of candy.*
>
> *I hope I get called to Washington soon, so I can do my small part!*

Published in the newspaper the next day was the following:

> *We wish to express our sincere appreciation to the Okmulgee High School band and former members of the band for the beautiful Memorial Plaque presented to us in memory of their classmate and our son and brother, Clyde Richard Williams.*
>
> *Knowing that we have the sympathy and moral support of the members and former members of the High School Band helps us a great deal to carry on in this, the darkest hour of our life.*
>
> *We are indeed grateful.*
> *Mr. and Mrs. R. B. Williams, Ruth Mae Williams.*[1]

My brother was just the first. Okmulgee was especially hard-hit by casualties in that horrible war. There seemed to be no end to the telegrams which showered down on our small town, as we heard that friend after friend would not be coming home, after all.

There is a circle at the Okmulgee Cemetery around the flagpole. There are placed the memorial headstones for our local servicemen who were killed in the war but whose bodies were never recovered. When I walk along that circle, it is with a deep feeling of sorrow. In addition to my brother, there are so many of our friends from high school and from the high school band represented there.

On August 3, 1942, our family was presented posthumously the American Legion Gold Star Citation, which read: "By virtue of an act of the national executive committee of The American Legion, approved May 1, 1942, this gold star citation, emblem of devotion to the highest duty of citizenship, is awarded in the name of The American Legion to the next of surviving kin of Clyde Williams, who died while a member of the armed forces of the United States of America in the war period beginning December 7, 1941. This death occurred in order that others might live."

The citation included a large gold star, the emblem of the American Legion, and a notation: "This citation is presented by Edwin K. White Post Number 10 Department of Oklahoma as visible evidence of its respect and lasting gratitude."[2]

After World War I, the American Legion post in Okmulgee had been named the Edwin K. White Post Number 10, to honor the last man killed in World War I from our area. Now, the name of the post was changed to the White-Williams Post Number 10, to honor Clyde R. Williams, the first Okmulgee boy killed in World War II.

In 1942, members of the Okmulgee Business and Professional Women's club voted to present a defense bond each year to the most outstanding member of the Okmulgee High School band as a memorial to Clyde. The award, to be presented at the close of each school year for the duration of the war, was to be known as the Clyde Williams Award.[3]

My brother would have been pleased.

Clyde's picture was featured in newspapers many, many times, asking people to buy U.S. War Bonds and Stamps in his memory.

The Okmulgee Pony Girls presented a defense bond to our parents on March 9, 1942, in memory of Clyde.[4]

Since Okmulgee had never had a Gold Star Mothers nor a Navy Mothers club, Mate helped form the Williams-Reed Chapter of the Gold Star Mothers and the Williams-Reed-Peak Club Number 255 of the Navy Mothers Club of America in 1942. Both clubs were named for Okmulgee area boys who had died at Pearl Harbor on December 7. In addition to my brother, Seaman Ray E. Reed of Nuyaka was killed on the *Arizona* and Marine Robert H. Peak was killed on another battleship.

In September 1942, in answer to an appeal from Secretary of the Navy Frank Knox for assistance with enlistment of recruits for the Navy, the Civilian Navy Recruiting Committee was formed in Okmulgee. Mate, as President of the Navy Mothers Club, was appointed to that committee.[5]

On May 22, 1946, a citation was presented to our parents from the local high school. It read: "In Memoriam, Okmulgee High School. His fellow students, teachers, and the citizens of this community hold in reverent memory Clyde Richard Williams, who gave his life for his country. May the great sacrifice he has made help to promote perpetual peace and further the welfare of our nation and the freedom and security of mankind. He shall be remembered as long as time shall endure. May 23, 1946".[6]

Similar honors were bestowed on the other *Arizona* musicians over the years by their hometowns. Each time, their families were proud.

Each state honored its own member of the *Arizona* band. On December 31, 1946, the State of Oklahoma issued a citation to my brother, expressing "appreciation for the supreme sacrifice for country and mankind made in World War II." The citation was signed by Robert S. Kerr, the Governor of Oklahoma, and by Katherine Manton, the Secretary of State.[7]

The two members of the *Arizona* band who were from Oklahoma, Wayne Bandy and Clyde Williams, were featured in the Spring 1944 issue of the *Chronicles of Oklahoma*, published quarterly by the Oklahoma Historical Society.[8]

The United States Government also honored all the members of *Arizona*'s band many times.

A memorial, signed by President Roosevelt, was sent to our family, stating: "In grateful memory of Clyde Richard Williams, who died in the service of his country at Pearl Harbor, T.H., attached U.S.S. *Arizona*, 7 December 1941. He stands in the unbroken line of patriots who have dared to die that freedom might live, and grow, and increase its blessings. Freedom lives and through it he lives—in a way that humbles the undertakings of most men."[9]

On February 18, 1944, all the bandsmen were awarded the Purple Heart medal posthumously. Our citation read: "The United States of America, to all who shall see these presents, greeting. This is to certify that the President of the United States of America, pursuant to authority vested in him by Congress, has awarded the Purple Heart, established by General George Washington at Newburgh, New York, August 7, 1782, to Clyde Richard Wiliiams, Musician Second Class, United States Navy, for military merit and for wounds received in action, resulting in his death December 7, 1941. Given under my hand in the City of Washington, this 18th day of February 1944."

The citation was signed by Randall Jacobs and by Frank Knox.

Accompanying the certificate and the beautiful Purple Heart medal was another certificate, which read: "Let it be known that he who wears the Order of the Purple Heart has given of his blood in the defense of his homeland and shall forever be revered by his fellow countrymen. George Washington, August 7, 1782"[10]

All the families received an undated letter from The Secretary of the Navy in Washington. Ours read:

> *My dear Mr. Williams. I desire to offer to you my personal condolence in the tragic death of your son, Clyde Richard Williams, Musician second class, United States Navy, which occurred at the time of the attack by the Japanese on December seventh. It is hoped that you may find comfort in the thought that he made the supreme sacrifice upholding the highest traditions of the Navy, in the defense of his country.*
> *Very sincerely yours, James Forrestal.*[11]

In addition to the Purple Heart, the bandsmen were awarded posthumously the American Defense Service Medal, the World War II Victory Medal, the Asiatic-Pacific Campaign Medal with one bronze star, and the World War II Victory Medal. In 1991, they were awarded posthumously the Pearl Harbor Commemorative Medal.

A Gold Star lapel pin was given without charge by Congress to the families of the men who had been killed in the war.

Of course, by far the most famous memorial to the victims of Pearl Harbor has been the USS *Arizona* Memorial.

From the beginning, the families of the *Arizona* bandsmen waited for word about the disposition of our boys' bodies. They shared with each other every crumb of information they could find about the bodies which were still on the *Arizona*.

Mabel Burdette wrote on June 1, 1943, concerning an article she had read about the bodies still on the *Arizona* and the *Oklahoma*: "It sounds as though they haven't taken any bodies from any of them— I don't see why not (with the exception of *Oklahoma*, of course). I would think that would be one of the first things to be done. But I do wish that they would let all the information out now and not bring it out little by little."[12]

And still trying to find out what the Navy planned to do with the bodies, Mabel wrote in September 1943 that one of the mothers had reported a sailor had told her that *Arizona* had been floated and was now at New Caledonia being refitted.[13] That ridiculous rumor shows what the families were still going through two years after the attack, as we kept trying to piece together the facts of the Pearl Harbor attack.

By March 1944, we knew better. Ernest Whitson's parents were working in Hawaii, and although their letters were censored, they were able to tell us some accurate facts. That led Mabel Burdette to write: "Some way I just wish that they would leave the *Arizona* just as it is and not disturb it, but my husband seems to think they won't."[14]

And so we went along for nearly twenty years, always watching the papers carefully for any information concerning the disposition of the bodies of our musicians.

In March 1950, when Admiral Arthur Radford ordered the Navy to raise and lower the American flag each day on *Arizona*, we were pleased.[15] Playing for colors on the *Arizona* had been one of our boys' duties when the ship was in port. *Arizona* was still in port, and we were glad the Navy had not forgotten her.

In 1956, we began receiving requests for donations toward an *Arizona* Memorial, and we read with interest the efforts of military and civilian groups to raise the necessary money with which to build it.

Finally, after much work by many people, the USS *Arizona* Memorial was dedicated on May 30, 1962.

We read all we could find about the Memorial. When friends went to Hawaii, they always took pictures of our boy's name which was engraved on the wall of the shrine.

We were especially touched by the Dedication Plaque, which repeated Admiral Radford's order of March 1950: "Dedicated to the eternal memory of our gallant shipmates in the USS *Arizona* who gave their lives in action 7 December 1941. 'From today on the USS *Arizona* will again fly our country's flag just as proudly as she did on the morning of 7 December 1941. I am sure the *Arizona*'s crew will know and appreciate what we are doing.' Admiral A. W. Radford, USN, 7 March 1950. May God make his face to shine upon them and grant them peace."[16]

On the marble wall of the Shrine Room is a list of the names of *Arizona*'s crewmen who were killed in the attack. In the center is engraved: "To the memory of the gallant men here entombed and their shipmates who gave their lives in action on December 7, 1941 on the USS *Arizona*."

My husband and I first visited my brother's grave in December 1976, on the occasion of the thirty-fifth anniversary of the Pearl Harbor attack. The visitors' center had not yet been built and the *Arizona* Memorial was operated by the U.S. Navy. We stood in a long line on wooden planks, waiting our turn to take a boat out to the Memorial.

To walk onto that Memorial was the most heartbreaking thing I have ever had to do. We all stood around and cried. Whether or not the visitors knew anyone who had been killed at Pearl Harbor, whether or not they had been born in 1941, everyone had heard of the attack on Pearl Harbor, and we all stood and grieved.

I had a distinct feeling that my brother was there beside me that day, trying to comfort me.

We took my mother to visit her son's grave in May 1982. By then, the beautiful visitors' center had been completed and the Memorial was operated by the National Park Service. As we watched the film of the attack, suddenly there was the photograph of the *Arizona* band which the Navy had sent us many years before. We three sat in the theater and stared into Clyde's eyes. We were stunned.

That was the first time we heard the inaccuracies being told about the band.

On the Memorial, strangers stood and cried with us. And again I felt my brother's presence near me.

The third time we went to Hawaii was in May 1994. We took the trip to celebrate our fiftieth wedding anniversary and to take our daughter and grandson to the Memorial.

We took flowers out to the Memorial to honor my brother, as we had always done, and we took a second floral tribute to honor the entire *Arizona* band.

That time I was very disappointed, both at the visitors' center and on the Memorial. I saw no tears, other than ours. What I did see was a woman standing in the hallowed Shrine Room, cursing over and over because she could not get a clear shot of the Marble Wall with her camera.

And on the Memorial, I saw people lined up to take the next boat back to the visitors' center. They were laughing and joking loudly.

I was distressed to see that people have evidently forgotten the meaning of that beautiful Memorial.

And I could not find my brother.

I walked over to the railing, took off my lei and threw it into the water toward turret two. The lei drifted slowly until it reached turret two, then paused and circled around and around the turret opening. I was very moved, and exclaimed, "Look at my flowers!"

When I realized that my family was not near me, as I had thought, I apologized for speaking aloud, but the young lady beside me asked me to finish what I had started to say. So I told her that my brother was in the band on the *Arizona* and that all the boys in the band had been killed that day. I told her they had been several decks below turret two, passing ammunition, when the magazines blew up. And I told her that my flowers were circling just above the place where the boys had died.

She murmured softly, "I'm so sorry!" I knew then that there are still some people who are moved by the experience of visiting the *Arizona* Memorial.

Suddenly a man standing beside me exclaimed, "Yes, and it was the best damn band in the whole Pacific Fleet!"

I told him that, although I was never able to hear them play, I had always heard that.

Then I looked around and saw that there were many people moving silently and reverently around the Memorial. And I realized I must not let a few slobs ruin my visit to the boys' graves.

So I walked back past the joking, laughing tourists, and past the cursing woman with the camera, and I stood again in the Shrine Room.

As I silently read the names of our musicians on the wall, I pictured each of them in my mind. I had been writing the band's story for eighteen months by then, and I felt I knew each of them very well.

I thought particularly of Neal Radford and his comments back in April 1941, as he described the military funerals at Arlington Cemetery. I remembered he had said: "Officers are the only ones that rate the band. Guys like me get the Seaman Guard to shoot over their graves."

And I had to smile as I thought of the many honors which have been heaped upon the crews of the *Arizona* and the other ships which were at Pearl Harbor that day. And I thought that very few top-ranking officers have received as much acclaim for as many years after their deaths as have the officers and enlisted men who were killed that day in Hawaii.

At last I could feel my brother and the rest of the band around me. I could hear their beautiful music, and I could hear them joking with each other.

And so I bid them farewell.

I told them that there are many people who still love them.

And I told them we would never forget that they were the best damn band in the whole Pacific Fleet!

CHAPTER 25

The *Arizona* Band Trophy

The families of the *Arizona* musicians first learned of the *Arizona* Band Trophy when Amelia Nadel, Alex's mother, received a letter from A. J. Homann, Commanding, USS *Arizona*, Pearl Harbor, which she shared with us. He stated:

> *During the short period of time Band Unit No. 22 served on board the USS* Arizona, *of which your son was a member, they acquired a very good reputation, and in the elimination contests of the "Battle of Music" held at Pearl Harbor, T. H., they won first prize in all contests as best band in the U.S. Pacific Fleet. An appropriate trophy, with all names of members of the* Arizona *band engraved thereon, is to be presented at a later date.*[1]

Shortly after, on April 2, 1942, the Navy released the following story which was carried in newspapers from coast to coast:

> *What becomes of the boys in the band when the guns begin to roar?*
>
> *Many a civilian has asked that question. Blowing a horn or beating a drum is not firing a gun. What becomes of the ship's musicians when the battle rages?*
>
> *The most dramatic answer to that question has been furnished by the incident of the ship's band of the battleship* Arizona.
>
> *On December 7 they went to their battle station, one of the most hazardous on the ship—down below, passing ammunition to the guns above.*

> *To a man, the* Arizona's *band was killed when the battleship's magazine exploded.*
>
> *Part of the program of recreation at Pearl Harbor last year was the Battle of Music, 1941. The bands of the ships in port contested. One of the best and near the top in scoring when the war began was the band of the* Arizona.
>
> *When its total loss was discovered, the other contestants unanimously agreed to award posthumously to the* Arizona's *band the trophy at stake.*
>
> *Great interest in the trophy has been expressed by the U.S. Navy School of Music at Washington, and in response to its request, a picture of the trophy was painted by Alfred Dupont, illustrator at the fleet recreation office, and sent to the national capital to be placed on permanent exhibit there.*
>
> *Henceforth the trophy will be known as the* Arizona *trophy.*
>
> *After the war, it will be put up again to be challenged, when the Battle of Music will be resumed.*

Following were the names of all the members of the *Arizona* band.[2]

Alfred Dupont's painting of the Trophy was beautiful. He depicted the Trophy standing in front of a drape. In the background was a ship's turret, representing turret two, the boys' death trap. In front of the turret was a sailor playing "Taps" on his bugle.

The Trophy itself was painted nearly exactly as it actually is.

The *Arizona* Band Trophy, which still exists, shows the figure of Liberty holding a torch. She is standing on a bronze cup, on which is inscribed "Grand Prize, Battle of Music, United States Navy 1941." At the base of the cup are two eagles with outstretched wings.

A bronze plate is affixed to the base, on which is engraved: "1941 Winning Orchestra 1941. USS *Arizona*. Sic Itur Ad Astra. F. W. Kinney, Bandmaster."

Below is listed the names of the twenty musicians of *Arizona*'s band.[3]

We were not surprised to hear that *Arizona*'s band had been chosen the best band. We had already heard about their excellence from many sources. Betty Kinney had written us: "My husband was so proud of all his boys in the band, and an excellent band it was. I never got to hear it, but I heard about it. Fred lived for his band and I'm sure he was happy going with his band."[4]

We were proud of that posthumous honor for our band, but we were saddened even more to think that the band had been eliminated from the Battle of Music in such a horrible way.

My parents received a letter written on the letterhead of the USS *Arizona*, c/o Postmaster, San Francisco, California, dated April 25, 1942:

> *The records of this office indicate that the late Clyde Richard WILLIAMS, Musician second class, U.S. Navy, had listed you as his beneficiary. This record also indicated that he was a member of the Ship's Band of the U.S.S. ARIZONA.*
>
> *During the latter part of 1941, the various ships' bands entered into a musical contest, known as the "BATTLE OF THE BANDS." The band of the U.S.S. ARIZONA was awarded first place in this contest, and an appropriate trophy has been awarded as a prize.*
>
> *As this trophy will be subject to future contests after the war, and in view of the fact that it could not be presented to the beneficiary of each of the members of the band, we have had photographs made of this trophy and the Supply Department of the Navy Yard at Pearl Harbor, T. H., is sending one copy of this picture to each beneficiary.*
>
> *This is a trophy that each of the members would have been proud of, and the officers and enlisted men of the U.S.S. ARIZONA were justly proud of their band.*
>
> *Very truly yours,*
> *HUGH MAC KAY,*
> *Lieutenant Commander, USN, Commanding Officer.*[5]

The Navy did indeed send a photograph of the Trophy to all the families in 1942. We thought it was exceptionally beautiful and from that moment on, the *Arizona* Band Trophy and Alfred Dupont's painting of it became the Holy Grails for the families of the *Arizona* band. They all expressed the hope that someday they would be able to see both of them.

We always kept track of the Trophy, as it traveled around for fifty years. We tried to keep track of the painting, but we were not successful.

As soon as the families heard that Dupont's painting of the Trophy had indeed been sent to the School of Music, I was, of course, delegated to go see it and to report back to them.

I did not have much faith in my ability to do that. Since we had not been allowed to attend the band's graduation exercise, I thought I would surely not be allowed into the Navy Yard, now that we were under wartime restrictions.

However, the usual coincidence occurred. My roommate and I went out to Glen Echo one evening, where I spotted two sailors with the familiar music lyre emblem on their sleeves.

With our usual wartime informality, I asked them if they were attending the School of Music, and told them that my brother had also gone to the School. One of the boys replied lightly, "He was not in the *Arizona* band, I hope!"

Then ensued the total silence common to such awkward situations. I knew he would feel so bad when I said "Yes, he was," but it had to be said.

We all rallied, and they went back to the school and told Boatswain Thurmond they had met me. He sent word by them that I should come out to the school to visit. Somehow, they worked out all the restrictions, and I went to see the memorial display at the school.

The painting was displayed prominently at the head of the first landing, as was the beautiful "Roll of Honor" which Boatswain Thurmond had asked one of his students to create.[6]

Painted in the center of the "Roll of Honor" plaque was a musical lyre, flanked by an American flag on the left, and a flag of stars on the right. Directly below were the words "Honor Roll," flanked by battleships on each side.

Under that was "U.S. Navy School of Music," and below were the names of *Arizona*'s bandsmen, painted on a background representing the sea. The boys were listed in the order of the instruments they played, and following each name was "Band 22."

Also listed was Eugene V. Lish, Band Number 17. Lish, a member of the *West Virginia* band, was in sick bay on the morning of December 7 and was killed.[7]

Thus, twenty-two former students of the School of Music were lost during the Pearl Harbor attack. Other School of Music graduates were killed during the war, but Thurmond hesitated to add their names to those first Pearl Harbor victims.[8]

Displayed with the painting of the Trophy and the "Roll of Honor" were the photographs of the *Arizona* musicians and of Lish. Thurmond had asked each family to send a photograph of its bandsmen and had proudly displayed those photographs on the wall at the school.

So all of us have known since 1942 about the four important memorials to our boys—The *Arizona* Band Trophy, Dupont's painting of the Trophy, the U.S. Navy School of Music Roll of Honor, and the display of our boys' photographs.

Pate wrote me in Washington in November 1942 that he had met a sailor whose home was in Henryetta and who was in Pearl Harbor on December 7. The sailor was a bugler on the *Pennsylvania* and had talked to Clyde for about thirty minutes on the evening of December 6.

I did not know that sailor's name for many years, but recently, through the help of Edward P. Strobak, a former *Pennsylvania* bandsman, I learned his name.[9]

Leonard Orville Yandle had received a leave in 1942 to go to Henryetta to be married. The officiating minister was our neighbor, W. M. Carter.[10] Reverend Carter knew Clyde's parents, of course, and was able to tell Yandle how to get in touch with my father.

Yandle told Pate that the *Pennsylvania* and the *Arizona* bands had both won in the semifinals of the Battle of Music, and were scheduled to battle it out for first place on Saturday night, December 20.

Because none of the *Arizona* band was left after the attack, the other bands had voted unanimously to concede first place to the *Arizona* band. Many of the musicians had remarked that *Arizona*'s band was the best band, anyway.

Yandle told my father that if Clyde's body was ever found and buried, he would like to blow taps over his grave.

Pennsylvania had pledged to sink five Jap battleships in retaliation for the sinking of the *Arizona*, and Yandle said they had already sunk two.[11]

I only hope Yandle knew how very much our family treasured his visit with my brother. And how much we appreciated his taking the trouble on his wedding day to find my father and tell him about their visit.

Bandmaster John Carey, who had been at Pearl Harbor on December 7, told the Burdettes in 1949 that four ships had won small cups, and it had been arranged to have the final contest for the trophy the week before Christmas. After the attack, the unanimous decision by the remaining three bands was that the *Arizona* band was by far the best in the Pacific Fleet and that the Trophy should be awarded to them.[12]

Later, the Navy did allow Ensign Thurmond to bring the *Arizona* Band Trophy to the School of Music. For many years, it was proudly displayed at the head of the stairway, along with the photographs of the bandsmen, the "Roll of Honor," and the painting of the Trophy.[13]

We were pleased that all four of our band's honors were now together in a safe place.

It was very fortunate for us that Ensign Thurmond persisted in obtaining the Trophy for the School of Music. It is now the only part of the memorial display at the School of Music which is still in existence.

The families of the *Arizona* band watched over the display at the School of Music for many years. Representatives of nearly every family eventually went to the school to view the memorial. Ensign Thurmond found each of their visits to be a very moving experience.[14]

It was gratifying to us that the school from which our boys had graduated still chose to honor them. And we were always grateful that Ensign Thurmond saw to it that we were all treated with respect and compassion whenever we visited the school in Washington.

The display to honor the *Arizona* band was still in a prominent place at the school when Mabel and Harry Burdette went to visit in

1949, and all four of our precious items were still there.[15]

When next I visited the School of Music in 1981, the school had been moved to Little Creek, Virginia, near Norfolk. I received permission to visit the school, but was dismayed to see there was no painting of the Trophy, no "Roll of Honor," and no photographs of the *Arizona* musicians.

I was relieved, however, to see that the *Arizona* Band Trophy had survived and was prominently displayed in the hall.

But by 1993, when I next visited the school, there was nothing left. I was assured, however, that the Trophy had not been lost, but had been sent to the USS *Arizona* Memorial in 1989.

Unfortunately, when my family visited the *Arizona* Memorial in Pearl Harbor in 1994, there was no sign of the Trophy. Again, I was told that it had not been lost, but was only in storage.

Apparently the Dupont painting of the Trophy has been lost, along with the photographs of our boys and the School of Music's "Roll of Honor."

So, although we watched carefully over our band's honors for many years, ultimately we lost.

The Battle of Music 1941 was never set up to be a scientific contest. Since the judges were not even trained musicians, the Battle could have been no more than a popularity contest between eighteen extremely fine bands.

The families of the *Arizona* bandsmen had no way of knowing which band was the best. We have always been justly proud of our *Arizona* band and let it go at that.

Therefore, I was not prepared for the reaction of the former servicemen whom I interviewed for this book, and to hear how very strongly they still feel about that Battle of Music 1941 after fifty years. Almost without exception, when I told them I was writing a history of *Arizona*'s last band, they stated emphatically that the *Arizona* band was the best band in the Pacific Fleet!

It has always been my fear that in a few years, all the people who knew *Arizona*'s musicians will be gone.

And that all the honors which have been awarded to them will be lost.

And that *Arizona*'s band will be forgotten.

So I was encouraged to hear those remarks from men who had heard the band play.

There is no happy ending to this story. *Arizona* did not ever come back to her home port in San Pedro.

Her crew did not ever get that leave.

The families did not ever find our musicians, wandering around with amnesia. Nor did we ever find them lying unidentified in some hospital.

They were gone, and they were gone forever.

As soon as we could accept that, we began our journey toward healing. It has been a long, painful trip.

In the beginning, we lost all our faith, and we lost all our hope.

So when, as early as 1942, a newspaper reporter lamented that all *Arizona*'s musicians had been killed at once, and there was none left to play them Taps, we agreed.

But he was wrong.

Although United States Navy Band Number 22 was silenced forever before it could complete its song, many, many men have stepped forward over the years to play Taps over them.

By the time a Pearl Harbor survivor remarked to me in 1993 that there is nothing left now of *Arizona*'s bandsmen except their teeth, I could disagree.

They may have killed them physically, but they could never wipe out our memories of them. So long as one person remembers the *Arizona* musicians, they are not gone.

And so long as one person remembers the bitter lessons we learned at Pearl Harbor that day, we can dare hope the deaths of *Arizona*'s musicians and the deaths of all the other Pearl Harbor victims will have served some purpose.

"Let it be known that he who wears the Order of the Purple Heart has given of his blood in the defense of his homeland and shall forever be revered by his fellow countrymen."[16]

"May the sacrifice he has made help to promote perpetual peace and further the welfare of our nation and the freedom and security of mankind. He shall be remembered as long as time shall endure."[17]

For the twenty-one members of USS *Arizona*'s last band, we can only repeat the words which are inscribed on the *Arizona* Band Trophy:

SIC ITUR AD ASTRA.

Such is the way to the stars, or to immortality.[18]

"God grant that I may sometime find that place where you have gone."[19]

"Wake not, O heroes—sleep ye on."[20]

Notes

Preface

1. "*Arizona*'s Band Killed Dec. 7, Awarded Trophy," *Honolulu Star-Bulletin*,
2. April 1942.

Chapter 1: They Didn't Have a Chance!

1. *Navy Times*, 10 December 1958.
2. Dr. James M. Thurmond, interview with author, 6 February 1994.
3. Thomas M. Leonard, *Day By Day: The Forties*, 447.
4. Richard A. Wisniewski, *Pearl Harbor and the USS Arizona Memorial: A Pictorial History*, 23.
5. Ibid, 26.
6. Paul Stillwell, *Battleship Arizona*, 275.
7. Ibid, 276-277.
8. Gordon W. Prange, *Pearl Harbor: The Verdict of History, xxxvi*.

Chapter 2: The Early Years

1. *The Washington Post*, 18 January 1942.

Chapter 3: 1940—The Year of Decision

1. "Information Regarding Enlistment and Application for the U. S. Navy School of Music." NRB-22064-3-22-38-25 M. (E-44, 45, 46.)
2. *Okmulgee (Oklahoma) Torchlight*, May 1939.
3. Ibid, May 1940.

Chapter 4: Enlistment

1. Leonard, *Day By Day: The Forties*, 40-41.
2. Ibid, 41.
3. Ibid, 47.
4. Lieutenant W. P. Grieves, postcard to Richard B. Williams, Jr., 9 July 1940.
5. *Okmulgee (Oklahoma) Daily Times*, 22 July 1940, 1.
6. Lieutenant Charles Benter, letter to Clyde Richard Williams, 11 July 1940.
7. "Information Regarding Enlistment and Application for the United States Navy School of Music." NRB-22064-3-22-38-25M. (E-44, 45, 46.)

8. Divine Worship Service program, Citizens' Military Training Camp, Fort Sill, Oklahoma, 4 August 1940.
9. Lieutenant Commander R. M. Little, U.S. Navy Recruiting Station, Dallas, Texas, letter to C. R. Williams, 15 August 1940.
10. Lieutenant Colonel Frank G. Forgione, interview with author, 3 July 1993.
11. Admiral C. W. Nimitz, letter to Honorable Jack Nichols, 14 October 1940.
12. Ibid.

Chapter 5: Boot Camp and Leave

1. "Information Regarding Enlistment and Application for the U. S. Navy School of Music." NRB-22064-3-22-38-25M. (E-44, 45, 46.)
2. Randall Jacobs, Chief of Bureau of Navigation, letter to R. B. Williams, 27 March 1942.
3. Thurmond, interview with author, 4 July 1993.
4. Forgione, interview with author, 3 July 1993.
5. Omer S. Kent, interview with author, 13 March 1993.
6. Captain H. A. McClure, Naval Training Station, Norfolk, Virginia, undated letter to R. B. Williams, (ca. December 1940). "Information Regarding Training Period for Apprentice Seamen," U.S. Naval Training Station. NTSNV-11-2-40-30 M.
7. Joan Watson, letter to C. R. Williams, 6 December 1940.
8. Ibid.
9. Ibid, 28 December 1940.
10. Christmas Menu, U.S. Navy Receiving Station, Washington, D.C., 25 December 1940.
11. Anita Berry, letter to C. R. Williams, 30 November 1940.

Chapter 6: The United States Navy School of Music

1. Charlene Cason, "Clinics Draw Musicians From Across U.S.," *The Clipper (Chesapeake, Virginia)*, 22/23 April 1993, E13a.
2. Robert Ruark, "They Don't Just Toot a Horn in the Navy," *The Washington Daily News*, 26 June 1942, 31.
3. *Our Navy*, 1944.
4. Gerald G. Gross, "Mister, Are You Musical?", *The Washington Post*, 4 May 1941.
5. *The Washington Post*, 29 December 1941.
6. Ibid.
7. Ibid.
8. Gross, "Mister, Are You Musical?", *The Washington Post*, 4 May 1941.
9. Thurmond, interview with author, 4 July 1993.
10. Ibid, 11 July 1994.
11. Ruark, "They Don't Just Toot a Horn in the Navy," *The Washington Daily News*, 26 June 1942, 31.
12. Ibid.
13. Gross, "Mister, Are You Musical?", *The Washington Post*, 4 May 1941.
14. Thurmond, interview with author, 6 February 1994.

15. Gross, "Mister, Are You Musical?", *The Washington Post*, 4 May 1941.
16. Ruark, "They Don't Just Toot a Horn in the Navy," *The Washington Daily News*, 26 June 1942, 31.
17. Ibid.
18. Forgione, interview with author, 3 July 1993.
19. Mabel Burdette, letter to M. J. Williams, 5 January 1949.
20. John W. Crawford, interview with author, 3 July 1993.
21. Ibid.
22. Ruark, "They Don't Just Toot a Horn in the Navy," *The Washington Daily News*, 26 June 1942, 31.
23. Ibid.
24. Ibid.
25. Gross, "Mister, Are You Musical?", *The Washington Post*, 4 May 1941.
26. Ruark, "They Don't Just Toot a Horn in the Navy," *The Washington Daily News*, 26 June 1942, 31.
27. Ibid.
28. Ibid.
29. "Navy School of Music," *Our Navy*, July 1941.
30. Ruark, "They Don't Just Toot a Horn in the Navy," *The Washington Daily News*, 26 June 1942, 31.
31. Gross, "Mister, Are You Musical?", *The Washington Post*, 4 May 1941.
32. Ibid.
33. Ruark, "They Don't Just Toot a Horn in the Navy," *The Washington Daily News*, 26 June 1942, 31.
34. *The Washington Post*, 29 December 1941.
35. Thurmond, interview with author, 4 July 1993.
36. Ruark, "They Don't Just Toot a Horn in the Navy," *The Washington Daily News*, 26 June 1942, 31.
37. Thurmond, interview with author, 6 February 1994.
38. Cason, "Clinics Draw Musicians From Across U.S.," *The Clipper (Chesapeake, Virginia)*, 22/23 April 1993, E13a.
39. Ibid.
40. Jack Dorsey, "Navy Changes Its Tune, Keeps Music School Open," *Norfolk Virginian-Pilot*, 3 November 1993.
41. Benter, *Excerpts from "Station Orders, Receiving Station, Washington, D.C." and Standing Orders of the Navy School of Music and the Navy School of Music Barracks*, 1 December 1939, 1-16.

Chapter 7: The Band Is Born

1. *The Bremerton Sun*, 22 December 1941. Los Angeles County, California Marriage License, 10 June 1938. Clara Kenney, interview with author, 11 June 1994. William Harten, interview with author, 26 November 1993. USS *Arizona*, 17 June 1941 deck log.
2. Jack L. Scruggs, letter to family, 30 March 1941.
3. Ibid, 9 February 1941.
4. Ibid.
5. Betty Kinney, letter to R. B. and M. J. Williams, 22 January 1942.
6. Kenneth Paul Bandy, letter to author, 29 July 1993. Ruth Cadwell Sanders, letter to author, 20 July 1993. USS *Arizona*, 17 June 1941 deck log.

7. *The Nassau Daily Review-Star*, 21 December 1941. Violet Brabbzson, letter to M. J. Williams, 24 May 1943. USS *Arizona*, 17 June 1941 deck log.

8. *Central New Jersey Home News*, 2 April 1942. Mabel Burdette, letter to M. J. Williams, 25 February 1942. Wendell R. Hurley, photograph album, 1941. USS *Arizona*, 17 June 1941 deck log.

9. *The Nassau Daily Review-Star*, 21 December 1941. Mrs. H. H. Chernucha, letter to M. J. Williams, 25 February 1942. N. J. Radford, letter to family, 13 July 1941. USS *Arizona*, 17 June 1941 deck log.

10. *Moline (Illinois) Daily Dispatch*, 11 April 1942. Amy Cox, letter to M. J. Williams, 11 April 1942. USS *Arizona*, 17 June 1941 deck log.

11. *Chicago Tribune*, 2 April 1942. Warren O. H. Floege, letter to M. J. Williams, 21 February 1942. USS *Arizona*, 17 June 1941 deck log.

12. *The Kansas City Times*, 24 December 1941. Betty Jane Brown Miller, interview with Edna Mae Scharz, 18 November 1993. Elizabeth Haas Landeweer, interview with author, 18 November 1993, 17 December 1993. *North Kansas City, Missouri, High School Yearbook*, 1937. USS *Arizona*, 17 June 1941 deck log.

13. *The Evening Times (Sayre, Athens, South Waverly, Pennsylvania)*, 22 July 1942. Gertrude Hughes, letter to Bonnie Moorhouse, December 1947. USS *Arizona*, 17 June 1941 deck log.

14. Donald L. Hurley, interview with author, 19 October 1993. Raymond Hurley, letter to R. B. and M. J. Williams, 9 February 1942. Wendell R. Hurley, photograph album, 1941. USS *Arizona*, 17 June 1941 deck log.

15. Pauline Scruggs Ellis, letter to author, 3 May 1993. John Crawford, interview with author, 3 September 1993. Betty Kinney, letter to R. B. and M. J. Williams, 22 January 1942. Prince George's County, Maryland, Marriage License, 8 February 1941. Howard Hare, interview with author, 17 September 1994. USS *Arizona*, 17 June 1941 deck log.

16. *The Birmingham News*, 22 December 1941, 18 January 1942, 1 February 1942. W. R. Hurley, photograph album, 1941. USS *Arizona*, 17 June 1941 deck log.

17. *The Erie (Pennsylvania) Daily Times*, January 1942, 2 April 1942. The *Wichita (Kansas) Eagle* 2 April 1942. Bonnie Moorhouse, letter to M. J. Williams, 16 January 1942, 19 February 1942, 28 April 1942, 18 September 1942. USS *Arizona*, 17 June 1941 deck log.

18. Amelia Nadel, letter to M. J. Williams, 27 January 1943. W. R. Hurley, photograph album, 1941. USS *Arizona*, 17 June 1941 deck log.

19. N. J. Radford, letter to family, 29 November 1940. Robert Radford, letter to author, 10 February 1993, 8 April 1993. Edna Radford, letter to M. J. Williams, 19 February 1942. W. R. Hurley, photograph album, 1941. USS *Arizona*, 17 June 1941 deck log.

20. Anna Sanderson, letter to M. J. Williams, 20 March 1942. USS *Arizona*, 17 June 1941 deck log.

21. *Long Beach Press-Telegram*, 6 January 1950. Pauline Scruggs Ellis, letter to author, 3 May 1993. USS *Arizona*, 17 June 1941 deck log.

22. *The Houston Post*, January 1941. Edna Shaw, letter to M. J. Williams, 14 February 1942. USS *Arizona*, 17 June 1941 deck log.

23. *The Salt Lake City Tribune,* 8 February 1942. Catherine White, letter to

M. J. Williams, 12 March 1942. USS *Arizona*, 17 June 1941 deck log.
24. *The Enquirer, Cincinnati*, 22 December 1941. Elizabeth Whitson, letter to M. J. Williams, 20 February 1942. USS *Arizona*, 17 June 1941 deck log.
25. Family records of author. W. R. Hurley, photograph album, 1941. USS *Arizona*, 17 June 1941 deck log.

Chapter 8: Winter in Washington

1. John W. Crawford, letter to author, 6 August 1993.
2. Thurmond, interview with author, 11 June 1994.
3. William E. Bohuslaw, interview with author, 22 November 1993.
4. Forgione, interview with author, 3 July 1993.
5. Gross, "Mister, Are You Musical?", *The Washington Post*, 4 May 1941.
6. Benter, "Excerpts from Station Orders, etc.", 5.
7. *The Houston Post*, date unknown.
8. Ruth Sanders, letter to author, 15 October 1993.
9. D. L. Hurley, interview with author, 19 October 1993.
10. Leonard, *Day By Day: The Forties*, 91.
11. Ibid, 94-95.
12. Benter, "Excerpts from Station Orders, etc.", 6.
13. *The Houston Post*, date unknown.
14. *The Birmingham News*, 22 December 1941.
15. Ruark, "They Don't Just Toot a Horn in the Navy," *The Washington Daily News*, 26 June 1942, 31.
16. J. E. "Duke" Bolen, interview with author, 18 September 1993. Gerald E. Wentworth, interview with author, 23 October 1993. Frank W. Schwarz, interview with author, 3 October 1993.
17. Gross, "Mister, Are You Musical?", *The Washington Post*, 4 May 1941.
18. Wentworth, interview with author, 19 March 1994.
19. Joan Watson, letter to C. R. Williams, 10 February 1941.
20. Joyce Billington, letter to C. R. Williams, 16 February 1941.
21. Prince George's County, Maryland, Marriage License, 8 February 1941.
22. John Crawford, interview with author, 24 November 1993.

Chapter 9: Spring in Washington

1. Larry Conley, interview with author, 11 September 1993.
2. Ibid.
3. *The Washington Post*, 2 April 1941.
4. Joseph R. Lucàs, letter to C. R. Williams, 3 March 1941.
5. *The Washington Post*, 8 April 1941.
6. Ibid, 10 April 1941.
7. Amy Cox, letter to M. J. Williams, 11 April 1942.
8. June Brabbzson, letter to M. J. Williams, 7 February 1942.
9. Reginald Carter, letter to C. R. Williams, 29 April 1941.

Chapter 10: Graduation

1. *The Washington Post*, 2 May 1941.
2. Ibid.

3. Ibid, 9 May 1941.
4. Ibid. 6 May 1941.
5. Ibid, 14 May 1941.
6. Ibid.
7. Ibid, 18 May 1941.
8. Ibid.
9. Ibid, 4 May 1941.
10. Dr. Walter Wehner, letter to author, 1 October 1993.
11. William Harten, interview with author, 26 November 1993.
12. Howard G. Hare, letter to author, 29 August 1993.
13. Casper J. Gerace, interview with author, 9 January 1994.
14. Jim McCulloch, interview with author, 29 September 1993.
15. James Montgomery, interview with author, 3 September 1993.
16. Paul Holdaway, interview with author, 28 September 1993.
17. Wendell Hurley, 1941 photograph album.
18. Raymond Hurley, letter to R. B. and M. J. Williams, 22 May 1942.
19. Roger Snyder, interview with author, 18 September 1993.
20. Richard Duryea, letter to author, 11 September 1993.
21. Wehner, letter to author, 1 October 1993.
22. Forgione, interview with author, 6 June 1993.
23. Wentworth, interview with author, 23 October 1993. Bolen, interview
    with author, 18 September 1993.
24. Schwarz, interview with author, 3 October 1993.
25. Raymond Hurley, letter to R. B. and M. J. Williams, 22 May 1942.
26. Betty Kinney, letter to R. B. and M. J. Williams, 22 January 1942.
27. Mabel Burdette, letter to M. J. Williams, 20 September 1943.
28. Elizabeth Whitson, letter to M. J. Williams, 20 February 1942.
29. "Navy School of Music," *Our Navy*, July 1941.
30. Ibid.
31. Wentworth, letter to the Pearl Harbor History Associates, Inc., 17 March
    1988.
32. L. B. Luckenbach, undated letter to John Crawford. Schwarz, letter to
    author, 27 September 1993.

Chapter 11: Our Trip

1. Reginald Carter, letter to C. R. Williams, 18 May 1941.
2. *The Washington Post*, 23 May 1941.
3. "Mother Steed," undated flyer.
4. *The Washington Post*, 15 May 1941.
5. "Mother Steed," undated flyer.
6. *The Washington Post*, 29 May 1941.

Chapter 12: USS *Lassen*

1. W. R. Hurley, 26 May to 7 July 1941 diary.
2. *Our Navy*, June 1941.
3. Ibid.
4. W. R. Hurley, 26 May to 7 July 1941 diary.
5. *The Washington Post*, 9 December 1941.

6. W. R. Hurley, 26 May to 7 July 1941 diary.
7. Ibid.
8. Mabel Burdette, letter to M. J. Williams, 5 January 1949.
9. *Our Navy*, 1944, 11.
10. USS *Arizona* Band Concert program, 30 August 1941.
11. Schwarz, interview with author, 3 October 1993.
12. *The Birmingham News*, 1 February 1942.
13. Bolen, interview with author, 19 September 1993. Conley, interview with author, 11 September 1993.
14. Duryea, letter to author, 11 September 1993. Hare, interview with author, 17 September 1994. Harten, interview with author, 26 November 1993.
15. Clara Kenney, interview with author, 23 October 1993.
16. Luchenbach, undated statement to John Crawford.
17. Thurmond, interview with author, 4 July 1993. Wehner, letter to author, 13 October 1993.
18. W. R. Hurley, 26 May to 7 July 1941 diary.
19. Ibid.
20. *Our Navy*, June 1941.
21. W. R. Hurley, 27 May to 7 July 1941 diary.
22. Ibid.
23. Ibid.
24. Mabel Burdette, letter to M. J. Williams, 25 February 1942.
25. W. R. Hurley, 27 May to 7 July 1941 diary.
26. Ibid.

Chapter 13: USS *Arizona*

1. USS *Arizona*, 17 June 1941 deck log.
2. Stillwell, *Battleship Arizona*, 6.
3. Ibid, 327, 330, 331.
4. USS *Arizona*, 17 June 1941 deck log.
5. Ibid.
6. John Crawford, interview with author, 15 October 1993.
7. John W. Doucett, interview with author, 12 February 1994.
8. Snyder, interview with author, 18 September 1993.
9. Stillwell, *Battleship Arizona*, 217.
10. Bonnie Moorhouse, letter to M. J. Williams, 16 January 1942.
11. Elizabeth Whitson, letter to M. J. Williams, 20 February 1942.
12. Harvey Milhorn, interview with author, 4 July 1993.
13. Hare, interview with author, September 1993.
14. Doucett, interview with author, 12 February 1994.
15. Montgomery, interview with author, 28 November 1993.
16. Hugh Wright, interview with author, 15 January 1994. Doucett, interview with author, 12 February 1994.
17. Wright, interview with author, 15 January 1994. Milhorn, interview with author, 6 February 1994.
18. Milhorn, interview with author, 6 February 1994.
19. Louis Conter, interview with author, 3 October 1993.
20. Snyder, interview with author, 3 October 1993. Doucett, interview with

author, 12 February 1994.

21. Thurmond, interview with author, 4 July 1993.
22. USS *Arizona* Band Concert program, 25 June 1941.
23. Mae Scruggs, letter to M. J. Williams, 30 April 1942. Pauline Scruggs Ellis, letter to author, 19 October 1993.
24. Edna Shaw, letter to M. J. Williams, 14 February 1942. Bonnie Moorhouse, letter to M. J. Williams, 19 February 1942.
25. Mae Scruggs, letter to M. J. Williams, 30 April 1942.

Chapter 14: "The Land of Sunshine and Beautiful Flowers"

1. W. R. Hurley, 26 May to 7 July 1941 diary.
2. Wehner, letter to author, 13 October 1993.
3. W. R. Hurley, 26 May to 7 July 1941 diary.
4. *The Bremerton Sun*, 27 October 1941, 11.
5. R. C. Bastian, letter to author, 22 August 1993.
6. Prange, *At Dawn We Slept*, 47.
7. Leonard, *Day By Day: The Forties*, 132-133.
8. *The Evening Times (Sayre, Athens, South Waverly, Pennsylvania)*,22 July 1942.
9. Stillwell, *Battleship Arizona*, 219. Hare, interview with author, 12 September 1993.

Chapter 15: Faded Blooms

1. Stillwell, *Battleship Arizona*, 332.
2. Mrs. M. Tragella, letter to R. B. and M. J. Williams, 9 September 1942.
3. USS *Arizona* Band Concert program, 30 August 1941.
4. Ralph Burdette, letter to family, 31 August 1941.

Chapter 16: The Battle of Music 1941

1. *The Evening Times (Sayre, Athens, South Waverly, Pennsylvania)*, 22 July 1942.
2. Stillwell, *Battleship Arizona*, 332.
3. Ibid.
4. Colonel C. C. Smith, interview with author, 6 February 1994.
5. Forgione, interview with author, 6 June 1993.
6. Battle of Music 1941 program, 13 September 1941.
7. Snyder, interview with author, 18 September 1993.
8. Hare, interview with author, 12 September 1993.
9. Wentworth, letter to Pearl Harbor History Association, Inc., 17 March 1988.
10. Battle of Music 1941 program, 13 September 1941.
11. J. L. "Kid" Reed, letter to author, 27 September 1941.
12. Hare, interview with author, 12 September 1993.
13. Stillwell, *Battleship Arizona*, 332.
14. Gertrude Hughes, letter to Bonnie Moorhouse, December 1947.
15. Stillwell, *Battleship Arizona*, 332.
16. Captain F. Van Valkenburgh, letter to The Chief of the Bureau of Ships, 2 October 1941.

17. Stillwell, *Battleship Arizona*, 332.
18. Charles E. Chase, article in *Pearl Harbor Survivors Book*, 176.
19. *The Bremerton Sun*, 10 October 1941.
20. Ibid, 10 October 1941, 11 October 1941.
21. Ibid, 11 October 1941.
22. Stillwell, *Battleship Arizona*, 332.
23. *The Bremerton Sun*, 24 October 1941.
24. Stillwell, *Battleship Arizona*, 332.
25. Battle of Music 1941 program, 25 October 1941.
26. Ibid.
27. *The Bremerton Sun*, 27 October 1941.
28. Ibid, 31 October 1941.

Chapter 17: "We Won't Be Home for Christmas"

1. Doucett, interview with author, 12 February 1994.
2. Snyder, interview with author, 18 September 1993.
3. *The Washington Post*, 26 June 1942.
4. Stillwell, *Battleship Arizona*, 332.
5. *The Bremerton Sun*, 5 November 1941.
6. Ibid.
7. Battle of Music 1941 program, 8 November 1941.
8. A. E. Streight, interview with author, 24 April 1993.
9. Raymond Hurley, 1942 statement.
10. James Clelland, interview with author, 16 January 1994.
11. Bastian, letter to author, 22 August 1993.
12. Frank Worden, interview with author, 10 June 1993.
13. Loren Bailey, interview with author, 24 June 1993.
14. *The Evening Times (Sayre, Athens, South Waverly, Pennsylvania)*, 22 July 1942.
15. Stillwell, *Battleship Arizona*, 126.
16. Don Bright, interview with author, 1 July 1993.
17. Leonard, *Day By Day: The Forties*, 165.
18. *The Washington Post*, 24 January 1941.
19. Leonard, *Day By Day: The Forties*, 164.
20. *The Bremerton Sun*, 26 November 1941.
21. Barbara Reid, letter of 18 October 1985 to Nina Hart, editor, *Arizona's Heart Beats*, Volume 1, 95.
22. Kenneth Paul Bandy, letter to author, 19 July 1993. Ruth Cadwell Sanders, letter to author, 20 July 1993.
23. Joan Watson Peters, interview with author, 26 February 1994.
24. *The Wichita (Kansas) Eagle*, 2 April 1942.
25. *The Enquirer, Cincinnati*, 22 December 1941.
26. Edna Shaw, letter to M. J. Williams, 14 February 1942.
27. Raymond Hurley, letter to R. B. and M. J. Williams, 9 February 1942.
28. W. R. Hurley, photograph album, 1941.
29. Stillwell, *Battleship Arizona*, 336-350.
30. W. R. Hurley, photograph album, 1941.
31. Ibid.
32. *The Birmingham News*, 1 December 1941.

33. *The Bremerton Sun*, 1 December 1941.
34. Ibid, 4 December 1941.
35. Stillwell, *Battleship Arizona*, 228.
36. Streight, interview with author, 24 April 1993.
37. Ibid.
38. Edwin E. Sharp, account in *Pearl Harbor Survivors*, 386.
39. J. L. "Kid" Reed, letter to author, 5 December 1941.

Chapter 18: December 6, 1941

1. Stillwell, *Battleship Arizona*, 228.
2. James Kennedy, interview with author, 11 December 1993.
3. Stillwell, *Battleship Arizona*, 228.
4. Kennedy, interview with author, 11 December 1993.
5. Ralph H. Goold, interview with author, 6 February 1994. Frank Peter Stock, interview with author, 6 February 1994.
6. Morris W. Van Korlaar, interview with author, 19 February 1994.
7. Stillwell, *Battleship Arizona*, 228.
8. Edna Shaw, letter to M. J. Williams, 14 February 1942. *The Enquirer, Cincinnati*, 22 December 1941.
9. Catherine White, letter to M. J. Williams, 24 April 1942.
10. Ruth Cadwell Sanders, letter to author, 20 July 1993.
11. Joan Watson Peters, interview with author, 26 February 1994.
12. *The Courier-Journal (Louisville, Kentucky)*, 9 December 1941.
13. Bonnie Moorhouse, letter to M. J. Williams, 28 April 1942.
14. Ruth Cadwell Sanders, letter to author, 15 October 1993.
15. L. H. Brown, interview with R. B. and M. J. Williams, January 1942. Chase, account in *Pearl Harbor Survivors*, 176.
16. Harold Breen, interview with author, 7 January 1995.
17. Worden, interview with author, 10 June 1993.
18. Hare, interview with author, 12 September 1993.
19. Eugene B. Crawford, interview with author, June 1993.
20. Prange, *December 7, 1941*, 43.
21. L. H. Brown, interview with R. B. and M. J. Williams, January 1942.
22. H. C. Kane, letter to M. J. Williams, 24 April 1942.
23. R. B. Williams, letter to author, 28 November 1942.
24. Ibid.
25. Snyder, interview with author, 18 September 1993.
26. Wentworth, letter to Pearl Harbor History Associates, Inc., 17 March 1988.
27. Anna Sanderson, letter to M. J. Williams, 20 March 1942.
28. Ibid.
29. Bolen, interview with author, September 1993.
30. Montgomery, interview with author, 28 November 1993.
31. Wentworth, letter to Pearl Harbor History Associates, Inc., 17 March 1988.
32. Ibid.
33. John W. Crawford, interview with author, 15 October 1993.
34. Ibid.
35. Lamar S. Crawford, interview with author, 30 January 1994.
36. Milhorn, interview with author, 6 February 1994.

Chapter 19: December 7, 1941

1. Milhorn, interview with author, 6 February 1994.
2. Doucett, interview with author, 12 February 1994.
3. Stillwell, *Battleship Arizona*, 228.
4. Mabel Burdette, interview with Warrant Officer John Carey, 5 January 1949.
5. Streight, interview with author, 24 April 1993.
6. Montgomery, interview with author, 28 November 1993.
7. Ibid.
8. John Crawford, interview with author, 15 October 1993.
9. Anna Sanderson, letter to M. J. Williams, 20 March 1942.
10. Wentworth, letter to Pearl Harbor History Associates, Inc., 17 March 1988.
11. Raymond Hurley, letter to R. B. and M. J. Williams, 9 February 1942.
12. Walter Lord, *Day of Infamy*, 62.
13. Forgione, interview with author, 6 June 1993.
14. John Crawford, interview with author, 11 September 1993.
15. Duryea, interview with author, 16 October 1993.
16. Mike Palchefsky, interview with author, 11 September 1993.
17. Richard A. Giglio, account in *Pearl Harbor Survivors*, 229.
18. Edward P. Strobak, interview with author, 16 December 1993.
19. Omer S. Kent, interview with author, 6 June 1993.
20. Conter, interview with author, 3 October 1993.
21. Ray Bowden, account in *Pearl Harbor Survivors*, 101.
22. Clay H. Musick, interview with author, 3 August 1993.
23. Jimmy C. Burcham, interview with author, 3 August 1993.
24. Conter, interview with author, 3 October 1993.
25. Milhorn, interview with author, 4 July 1993.
26. James Kennedy, interview with author, 11 December 1993.
27. Jack E. Rininger, interview with author, 19 February 1994.
28. John Crawford, interview with author, 15 October 1993.
29. Forgione, interview with author, 6 June 1993.
30. Bowden, account in *Pearl Harbor Survivors*, 101.
31. Snyder, interview with author, 18 September 1993.
32. Bohuslaw, account in *Pearl Harbor Survivors*, 154.
33. Duryea, letter to author, 11 September 1993. Holdaway, interview with author, 28 September 1993.
34. Montgomery, interview with author, 3 September 1993. Snyder, interview with author, 18 September 1993.
35. Hare, letter to author, 29 August 1993.
36. Ibid. Harten, interview with author, 26 November 1993. Sol Blain, interview with author, 15 January 1994.
37. R. J. Tippets, 7 December 1941 diary.
38. Ibid.
39. William W. Bucher, interview with author, 15 January 1994.
40. Bowden, account in *Pearl Harbor Survivors*, 101.
41. Charles Risher, interview with author, 2 January 1994.
42. Robert S. La Forte and Ronald E. Marcello, *Remembering Pearl Harbor*, 83.
43. Conley, interview with author, 11 September 1993.

44. Palchefsky, interview with author, 11 September 1993.
45. Henry Lachenmeyer, 8 December 1941 diary.
46. Ibid.
47. James W. Henry, account in *Pearl Harbor Survivors*, 250.
48. Dean R. Kreek, interview with author, 10 July 1993, 24 July 1993.
49. Ibid. Clyde S. Griffin, account in *Pearl Harbor Survivors*, 237.
50. William E. Clemons, interview with author, August 1993.
51. Guy Flannigan, account to Nina Hart, editor, *Arizona's Heart Beats*, volume 1, 105.
52. Betty Kinney, letter to R. B. and M. J. Williams, 22 January 1942.
53. Milhorn, interview with author, 4 July 1993.
54. John H. Birmingham, account in *Pearl Harbor Survivors*, 151 and interview with author, 9 January 1994.
55. Burcham, interview with author, 3 August 1993.
56. Jack E. Rininger, interview with author, 19 February 1994.
57. Lamar S. Crawford, interview with author, 30 January 1994.
58. Captain Jim Dick Miller, letter to Lorraine Marks, 14 June 1991.
59. Lamar S. Crawford, interview with author, 30 January 1994.
60. Doucett, interview with author, 12 February 1994.
61. Ibid.
62. Paul Faulkner, interview with author, 19 February 1994.

Chapter 20: We Hear

1. *The Kansas City Star Magazine*, 21 November 1993.
2. Ibid.
3. *The Courier-Journal (Louisville, Kentucky)*, 7 December 1941.
4. Ibid, 8 December 1941.
5. *Okmulgee (Oklahoma) Daily Times*, 9 December 1941.
6. *The Enquirer, Cincinnati*, 9 December 1941.
7. *The Courier-Journal (Louisville, Kentucky)*, 11 December 1941.
8. *Okmulgee (Oklahoma) Daily Times*, 16 December 1941.
9. Ibid, 23 December 1941.
10. D. E. Handy, Okmulgee, Oklahoma, 23 December 1941.
11. Edith White, Okmulgee, Oklahoma, 26 December 1941.
12. Fred Watson, Okmulgee, Oklahoma, 20 December 1941.

Chapter 21: We Search

1. *The Courier-Journal (Louisville, Kentucky)*, 10 December 1941.
2. Ibid.
3. *At 'Em Arizona*, June 1941.
4. Bonnie Moorhouse, letter to Next of Kin of C. R. Williams, 7 January 1942.
5. June Brabbzson, letter to R. B. and M. J. Williams, 14 January 1942.
6. Mabel Burdette, letter to R. B. and M. J. Williams, 25 February 1942.
7. Bonnie Moorhouse, letter to M. J. Williams, 16 January 1942.
8. Bright, letter to author, 27 June 1993.
9. Ibid.
10. Ibid.
11. U.S. Navy List of Dead, as of 7 December 1941, 3.

12. *At 'Em Arizona*, Summer Edition 1993, 7.
13. Edna Shaw, letter to M. J. Williams, 2 August 1942.
14. U.S. Navy List of Dead, as of 7 December 1941, 8.
15. *At 'Em Arizona*, Summer Edition 1993, 7.
16. Mae Scruggs, letter to M. J. Williams, 13 August 1949.
17. Ibid.
18. *Long Beach Press Telegram*, 6 January 1950.
19. Mae Scruggs, letter to M. J. Williams, 13 August 1949.
20. *The Courier-Journal (Louisville, Kentucky)*, 2 February 1942.
21. Betty Kinney, letter to R. B. and M. J. Williams, 22 January 1942.
22. Duryea, interview with author, October 1993.
23. Betty Kinney, letter to M. J. Williams, 22 January 1942.
24. Ibid.
25. Ibid.
26. Ibid.
27. Ibid.
28. L. Henry Brown, interview with R. B. and M. J. Williams, January 1942.
29. H. C. Kane, letter to M. J. Williams, 24 April 1943.
30. Catherine White, letter to M. J. Williams, 4 April 1942.
31. Mabel Burdette, letter to M. J. Williams, 22 April 1942.
32. Bonnie Moorhouse, letter to M. J. Williams, 28 April 1942.
33. Edna Shaw, letter to M. J. Williams, 2 August 1942.
34. Mabel Burdette, letter to M. J. Williams, 22 September 1942.
35. Ibid.
36. Stillwell, *Battleship Arizona*, 350.
37. Bonnie Moorhouse, letter to M. J. Williams, 28 April 1942.
38. Mabel Burdette, letter to M. J. Williams, 5 January 1949.
39. Elizabeth Whitson, letter to M. J. Williams, 3 September 1943.
40. Alexander F. Jones, letter to M. J. Williams, 10 March 1942.
41. *Honolulu Star-Bulletin*, 2 May 1942.
42. Mrs. M. Tragella, Manager Moana Hotel, letter to M. J. Williams, 9 September 1942.
43. Don Senick, letter to R. B. Williams, 27 May 1942.
44. Elizabeth Whitson, letter to M. J. Williams, 11 November 1943.
45. James Leamon Forbis, interview with author, 22 January 1994.
46. Edward A. Teats, account in *Pearl Harbor Survivors*, 412.
47. Ibid.
48. Mabel Burdette, letter to M. J. Williams, 16 December 1942.

Chapter 22: We Grieve

1. *The Enquirer, Cincinnati*, 22 December 1941.
2. Elizabeth Haas Landeweer, interview with author, 23 November 1993.
3. *The Washington Post*, 3 February 1942.
4. *The Enquirer, Cincinnati*, 22 December 1941.
5. R. B. Williams, Jr., letter to Frank Knox, 17 June 1942.
6. Navy Department, Bureau of Naval Personnel (Randall Jacobs, Rear Admiral, U.S. Navy), letter to R. B. Williams, Jr., 13 November 1942.
7. Navy Department, Public Voucher to R. B. Williams, Jr., 19 November 1942.

Chapter 23: Obituaries

1. *The Bremerton Sun*, 22 December 1941. Elizabeth Kinney, letter to R. B. and M. J. Williams, 22 January 1942. Los Angeles County, California, Marriage License, 10 June 1938. William Harten, interview with author, 26 November 1993. Clara Kenney, interview with author, 23 October 1993. USS *Arizona*, 17 June 1941 deck log.

2. Mattie Mae Bandy, letter to R. B. and M. J. Williams, 13 May 1942. Dolores Bertels, letter to author, 20 June 1993. Kenneth Paul Bandy, letter to author, 29 July 1993. Ruth Cadwell Sanders, letters to author, 20 July 1993, 15 October 1993, 2 November 1993. Jack Leo Scruggs, letter to family, 24 July 1941. *The Chronicles of Oklahoma*, Oklahoma Historical Society Quarterly, Spring 1944, 13. USS *Arizona*, 17 June 1941 deck log.

3. *The Nassau Daily Review-Star*, 21 December 1941, 30 March 1942. June Brabbzson, letters to M. J. Williams, various dates, 1942. *The National Legionnaire*, 1942. Violet Brabbzson, letters to M. J. Williams, various dates, 1942 and 1943. Mabel Burdette, letter to M. J. Williams, 25 February 1942. USS *Arizona*, 17 June 1941 deck log.

4. *Central New Jersey Home News*, 2 April 1942. Mabel Burdette, letters to M. J. Williams, various dates, 1942-1949. USS *Arizona*, 17 June 1941 deck log.

5. *The Nassau Daily Review-Star*, 21 December 1941. Mrs. H. H. Chernucha, letters to M. J. Williams, 25 February 1942, 15 April 1942. N. J. Radford, letter to family, 13 July 1941. USS *Arizona*, 17 June 1941 deck log.

6. *Moline (Illinois) Daily Dispatch*, 11 April 1942. Amy Cox, letter to M. J. Williams, 11 April 1942. Lorraine Marks Haislip, letter to author, 26 September 1993. USS *Arizona*, 17 June 1941 deck log.

7. *Chicago Tribune*, 2 April 1942. Warren O. H. Floege, letter to M. J. Williams, 21 February 1942. USS *Arizona*, 17 June 1941 deck log.

8. *The Kansas City Times*, 24 December 1941. *Adrian (Missouri) Journal*, 25 December 1941. Elizabeth Haas Landeweer, interviews with author, 18 November 1993, 23 November 1993, 17 December 1993. *North Kansas City, Missouri, High School Yearbook*, 1937. Edna Mae Schwarz, interviews with author, 18 November 1993, 23 November 1993. Betty Jane Brown Miller, interview with Edna Mae Scharz, 18 November 1993. *Kansas City, Missouri, City Directory*, 1941. USS *Arizona*, 17 June 1941 deck log.

9. *The Evening Times (Sayre, Athens, South Waverly, Pennsylvania)*, 22 July 1942. Gertrude Hughes, letters to M. J. Williams, December 1951, 14 December 1962. Amelia Nadel, letter to M. J. Williams, 27 January 1943. Gertrude Hughes, letter to Bonnie Moorhouse, December 1947. USS *Arizona*, 17 June 1941 deck log.

10. Raymond Hurley, letters to R. B. and M. J. Williams, 9 February 1942, 22 May 1942. Donald L. Hurley, interview with author, 19 October 1993. Donald L. Hurley, letter to author, 7 December 1993. Wendell Ray Hurley, 1 March-28 November 1941 photograph and autograph album. Wendell Ray Hurley, 26 May-7 July 1941 diary. Raymond Hurley, 1 February 1942 statement. Funeral Card, Wendell Ray Hurley, 1 Febru-

ary 1942. USS *Arizona*, 17 June 1941 deck log.

11. Elizabeth Von Babo Kinney, letter to R. B. and M. J. Williams, 22 January 1942. Pauline Scruggs Ellis, letter to author, 3 May 1993. Howard Hare, interview with author, 17 September 1994. John Crawford, interview with author, 3 September 1993. Prince George's County, Maryland, Marriage License, 8 February 1941. USS *Arizona*, 17 June 1941 deck log.

12. *The Birmingham News*, 17 December 1941, 22 December 1941, 18 January 1941, 1 February 1941. Edna Shaw, letter to M. J. Williams, 2 August 1942. Wendell Ray Hurley, 1 March-28 November 1941 photograph and autograph album. *Birmingham, Alabama, City Directory*, 1941. USS *Arizona*, 17 June 1941 deck log.

13. *The Wichita (Kansas) Eagle*, 2 April 1942. *Erie (Pennsylvania) Daily Times*, 2 April 1942. Bonnie Moorhouse, letters to M. J. Williams, various dates, 7 January 1942 to 19 December 1944. Elizabeth Kinney, letter to R. B. and M. J. Williams, 22 January 1942. USS *Arizona*, 17 June 1941 deck log.

14. Amelia Nadel, letters to M. J. Williams, 31 March 1942, 17 December 1942, 27 January 1943. Wendell Ray Hurley, 1 March-28 November 1941 photograph and autograph album. USS *Arizona*, 17 June 1941 deck log.

15. Edna Radford, letters to M. J. Williams, 19 February 1942, 17 January 1943. Neal J. Radford, letters to family, various dates, 29 November 1940-25 November 1941. Robert Radford, letters to author, various dates, 15 February 1993-22 January 1994. Robert Radford, interview with author, August 1993. Wendell Ray Hurley, 1 March-28 November 1941 photograph and autograph album. USS *Arizona*, 17 June 1941 deck log.

16. Anna Sanderson, letters to M. J. Williams, 20 March 1942, 20 April 1942. Tombstone Inscription, Lindsay Strathmore Cemetery, Lindsay, California. USS *Arizona*, 17 June 1941 deck log.

17. *Long Beach Press-Telegram*, 6 January 1950. Mac Scruggs, letters to M. J. Williams, 30 April 1942, 13 August 1949. Pauline Scruggs Ellis, letters to author, various dates, 3 May 1993-5 May 1994. Pauline Scruggs Ellis, interviews with author, various dates, 15 February 1993-7 December 1994. Funeral Card, Jack Leo Scruggs, 7 January 1950. Jack Leo Scruggs, letters to family, 9 February 1941-23 November 1941. USS *Arizona*, 17 June 1941 deck log.

18. *The Houston Post*, January 1941. Edna Shaw, letters to M. J. Williams, various dates, 14 February 1942-12 September 1944. Elizabeth Kinney, letter to R. B. and M. J. Williams, 22 January 1942. USS *Arizona*, 17 June 1941 deck log.

19. *The Salt Lake City Tribune*, 8 February 1942. Catherine White, letters to M. J. Williams, 12 March 1942, 24 April 1942. Bonnie Moorhouse, letter to M. J. Williams, 19 February 1942. USS *Arizona*, 17 June 1941 deck log.

20. *The Enquirer, Cincinnati*, 16 December 1941, 22 December 1941. Elizabeth Whitson, letters to M. J. Williams, 20 February 1942-17 November 1943. USS *Arizona*, 17 June 1941 deck log.

21. Family records in collection of author. C. R. Williams, letters to family,

20 May 1940-26 November 1941. R. B. and M. J. Williams and author, letters to C. R. Williams, various dates, 9 July 1940-15 May 1941. *The Chronicles of Oklahoma*, Oklahoma Historical Society Quarterly, Spring 1944, 39,40. USS *Arizona*, 17 June 1941 deck log.

Chapter 24: Honors

1. *Okmulgee (Oklahoma) Daily Times*, 9 January 1941.
2. The American Legion Gold Star Citation, 9 August 1943.
3. *Okmulgee (Oklahoma) Daily Times*, 29 May 1942.
4. Ibid, 10 March 1942.
5. Joe Croom, letter to M. J. Williams, 9 September 1942.
6. Citation, Okmulgee, Oklahoma, High School, 23 May 1946.
7. Citation, State of Oklahoma, 31 December 1946.
8. *The Chronicles of Oklahoma*, Oklahoma Historical Society Quarterly, Spring 1944, 39,40.
9. President Franklin D. Roosevelt, Citation. Undated.
10. Citation, Purple Heart, 18 February 1944.
11. James Forrestal, Secretary of the Navy, undated letter to R. B. Williams.
12. Mabel Burdette, letter to M. J. Williams, 1 June 1943.
13. Ibid, 20 September 1943.
14. Ibid, 16 March 1944.
15. Wisniewski, *Pearl Harbor and the USS Arizona Memorial*, 55.
16. Ibid, 58.

Chapter 25: The *Arizona* Band Trophy

1. Amelia Nadel, letter to M. J. Williams, 31 March 1942.
2. *The Honolulu Star-Bulletin*, 2 April 1942.
3. Alfred Dupont, painting of "*Arizona* Trophy," April 1942.
4. Betty Kinney, letter to R. B. and M. J. Williams, 22 January 1942.
5. Lieutenant Commander Hugh McKay, letter to R. B. Williams, 25 April 1942.
6. Mabel Burdette, letter to M. J. Williams, 17 February 1943.
7. Ibid.
8. Ibid.
9. Edward P. Strobak, interview with author, 16 December 1993.
10. Okmulgee County, Oklahoma, Marriage License, 29 November 1942.
11. R. B. Williams, letter to author, 28 November 1942.
12. Mabel Burdette, letter to M. J. Williams, 17 February 1943.
13. John W. Crawford, interview with author, 24 November 1993.
14. Thurmond, interview with author, 4 July 1993.
15. Mabel Burdette, letter to M. J. Williams, 5 January 1949.
16. Citation, Purple Heart, 18 February 1944.
17. Citation, Okmulgee, Oklahoma, High School, 23 May 1946.
18. *Arizona* Band Trophy.
19. Fred Watson, Okmulgee, Oklahoma, 20 December 1941.
20. J. L. Scruggs, Apprentice Seaman, 13 March 1941.

Sources

Interviews with Author

Alverson, Lieutenant Commander Mike, USN. Norfolk, Virginia, 21 May 1993. By telephone, 14 June 1993, 5 July 1994.

Bandy, Kenneth Paul. By telephone, 23 June 1993.

Bandy, Kenneth Wayne. By telephone, 23 June 1993.

Bastian, Chief Petty Officer Russell C., USN (Ret.). By telephone, 21 August 1993.

Birmingham, John H. By telephone, 9 January 1994.

Blaine, Sol. By telephone, 2 September 1993.

Bohuslaw, William E. By telephone, 18 September 1993, 22 September 1993.

Bolen, J. E. "Duke". By telephone, 18 September 1993.

Breen, Harold. By telephone, 7 January 1995.

Bright, Don. By telephone, 1 July 1993, 10 July 1993, 2 January 1994.

Bucher, William W. By telephone, 15 January 1994.

Burcham, Jimmie Charles. By telephone, 3 August 1993.

Cabiness, Frank R. By telephone, 30 January 1994.

Christiansen, Harlan Carl. By telephone, 2 January 1994.

Clelland, Master Sergeant James, USMC (Ret.). By telephone, 16 January 1994.

Clemons, William E. By telephone, 31 July 1993.

Cockburn, John L. By telephone, 10 January 1994.

Conley, Data Processing Chief Larry, USN (Ret.). By telephone, 2 September 1993, 11 September 1993, 21 January 1994.

Conter, Louis. By telephone, 3 October 1993.

Cozad, Reymon. By telephone, 11 December 1993, 5 January 1994.

Crawford, Eugene B. By telephone, 10 June 1993, 29 December 1993.

Crawford, John W. By telephone, 3 July 1993, 15 October 1993, 24 November 1993.

Crawford, Lamar. By telephone, 30 January 1994.

Doucett, John. W. By telephone, 12 February 1994.

Doughty, Virginia. By telephone, May 1993.

Duryea, Richard T. By telephone, 16 October 1993.

Ellis, Pauline Scruggs. By telephone, various dates, 2 May 1993 to present.

Emelander, Henry. By telephone, 8 January 1994.

Faulkner, Paul Harding. By telephone, 19 February 1994.

Ferri, Ambrose F. By telephone, 6 February 1994.

Forbis, Chief Boatswain's Mate James Leamon, USN (Ret.). By telephone, 22 January 1994.

Forgione, Lieutenant Colonel Frank G., USA. By telephone, 6 June 1993, 3 July 1993, 2 January 1994.

Gerace, Casper J. By telephone, 9 January 1994.

Goold, Ralph H. By telephone, 6 February 1994.

Hackett, Daniel Vernon. By telephone, 6 February 1994.

Hall, Harold. By telephone, 21 June 1993.

Hare, Howard G. By telephone, 12 September 1993.

Harten, William. By telephone, 26 November 1993, 27 November 1993.

Hetrick, Clarendon Robert. By telephone, 21 August 1993.

Holdaway, Paul. By telephone, 28 September 1993.

Houchin, Lawrence. By telephone, various dates.

Hurley, Donald Lee. By telephone, 19 October 1993, 1 November 1993, 23 November 1993.

Hurley, Robert Delmar. By telephone, 18 October 1993.

Kennedy, James H. By telephone, 11 December 1993, 8 February 1994.

Kenney, Clara. By telephone, 16 October 1993, 23 October 1993, 11 June 1994.

Kent, Omer S. Kansas City, Kansas, various dates, 1943 to present.

Kreek, Dean R. By telephone, 10 July 1993, 25 July, 1993.

Kropf, Fred F. By telephone, various dates 1993 and 1994.

Lachenmayer, Musician Henry A., USN (Ret.). By telephone, 27 September 1993, 15 October 1993, 15 January 1994.

Landeweer, Elizabeth Haas. By telephone, various dates, 1993 and 1994.

Langdell, Joseph Kopcho. Tuscon, Arizona, 4 December 1992.

Marks, Lorraine E. Tuscon, Arizona, 4 December 1992. By telephone, January 1993.

McCulloch, James W. By telephone, 29 September 1993.

Milhorn, Harvey Hollis, USN (Ret.). By telephone, 4 July 1993, 6 February 1994.

Mitchell, Glen H. By telephone, 15 January 1994.

Montgomery, James W. By telephone, 2 September 1993, 28 November 1993.

Musick, Clay Henry. By telephone, 3 August 1993.

Palchefsky, Mike. By telephone, 11 September 1993, 3 October 1993.

Peters, Joan Watson. By telephone, 26 February 1994.

Radford, Robert. By telephone, 20 February 1993, 31 August 1993.

Rininger, Senior Chief Jack E., USNR (Ret.). By telephone, 19 February 1994.

Risher, Charles. By telephone, 2 January 1994.

Scharz, Edna Mae. By telephone, 18 November 1993, 23 November 1993.

Schwarz, Frank W. By telephone, 3 October 1993, 2 January 1994.

Seitz, Lieutenant Gary, USN. By telephone, 2 October 1994.

Smith, Colonel C. C., USMC (Ret.). By telephone, 6 February 1994.

Smith, Marion. By telephone, 4 January 1994.

Snyder, Roger. By telephone, 18 September 1993, 3 October 1993.

Stock, Frank Peter. By telephone, 6 February 1994.

Stratton, Donald. By telephone, 12 February 1994.

Streight, Asa E. By telephone, 23 January 1993, 24 April 1993, 10 July 1993.

Strobak, Edward P. By telephone, 16 December 1993.

Sudduth, Joe. By telephone, 15 January 1994, 16 January 1994.

Swain, Donald K. By telephone, 21 August 1993.

Thomas, Jerry. By telephone, 23 November 1993.

Thurmond, Boatswain's Mate James M., USN. Washington, D.C., various dates, 1942 to 1943.

Thurmond, Dr. James M., USN (Ret.). By telephone, 4 July 1993, 6 February 1994.

Von Korlaar, Morris W. By telephone, 19 February 1994.

Webb Sanders Funeral Home. By telephone, 1 December 1993.

Wentworth, Gerald. By telephone, 29 September 1993, 23 October 1993, 19 March

1994, 24 October 1994.
Worden, Frank. By telephone, 3 July 1993, 10 July 1993, 31 July 1993.
Wright, Hugh. By telephone, 15 January 1994.

Other Interviews

Brown, Musician Second Class Luther Henry, USN. With R. B. and M. J. Williams, various dates, 1942 to 1945.
Carey, Warrant Officer John, USN. With Harry and Mabel Burdette, United States Navy School of Music, Washington, D. C., 2 January 1949.
Miller, Betty Jane Brown. With Edna Mae Scharz, 18 November 1993.
Murphey, Chief Quartermaster P. L. "Spud", USN (Ret.). With Mabel Burdette, Kansas City, Missouri, 20 September 1942.
Nichols, Radioman First Class John Edward, USN. With Arthur S. White, Salt Lake City, Utah, 24 April 1942.
Smith, Bandmaster James Lamar, USN. With Elizabeth Marie Kinney, Bremerton, Washington, January 1942.
Thurmond, Ensign James T., USN. With Mabel Burdette, United States Navy School of Music, Washington, D. C., 16 January 1943.
Thurmond, Lieutenant James T., USN. With Harry and Mabel Burdette, United States Navy School of Music, Washington, D. C., 2 January 1949.
Yandle, Seaman Second Class Leonard Orville, USN. With R. B. Williams, 28 November 1942.

Booklets

American Battle Monuments Commission. *American Memorials and Overseas Military Cemeteries*, (1980).
American Battle Monuments Commission. *Honolulu Memorial, National Memorial Cemetery of the Pacific, Honolulu, Hawaii*, (1964).
Dictionary of American Naval Fighting Ships.
Yearbook, North Kansas City, Missouri, High School, 1937. Courtesy Gus Leimkuler.
Yearbook, Okmulgee, Oklahoma, High School, 1939, 1940.

Books

Arizona, USS Reunion Association. *Membership Roster*, 1992.
Brinkley, David. *Washington Goes to War*. New York: Ballantine Books, 1988.
Friedman, Norman, Arthur D. Baker, III, Arnold S. Lott, and Robert F. Sumrall. *USS Arizona (BB 39)*. Annapolis: Leeward Publications, 1978.
Goldstein, Donald M. and Katherine V. Dillon. *The Way it Was: Pearl Harbor— The Original Photographs*. Brassey's (U.S.) Inc. 1991.
Hart, Nina, editor. *Arizona's Heart Beats*, two volumes. Lake Henry, Florida: privately published, 1986 and 1987.
LaForte, Robert S. and Ronald E. Marcello. *Remembering Pearl Harbor*.Scholarly Research, 1991.

Leonard, Thomas M. *Day By Day: The Forties*. Facts on File, New York, 1977.

Lord, Walter. *Day of Infamy*. New York: Bantam Books, 1957.

Moffitt, James W., Editor. *The Chronicles of Oklahoma*. Oklahoma Historical Society Quarterly, Spring, 1944.

Palmer, Norman and Thomas B. Allen. *World War II—America at War 1941-1945*. New York: Random House, 1991.

Parish, Thomas and S. L. A. Marshall, Editors. *The Simon & Schuster Encyclopedia of World War II*. Simon and Schuster, New York, 1978.

Pearl Harbor Survivors. Turner Publishing Company, 1992.

Prang, Gordon W. *At Dawn We Slept*. New York: Penguin Books, 1986.

_____ *December 7, 1941. The Day the Japanese Attacked Pearl Harbor*. New York: Warner Book, Inc., 1989.

_____ *Pearl Harbor: The Verdict of History*. New York: McGraw-Hill, 1986.

Rice, Captain William T., USNR (Ret.). *Pearl Harbor Story*. Honolulu: Swak, Inc., 1974.

Stillwell, Paul. *Air Raid: Pearl Harbor!* Annapolis: Naval Institute Press, 1981.

_____ *Battleship Arizona*. Annapolis: Naval Institute Press, 1991.

Toland, John. *Infamy: Pearl Harbor and Its Aftermath*. Garden City, NY: Doubleday & Co., Inc., 1982.

Warner, Denis & Peggy Warner. *The Sacred Warriors: Japan's Suicide Legions*. New York: Avon Books, 1982.

Wells, Arthur W. *The Quack Corps*. Chico, California: Dol Art Published, 1992.

Wisniewski, Richard A. *Pearl Harbor and the USS Arizona Memorial: A Pictorial History*. Honolulu, Hawaii: Pacific Basin Enterprises, revised edition.

Brochures

Arizona, USS Memorial. 14 ND-DISTAFF-P-5723/1 (Rev 9-67).

Navy Family Chapel, Long Beach, California.

Pearl Harbor Cruise on Adventure V.

Pearl Harbor Cruise on the M/V Kaimanu II. (1959.)

Reproduction of Official U.S. Navy Photographs, Pearl Harbor. Plane Facts Company, New York.

Steed, Mrs. J. Nathaniel. Undated.

Citations

American Legion Gold Star Citation. In memory of Clyde R. Williams, 3 August 1943.

Chambers, Superintendent W. W. and Principal Guy B. Blakey, Okmulgee High School. Certificates of Attendance to Clyde R. Williams. Various dates.

Chambers, Superintendent W. W. and Principal Guy B. Blakey, Okmulgee High School. Certificate of Letter Award in Instrumental Music to Clyde R. Williams. 22 May 1940.

Jacobs, Rear Admiral Randall. Purple Heart to Clyde Richard Williams, Musician 2 Class, USN. 18 February 1944.

Okmulgee, Oklahoma, High School. Citation in memory of Clyde R. Williams, 23 May 1946.

Roosevelt, President Franklin D. Citation in Memory of Clyde Richard Williams. Undated.

Letters

Arizona, USS (BB-39). Postcards, collections of Hurley family and of author, various dates, 1940 and 1941. Courtesy Donald Hurley.

Ascione, Commander Raymond A., USN. To author, 4 March 1993.

Author. To Commandant Navy Yard, Pearl Harbor, T. H., 8 May 1943.

Author. To Gary T. Cummins, USS *Arizona* Memorial. 21 September 1982.

Author. To Clyde Richard Williams, various dates, 1940-1941.

Bailey, E. L., Veterans Administration. To Martha Jane Williams, 5 March 1942.

Bailey, E. L., Veterans Administration. To Richard B. Williams, Jr., 20 February 1942, 5 March 1942.

Bailey, Loren. To author, 24 June 1993.

Bandy, Reverend John L. To Bonnie Moorhouse, January 1942.

Bandy, Reverend Kenneth Paul. To author, 29 June 1993 and 29 July 1993.

Bandy, Mattie Mae. To M. J. Williams, 11 May 1942.

Bastian, Chief Petty Officer Russell C., USN (Ret.). To author, 22 August 1993.

Bennett, Lieutenant Commander D. A., USNR, Navy Department, Bureau of Naval Personnel. To R. B. Williams, 16 July 1947, 11 August 1947.

Benter, Lieutenant Charles, USN. To C. R. Williams, 11 July 1940.

Berry, Anita. To Clyde R. Williams, various dates, 29 August 1940 to 30 November 1940.

Bertels, Dolores A. To author, 30 April 1993, 9 May 1993, 17 May 1993, 20 June 1993 and 25 June 1993.

Billington, Joyce. To Clyde R. Williams, various dates, 1 October 1940 to 19 May 1941.

Blaine, Sol. To author, 27 August 1993 and 2 September 1993.

Blakey, Guy B., Principal Okmulgee High School. To Commanding Officer, The United States Naval School of Music, Washington, D. C., 15 June 1940.

Blakey, Ruth. To Richard B. and M. J. Williams, undated. (ca. December 1941.)

Bohuslaw, William E. To author, 13 September 1993 and 22 November 1993.

Brabbzson, June. To M. J. Williams, various dates, 14 January 1942 to 15 May 1943.

Brabbzson, Violet. To M. J. Williams, various dates, 15 May 1943 to 18 June 1944.

Bright, Don. To author, 27 June 1993.

Burdette, Mabel. To R. B. and M. J. Williams, various dates, 25 February 1942 to 5 January 1949.

Carter, Reginald. To Clyde R. Williams, 7 June 1938, 7 March 1941, 29 April 1941 and 19 May 1941.

Chambers, Superintendent W. Max, Okmulgee High School. To Mr. and Mrs. R. B. Williams, 18 May 1946.

Chernucha, Mrs. H. H. To M. J. Williams, 25 February 1942 and 15 April 1942.

Conley, Data Processing Chief Larry M., USN (Ret.). To author, 27 August 1993.

Cox, Amy. To Bonnie Moorhouse, January 1942.

Cox, Amy. To M. J. Williams, 11 April 1942.

Crawford, John W. To author, 6 August 1993 and 14 September 1993.

Croom, Editor Joe N. To Mrs. R. B. Williams, 9 September 1942.

De Rouin, Lieutenant E., USN, Navy Department, Bureau of Naval Personnel. To R. B. and M. J. Williams, 27 September 1946.

Dole, Senator Bob, United States Senate. To author, 11 November 1991 and 12 May 1993.

Duryea, Richard T. To author, 11 September 1993.

Earle, Colonel John H., USN (Ret.). To author, 2 July 1993.

Ellis, Pauline Scruggs. To author, various dates, 1993 to present.

Emelander, Henry. To author, 28 January 1994.

Emery, Karolyn K., Chief Operations Division, The American Battle Monuments Commission. To Mrs. M. J. Williams, 21 July 1982.

Field, P. H. To Musician H. A. Lachenmayer, USN (Ret.), 30 March 1987. Courtesy H. A. Lachenmayer.

Floege, Warren O. H. To M. J. Williams, 21 February 1942 and 3 June 1942.

Forrestal, Secretary of the Navy James, USN. To Mr. Richard B. Williams, Jr., Undated. (ca. January 1942.)

Gerace, Casper J. To author, 15 January 1994.

Gerard, Mrs. John C., Okmulgee Pony Girls. To Mr. and Mrs. R. B. Williams, 9 March 1942.

Gerow, Betty. To Apprentice Seaman Clyde R. Williams, USN, 2 February 1941 and 26 February 1941.

Glickman, Representative Dan, United States House of Representatives. To author, 13 November 1991.

Grieves, First Lieutenant W. P., USA. Postcard to Mr. R. B. Williams, Jr, 9 July 1940. CMTC Form No. 1. F.A.S. Ft. Sill, Oklahoma. (2-14-38-1500) 19216 66-a.

Hare, Howard G. To author, 29 August 1993.

Harten, William. Undated letter to author.

Homann, A. J., USN. To Mrs. Amelia Nadel, 1942.

Hudson, Robert Stephen. To author, 10 June 1993.

Hughes, Gertrude. To Bonnie Moorhouse, December 1947.

Hughes, Gertrude. To M. J. Williams, 21 December 1942 and 14 December 1962.

Hurley, Donald Lee. To author, various dates, 1993 to present.

Hurley, Raymond. To R. B. and M. J. Williams, 9 February 1942 and 22 May 1942.

Jacobs, Rear Admiral Randall, USN, Chief, Bureau of Naval Personnel. To R. B. Williams, Jr., telegrams 20 December, 1941, 6 February 1942. Letters 27 March 1942, 8 June 1942, 13 November 1942.

Japanese Bazaar, Honolulu. To Mrs. R. B. Williams, Jr., 31 December 1941 (package).

Jones, Alexander F., Editor, *The Washington Post*. To Mrs. R. B. Williams, 10 March 1942.

Kane, Pharmacist's Mate Second Class H. C., USN. To M. J. Williams, various dates, beginning 1942.

Kinney, Elizabeth Marie. To R. B. and M. J. Williams, 22 January 1942.

Lachenmayer, Musician Henry A, USN (Ret.). To author, 16 October 1993.

Lachenmayer, Musician Henry A, USN (Ret.). To Curator for the Navy, Naval Historical Center, 10 January 1987. Courtesy H. A. Lachenmayer.

Lanham, Lieutenant J.G. Mark, USN. To Mr. R. B. Williams, Jr., 15 November 1946 and 19 September 1948.

Little, Lieutenant Commander R. M., USN, Navy Recruiting Station, Dallas, Texas. To Clyde R. Williams, 15 August 1940.

Lobien, Mrs. Frank. To Raymond Hurley, May 1942.

Lucas, Private Joseph R., USAC. To Apprentice Seaman Clyde R. Williams, USN, 3 March 1941.

MacKay, Lieutenant Commander Hugh, USN. To Mr. R. B. Williams, Jr., 25 April 1942.

Marks, Lorraine E. To author, 26 September 1993, 30 October 1993, 21 June 1993, 3 February 1993 and 11 April 1993.

Marks, Lorraine E. To Pat and Cecil Gates, 26 April 1993 and 20 June 1993. Courtesy Lorraine Marks.

McClure, Captain H. A., USN. To R. B. Williams, Jr., undated (ca. December 1941).

McCoy, H. L., Veterans Administration. To M. J. Williams, 25 February 1942.

McCoy, H. L., Veterans Administration. To R. B. Williams, Jr., 19 May 1943, 25 May 1943.

McMillan, Merrill. To Whom It May Concern, undated (ca. June 1940).

McNeil, Lieutenant Commander W. J., USNR, Bureau of Supplies and Accounts. To R. B. Williams, Jr., 11 March 1942.

Miller, Captain Jim Dick, USN (Ret.). To Lorraine E. Marks, 14 June 1991. Courtesy Lorraine Marks.

Moffatt, Lewis K. To Whom It May Concern, undated (ca. June 1940).

Montgomery, James W. To author, 15 September 1993.

Moorhouse, Bonnie. To M. J. Williams, various dates, 7 January 1942 to August 1943.

Nadel, Amelia. To M. J. Williams, 31 March 1942, 17 December 1942 and 27 January 1943.

Navy Department, Public Voucher. To R. B. Williams, Jr., 19 November 1942.

Nimitz, Admiral C. W., USN. To Honorable Jack Nichols, House of Representatives, 14 October 1940 and 4 November 1940.

Oshiro, Calvin T. To author, 25 May 1993.

Page, Chief Water Tender F. W., USN. To R. B. Williams, Jr., 9 October 1940.

Phillips, Captain William J., USN. To author, 9 June 1993 (by J. L. Barnes, Master Chief Musician, USN).

Phillips, Captain William J., USN. To Musician Henry A. Lachenmayer, USN (Ret.). 12 January 1987. Courtesy H. A. Lachenmayer.

Platts, Estelle. To M. J. Williams, various dates, 1942 to 1992.

Quinn, Ensign (S.C.) J. P., USNR. To M. J. Williams, 24 June 1942.

Radford, Edna. To Bonnie Moorhouse. January 1942.

Radford, Edna. To M. J. Williams, 19 February 1942 and 17 January 1943.

Radford, Apprentice Seaman, Seaman Second Class and Musician Second Class Neal Jason, USN. To his family, various dates, 29 November 1940 to 25 November 1941. Courtesy Robert Radford.

Radford, Robert. To author, 1993 to present.

Reed, Musician Second Class J. L. "Kid", USN. To author, 27 September 1941, 5 December 1941.

Ryan, Colonel William E., Jr., ADA. To M. J. Williams, 1 September 1982.

Sanders, Ruth Cadwell. To author, various dates, 1993 to present.

Sanderson, Anna. To M. J. Williams, 20 March 1942 and 20 April 1942.

Schwarz, Frank W. To author, 27 September 1993.

Scruggs, Apprentice Seaman, Seaman Second Class and Musician Second Class Jack Leo. To his family, various dates, 9 February 1941 to 23 November 1941. Courtesy Pauline Scruggs Ellis.

Scruggs, Mae. To R. B. and M. J. Williams, 30 April 1942, 15 July 1942, and 13 August 1949.

Senick, Don, Senick Photographic Studio, Honolulu. To R. B. Williams, 27 May 1942.

Shaw, Edna. To Bonnie Moorhouse, January 1942.

Shaw, Edna. To R. B. and M. J. Williams, various dates, 14 February 1942 to 12 September 1944.

Simms, F. B., Veterans Administration. To R. B. Williams, 11 March 1947.

Somervell, Lieutenant General Brehon, USA. To author, 18 October 1944.

Stark, Clifford L., Chamber of Commerce of Honolulu. To author, 6 February 1942.

Stoddard, Captain G. M., USN. To R. B. Williams, Jr., 4 April 1944.

Strobak, Ed. To author, 5 January 1994.

Supply Department, Navy Yard, Pearl Harbor, Hawaii. To R. B. Williams, Jr. 17 May 1942. (Package).

Thurmond, Dr. James M., USN (Ret.). To author, 15 July 1993 and December 1993.

Tragella, Margaret. To R. B. and M. J. Williams, 9 September 1942.

Van Valkenburgh, Captain F., USN. To the Chief of the Bureau of Ships, 2 October 1941. Courtesy Lorraine E. Marks.

Ward, Michael S., Social Security Board. To R. B. Williams, 15 May 1943.

Warren, Lindsay C., General Accounting Office. Letter 20 May 1942. Voucher to R. B. Williams, Jr., 20 March 1946.

Watson, Joan. To author, 17 January 1942.

Watson, Joan. To Clyde R. Williams, various dates, 16 July 1940 to 17 January 1942.

Wehner, Dr. Walter. To author, 1 October 1993, 13 October 1993, 10 January 1995.

Wells, Alvina. To author, 6 January 1994.

Wells, Arthur W. To author, 21 November 1993.

Wentworth, Gerald E. To author, 11 September 1993.

Wentworth, Gerald E. To The Pearl Harbor History Associates, Inc., 17 March 1988. Courtesy Gerald E. Wentworth.

White, Catherine. To M. J. Williams, 12 March 1942 and 24 April 1942.

Whitson, Elizabeth. To M. J. Williams, 20 February 1942, 23 July 1943, 3 September 1943 and 17 November 1943.

Williams, Apprentice Seaman Clyde Richard, USN. To Betty Gerow, 20 February 1941, 21 March 1941 and 23 June 1941.

Williams, Apprentice Seaman Clyde Richard, USN. To R. B. Williams. 24 December 1940. (Telegram).

Williams, Apprentice Seaman, Seaman Second Class, Musician Second Class Clyde Richard, USN. To his family, various dates, 6 August 1940 to 26 November 1941.

Williams, R. B. To author, 28 November 1942.

Williams, R. B. To Secretary of the Navy Frank Knox, 17 June 1942.

Williams, R. B. Jr. To Commanding Officer, The United States Navy School of Music, Washington, D. C., 29 June 1940.

Williams, R. B., Jr. To Oklahoma Historical Society, 28 August 1943.

Williams, R. B., M. J. and author. To Clyde R. Williams, Apprentice Seaman, Seaman Second Class, Musician Second Class, USN. Various dates, 9 July 1940 to May 1941.

Wright, Muriel H., Oklahoma Historical Society. To R. B. Williams, Jr., 23 August 1943.

Magazine Articles

"*Arizona* Condition Under Study." *Veterans of Foreign Wars Magazine* (December 1985).

Barnard, Charles N. "Ships to Stir Our Souls." *Modern Maturity* (April-May 1985).

DeLong, Kent. "More Important Than Life." *Veterans of Foreign Wars Magazine* (December 1991).

Heinz, Robert. "The Bombing of the *Arizona*." *Veterans of Foreign Wars Magazine* (December 1966).

"It Is Altogether Fitting and Proper." *Colliers* (3 June, 1950).
Life, (5 July 1943).
McKinley, JO 2 Mike, USN. "December 6, 1941. Pearl Harbor. The Last Day of Innocence." *All Hands* (December 1986). Courtesy Musician H. A. Lachenmayer, USN (Ret.).
Morison, Samuel Eliot. "The Lessons of Pearl Harbor." *The Saturday Evening Post* (1961).
"Navy School of Music." *Our Navy* (July 1941). Courtesy John Crawford and Dr. Walter Wehner.
Our Navy (1944). Courtesy John Crawford.
"Pearl Harbor: A Day of Loss." *Veterans of Foreign Wars Auxiliary* (November 1984).
"They Lie Where They Would Wish To Be." Reprinted from the *Atlanta Constitution*. *Readers' Digest*. Unknown date.
"Where Were You — ?" *Newsweek* (12 December 1966).
"World War II Commemorative Issue." *Veterans of Foreign Wars Magazine* (November 1991).

Newsletters

Pacific Memorial System, Honolulu, Volume 1, Number 3, 1962.

News Releases

Release No. 232-67 j d, 27 November 1967. *$7,500 USS Arizona Model to be Placed on Memorial*. 14 N D-DISTAFF-P-23.

Newspaper Articles

Adrian Journal (Missouri), 25 December 1941. Courtesy Alvina Wells.
At 'Em Arizona, various dates.
Birmingham News (Alabama), various dates, 1941, 1942.
Bremerton Sun (Washington), various dates, 1940, 1942.
Central New Jersey Home News, 6 February 1942, 2 April 1942.
Chicago Tribune, 2 April 1942.
Christian Science Monitor, various dates, beginning 1941.
Clipper (Chesapeake, Virginia), 22/23 April 1993. Courtesy Virginia Doughty.
Corvallis Gazette-Times (Oregon), 8 December 1993. Courtesy Estelle Platts.
Courier-Journal (Louisville, Kentucky), various dates, 1941, 1942.
Daily News, 1 December 1991. Courtesy William E. Bohuslaw.
Daily Oklahoman, 16 December 1941 and 2 April 1942.
Denver Post, 9 March 1975.
Enquirer (Cincinnati), various dates, 1941.
Erie Daily Times (Pennsylvania), January 1942, 6 February 1942.
Evening Star (Washington, D.C.), 16 December 1941 and 2 April 1942.
Evening Times (Sayre, Athens, South Waverly, Pennsylvania), 22 July 1942.
Honolulu Advertiser, various dates, beginning 7 December 1941. Courtesy Estelle Platts.
Honolulu Star-Bulletin, various dates, beginning 7 December 1941. Courtesy

Estelle Platts.
Houston Post, January 1941, 21 December 1941.
Kansas City Kansan, 12 November 1991.
Kansas City Star, various dates, beginning 1942.
Kansas City Times, 24 December 1941.
Long Beach (Calif.) Press-Telegram, 7 June 1947 and 6 January 1950.
Mirror, 23 December 1941.
Moline Daily Dispatch (Illinois), 11 April 1942.
Nassau Daily Review-Star (Long Ioland, New York), 21 December 1941, 30 March
    1942 and 17 July 1943.
National Legionnaire, undated.
Navy Times, 10 December 1958.
Newark Evening News (New Jersey), 22 December 1941.
Norfolk Virginian-Pilot, 3 November 1993. Courtesy Virginia Doughty.
Okmulgee Daily Times (Oklahoma), various dates, beginning 1940.
Okmulgee Torchlight (Oklahoma), various dates, beginning 1938.
Paradise News (Honolulu), June 1981.
Tourist News (Hawaii), 2-8 December 1976.
Tribune Newspapers (Phoenix, Arizona), 8 December 1992.
Tribune (Salt Lake City, Utah), 8 February 1942.
Tulsa Daily World, various dates, beginning 1941.
Tulsa Tribune, various dates, beginning 1941.
Veterans View (Chicago), 15 January 1992.
Washington Daily News, 26 June 1942.
Washington Post, various dates, 1941 to present.
Washington Star, No date.
Wichita Eagle (Kansas), 2 April 1942.
Wyandotte West (Kansas City, Kansas), 4 June 1987.

Official Publications and Records

Act of Congress, 18 August 1941.
Arizona USS (BB-39). Deck Log, 17 June 1941. Courtesy Lorraine Marks.
Benter, Lieutenant Charles, USN, Officer-in-Charge, U.S. Navy School of Music.
    Excerpts from "Station Orders" Receiving Station, Washington, D.C. United
    States Navy School of Music, Navy Yard, Washington, D. C., 1 December
    1939. Courtesy Pauline Scruggs Ellis.
Congressional Record-U.S. Senate. 5 February 1942.
Executive Order No. 9265 Establishing the Area Campaign Medals. Franklin D.
    Roosevelt, The White House, 6 November 1942 and Amendment, Harry S
    Truman, The White House, 15 March 1946.
H R 1544 (Report No. 674), 80th Congress 1st Session. An Act. 22 July 1947.
Information Regarding Enlistment and Application for the United States Navy
    School of Music. NRB-22064-3-22-38 - 25 M. (E-44, 45, 46.)
Information Regarding Training Period for Apprentice Seamen. United States
    Naval Training Station, Norfolk, Virginia. NTSNV-11-2-40-30 M.
Marriage Records:
    Los Angeles County, California, 10 June 1938.
    Prince George's County, Maryland, 8 February 1941.
    Okmulgee County, Oklahoma, 28 November 1942.

Narrative of the Pearl Harbor Attack. Headquarters Fourteenth Naval District. No date.

Navy Department, Bureau of Navigation. NAV 64-EVH.

Navy List of Dead, as of December 7, 1941. Second Report, Enclosure A, 3, 8. National Archives. Courtesy Lorraine Marks.

Outstanding Events in U.S. Naval History, (1929). NRB-28344-11-13-40-200 M.

Programs

American Legion, Edwin K. White-Clyde Williams Post Number 10, Okmulgee, Oklahoma. Memorial and Dedication Service, in Memory of Edwin K. White and Clyde Williams. 7 December 1944.

Arizona, USS (BB 39) Band Concert, 25 June 1941.

Arizona, USS (BB 39) Band Concert, 30 August 1941.

Arizona, USS Memorial Programs of Memorial Day and December 7 Services, various dates. Collection of author.

Citizens Military Training Camp, Fort Sill, Oklahoma. Divine Worship Service, 4 August 1940.

Navy Battle of Music, Bloch Recreation Center, 13 September 1941, 8 November 1941, 6 December 1941. *At 'Em Arizona,* Summer, 1993. Courtesy Lorraine Marks, Mary Day Wilson, and Barbara Kuhne.

Navy Battle of Music, Bloch Recreation Center, 25 October 1941. Courtesy Roger Snyder.

Navy Receiving Station, U. S. Navy Yard, Washington, D. C. Christmas Menu, 1940.

Pacific War Memorial Commission, Dedication Ceremonies of USS *Arizona* Memorial, 30 May 1962.

Pearl Harbor Survivors Association, 50th Anniversary Congressional Commemorative Medal Ceremonies. State Capitol Rotunda, Topeka, Kansas. 11 November 1991.

Unpublished Manuscripts

Author. 1941 and 1942 diary.

Author. January 1942 essay.

Author. Undated essay. *They Didn't Have A Chance.*

Bastian, Chief Petty Officer Russell C., USN (Ret.). 22 August 1993 remembrances. Courtesy Chief Petty Officer Russell C. Bastian, USN (Ret.).

Hurley, Raymond. 1942 statement.

Hurley, Wendell R. 1941 autograph and photograph album.

Hurley, Wendell R. 1941 diary.

Lachenmayer, Musician Second Class Henry A., USN. Remembrances, 8 December 1941. Courtesy Musician H. A. Lachenmayer, USN (Ret.).

Luckenbach, Bandmaster L. B. "Red", USN, (Ret.). Undated and untitled recollections of 7 December 1941. Courtesy John Crawford.

Tippets, Musician Second Class Russell J., USN. 7 December 1941 diary. Courtesy Sol Blaine.

Order Form

Silent Song Publishing
Molly Kent, Author
2122 North 49th Terrace
Kansas City, KS 66104-3103
(913) 287-5797

USS *Arizona*'s Last Band is a 6" x 9" hard-cover book, consisting of 384 pages, including 45 black and white photographs.

Please make check or money order, payable to Silent Song Publishing, in the amount of $27.50 ($25.00 per book, plus shipping and handling). (Kansas residents please add $1.72 sales tax per book.)

Please enter my order for _____ copies of
USS *Arizona*'s Last Band, and ship to:

Name_____

Address_____

City _____

State_____ Zip_____

Phone (_____)_____

(Please allow 4 to 6 weeks for delivery.)
Thank you for your order.